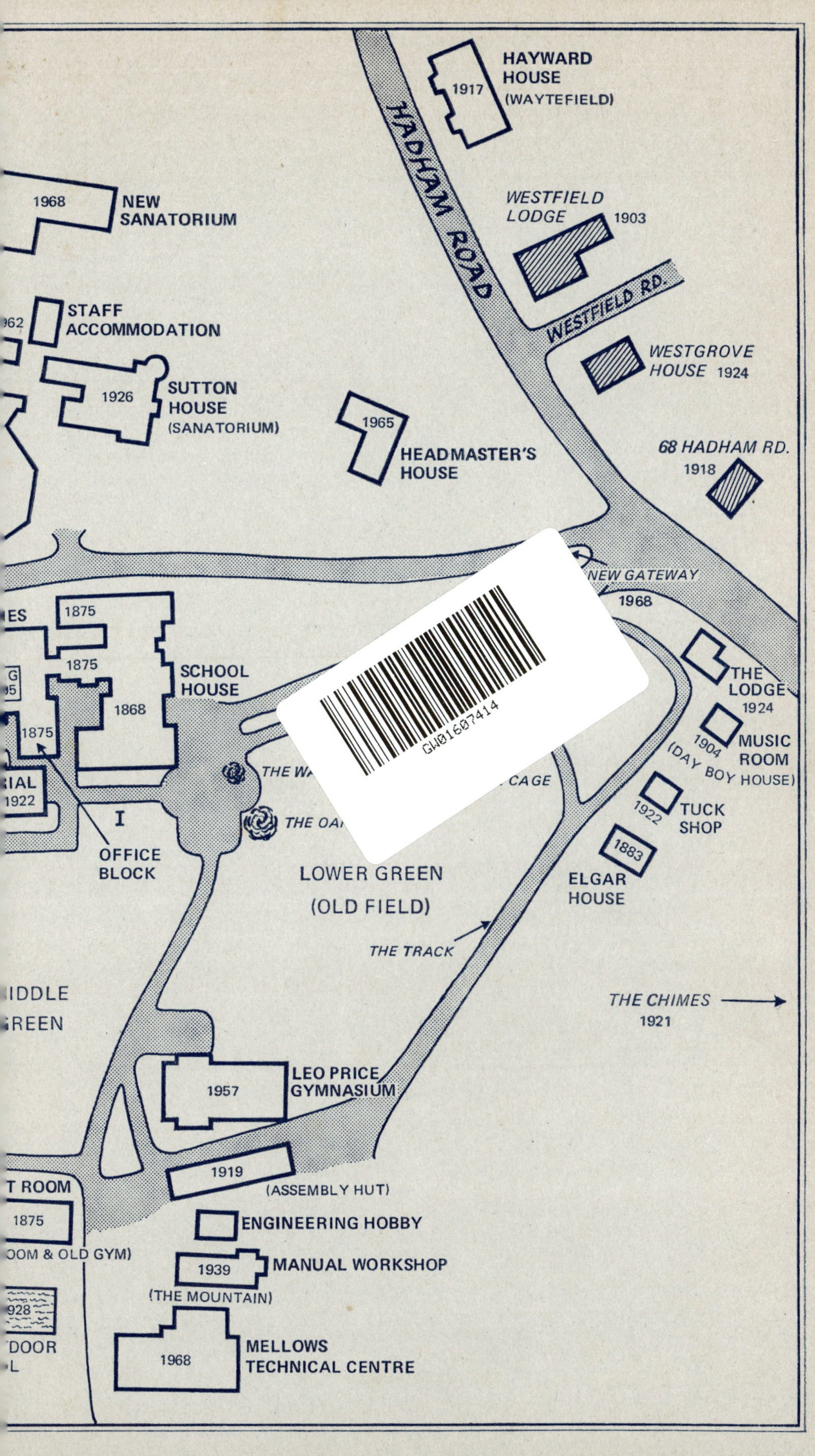

HAYWARD HOUSE
1917
(WAYTEFIELD)
HADHAM ROAD
1968
NEW SANATORIUM
WESTFIELD LODGE
1903
WESTFIELD RD.
STAFF ACCOMMODATION
WESTGROVE HOUSE 1924
1926
SUTTON HOUSE
(SANATORIUM)
1965
HEADMASTER'S HOUSE
68 HADHAM RD.
1918
NEW GATEWAY
1968
1875
1875
1868
SCHOOL HOUSE
1875
1922
THE LODGE
1924
1904
MUSIC ROOM
(DAY BOY HOUSE)
CAGE
1922
TUCK SHOP
1883
ELGAR HOUSE
OFFICE BLOCK
LOWER GREEN
(OLD FIELD)
THE TRACK
THE CHIMES
1921
1957
LEO PRICE GYMNASIUM
1919
(ASSEMBLY HUT)
1875
ENGINEERING HOBBY
1939
MANUAL WORKSHOP
(THE MOUNTAIN)
1968
MELLOWS TECHNICAL CENTRE

Bishop's Stortford College
1868–1968

Per fesse, the chief per pale; the dexter chief gules, on a mount vert a hart statant or; the sinister of the first, three seaxes in pale fesseways proper, pommelled and hilted of the third; in the base azure, an open bible bound of the first with two clasps of the third, thereon the words Verbum Dei

Bishop's Stortford College
1868–1968

A CENTENARY CHRONICLE

by

JOHN MORLEY

and

NORMAN MONK-JONES

ILLUSTRATED

J. M. DENT & SONS LTD
LONDON

Made in Great Britain
at the
Aldine Press • Letchworth • Herts
by
J. M. Dent & Sons Ltd
Aldine House • Bedford Street • London WC2
for the Governors of
Bishop's Stortford College
who commissioned and have
editorial responsibility for the work

First published 1969

SBN: 460 04801 5

We are persuaded that the friendships fostered at school are the School's richest legacy. We dare not think how easily we might never have known the people we met here. No doubt we should have found others but we should not be ourselves.

Contents

List of Illustrations ix
Foreword xiii
Acknowledgements xv
1 Our Origins 1
2 Richard Alliott and the N.G.S.: 1868–1899 10
3 Victorian Memories 23
4 F. S. Young: (1) 1900–1918 39
5 Some School Characters 57
6 F. S. Young: (2) 1918–1931 63
7 More Reminiscences 86
8 H. L. Price: 1932–1943 99
9 Scrapbook from the *Stortfordian* 120
10 A. N. Evans: 1944–1957 132
11 Some School Societies 157
12 P. W. Rowe: from 1957 171
13 Fifty Years in Retrospect 199
14 Centenary Year: 1968 207
'Heroes' 221

List of Illustrations

Between pages 16 and 17

The Collegiate School and the N.G.S.

R. Alliott; F. S. Young; School House.

1st XI Cricket, 1890; 1st XI Football, 1891–2.

Interiors of N.G.S., 1892, with C. D. Whittaker and A. H. Blandford.

The Staff, 1894; Alliott Memorial Library.

Newbury House; Preparatory School Group, 1902; 1st XI Cricket, 1906.

Masters, 1903; Monitors, 1903.

Racquets Court; Chemistry Laboratory; Cricket on New Field.

Between pages 48 and 49

Westfield Lodge; W. L. House Group, 1904; Day Boy House Group, 1906.

Orchestra, 1908; Choir, 1911.

F. M. Kingdon; C. S. Colman; F. S. Sutton; A. G. Tidmarsh; N. P. Wood.

Classroom Interiors, 1912, with C. Moser, R. G. Kelland and F. B. Shawe.

New Classroom Block and Purcell House, 1909; C. S. Colman teaching, 1914; View of B.S.C. *c.* 1910.

Grimwade House; Prize Giving in Schoolroom; Unveiling Alliott House Foundation Stone. (All 1913.)

George Mitchell; Albert Carter; Sergeant Salmon; Water Polo Team, 1914.

Alliott House; House Group, 1915.

Between pages 80 and 81

1st XI Football, 1915; Scouts, 1915.

Westfield Lodge Group, 1915; 1st XV, 1920; Preparatory School Group, 1921.

1st XI Football, 1921; School House Group, 1920.

Waytefield; House Group, 1919; House XV, 1930.

Jubilee, 1919: O.S. Cricket XI; Reunion Group.

The Hut, 1919; School House Interiors, 1920.

C. Mellows; A. D. Hayward; J. D. Craig; N. Monk-Jones; B. J. Adams.

View from Labs to School House, 1920.

Masters, Prize Day, 1921.

Opening of Memorial Hall, 1922; Choir; Masters.

The Memorial Hall.

The Roll of Honour, 1914–1918 and 1939–45.

Opening of Memorial Hall Doors, 1922; 68 Hadham Road Group, 1922; The Chimes Group, 1922.

Prep. watching cricket on New Field; Interiors of two former classrooms.

Gym with Sergeant Salmon and Interior of Old Gymnasium.

The Bath Club Cup: 1923, 1929, 1949.

Robert Pearce House; House Group, 1923.

Between pages 112 and 113

Classrooms and Labs, 1925; Athletic Team, 1925; A. I. Rae, Public Schools Half-Mile Champion, 1947.

Westgrove House Group, 1926; The Sanatorium; School House Fire Drill, 1930.

The Preparatory School, 1927; Grimwade House; W. Rogers.

Indoor and Outdoor Swimming Baths.

Enjoying the Outdoor Bath: 1939 and 1948.

H. L. Price; A. N. Evans; P. W. Rowe; Headmaster's House, 1965.

School House Group, 1932; The Library, 1933.

The Rock Gardens, 1932.

Between pages 128 and 129

Holiday Parties.

'Masters Off Duty.'

'Hasbro'.'

'Claremont.'

N.H.S. Expedition; Skating at Takeley.

Dramatic Group, 1925; 'All clear', 1939.

The Old Pavilion, 1928; The Doggart Pavilion, Whit Monday, 1933.

1st XI Cricket, 1933; Practising for Massed P.T.; Westfield Lodge Group, 1933.

Between pages 144 and 145

The Opening (1936) and Interior of the F. S. Young Memorial Library.

Yeo Cup, Senior Cross, 1937; Alliott House, 1938.

1st XV, 1937; Waytefield Reunion and Farewell Group, 1938.

Cadet Corps, 1915; C.C.F., 1942.

Robert Pearce House Dining Room; R.P. House Group, 1944.

School House Group, 1945; Manual Workshop, with P. Carlaw.

Alliott House Group, 1951; Robert Pearce House Group, 1951.

Day Boy House Group, 1951; C. Covill; Upper Field, 1st XV *v.* C. Mellows' XV, 1953.

Between pages 176 and 177

O.O.S. Group at B.S.C., 1954.

'Old Storts' Group, 1889; Past and Present Group, 1895.

1st XI Hockey, 1953; School House at Lunch.

Laboratory Interiors, with W. E. Clare, A. Darlington and H. D. J. McKeown.

Shooting Eight, 1955; Athletic Team, 1956.

School House Group, 1957; 1st XV, 1958.

Leo Price Gymnasium, 1957.

1st Swimming Team, 1960; 1st XI Cricket, 1964.

Between pages 208 and 209

Development of Library Block.

New Dining Hall, 1962.

1st XI Hockey, 1965; The 'Hard Surface', 1965.

Grimwade House New Wing, 1964; First School Council, 1966.

Miss G. E. Parsons; A. O. Ward; W. J. Strachan; H. E. Wall.

Language Laboratory; New Science Laboratories.

The Masters, 1968; School House Group, 1968.

Aerial Views, 1922 and 1968.

Preparatory School Group, 1968.

Hayward House Group, 1968.

Sutton House Group, 1968.

Alliott House Group, 1968; Robert Pearce House Group, 1968.

Administrative and Outside Staff, 1968; Preparatory School Assembly Hall.

Visit of H.M. Queen Elizabeth the Queen Mother, 1968.

Open Day, Lord Soper speaking; New Sanatorium; Charles Mellows Technical Centre. (All 1968.)

TAIL-PIECES

The Collegiate School. 9

From a Progress Report of the N.G.S. (1895). 22

School House Sundial. 38

Shield worn by 1st XV during 1939–45 War (G.H.R.). 56
C. S. Colman's Book-plate. 62
Lectern formerly in Memorial Hall. 85
Opening Bars of 'Heroes'. 98
Memorial Hall before alteration (A.J.H.). 119
Sculpture formerly on Fireplace of A.H. Common-room. 131
Shield on original Proscenium Arch of Memorial Hall. 156
Architectural Society Paper Heading (P.F.H.). 170
Preparatory School League Trophy. 198
From *New Wine*. 206
The 1968 Gateway (A.J.H.). 220

Foreword

In writing the story of Bishop's Stortford College we have been concerned not merely with the objective facts of its history, but even more with the personalities of those who have mainly helped to inspire the spirit and to build up the traditions of the School. And we have had in mind as our readers not only those seeking information about the School, but especially Stortfordians and friends of the School who already share the affection for Stortford that we ourselves feel.

This approach has involved us in two difficulties. A large part of this book is concerned with the activities of the School's successive headmasters and of such members of the staff as have devoted most of their working years to the School, or at least have stayed long enough to make a considerable contribution to its life. As any school exists primarily for the boys who pass through it, to concentrate so much on the masters may seem to imply a wrong sense of priorities on our part. But the fact remains that it is the staff who provide continuity in the life of a school, however much its traditions rest in the hands of its pupils. And in any case, the mere numbers of the latter make it impossible to mention by name more than a few individual boys.

Nor have we thought it advisable to attempt to recount here, except by way of an occasional reference in some special context, the doings of Old Stortfordians as such; and in this we had the full support of the Committee of the O.S.C. This is the story of the School, not of its Old Boys. Indeed Old Stortfordians have distinguished themselves in so many walks of life—in the civil and diplomatic services, in the armed forces of the Crown, in the legal and medical professions, in the worlds of industry and commerce, of literature and the arts, of education and science and technology—that it would need another volume to do justice to their varied achievements.

Our second difficulty arises from the essentially repetitive nature of the hundred and one incidents which, day by day, term by term, make up the life of a school. 'Each Old Boy's story of the School', wrote N. P. Wood in the Jubilee Booklet of 1919, 'would differ in many respects from that which would be related by any other; for the incidents which he cherishes were in many cases peculiar to him, and more or less consciously have influenced the whole of his life. Thus the real history of a great school is made up of hundreds of such stories that can never see the light of day.'

It has not been easy to decide which among the myriad details mentioned in the files of the school magazines are worth recording in a centenary chronicle. We have tried to base our story on what might be termed the highest common factor of the individual viewpoints to which Nevil Wood referred, and to produce a narrative which will be something more personal than a mere compilation of names, dates and events. Macaulay once wrote, 'I shall cheerfully bear the reproach of having descended below the dignity of History': if we too have descended at times to trivialities (and many of the events here recorded are indeed trivial), it is in the hope that such details may help to fill in the bare outlines of the School's development, and enable Old Stortfordians to recall more vividly their own days at school.

Our primary sources have naturally been the files of the *N.G.S.* and the *Stortfordian*, which we have felt free to quote, at times extensively, or to adapt for our purposes: to the writers thus quoted we are grateful. Professor J. Morley has done much painstaking research, especially for the earlier period but also up to the 1914–1918 war; N. Monk-Jones has made himself responsible for the years from then until the present day and also for the general arrangement of the book as a whole; I myself have chosen the illustrations and have helped to see the book through the press.

In dealing with such a mass of miscellaneous detail we can scarcely have avoided some minor mistakes, for which we apologize in advance; but we hope we have not been guilty of any major inaccuracies or omissions. With regard to the illustrations, considerations of space have made it impossible to include more than a limited selection: to all those O.S. who responded so kindly to our appeal for photographs we are none the less grateful.

We also wish to thank the following for their help in producing this book: Messrs J. M. Dent and Sons, especially F. J. M. Dent and R. J. Hall (both O.S.), who took such a personal interest in it; B. Blaxill and V. R. Price for reading the typescript and making valuable comments; Mrs Monk-Jones, for numerous helpful suggestions and for reading the proofs; R. W. Arend, for his calligraphy (a transcript from a *Stortfordian* editorial); P. J. Savidge, for the manuscript of the musical quotation; P. F. Horton, G. H. Rhoades, A. J. Hunt, C. J. Hewett, J. R. Harvey, and the B.S.C. Architectural and Typographical Societies, for tail-pieces; C. I. M. Jones, for help with the end-papers; I. D. Taylor, who took a number of photographs specially for this book; and D. A. Thomas of Bishop's Stortford for help with research.

H. E. WALL (*Editor*).

Acknowledgements

Our thanks are due to the following for illustrations reproduced in this book: Barratt's Photo Press; W. H. Beynon and Co. (etching by C. H. Boucher, Esq.); W. R. Bowman; Bertram Chapman; Cox Photography; Daisy Day; Elliott and Fry; the *Herts and Essex Observer*; Marshall Keene and Co.; Arthur Maxwell; Photo-Reportage Ltd, London; Raphael Tuck and Sons; Sports and General Press Agency; J. and G. Taylor; *The Times*; Topical Press Agency; Ernest Williams.

In addition we should like particularly to thank Messrs F. Harris and Sons of Bishop's Stortford, for photographs and for their invaluable help; Mr Ray Stebbings of Epping, for two aerial photographs, that on the book-jacket (1959) and the one in the book, which he took specially for us (1968); also the Editor of the *Observer*, for permission to reprint the article on H. L. Price at Oxford.

We apologize for any illustrations inadvertently left unacknowledged: it has been difficult to trace the originals of some in the school records.

H. E. W.

1. Our Origins

THE Nonconformist Grammar School, Bishop's Stortford, which was later to become Bishop's Stortford College, was founded in 1868, and was housed in the buildings of a previous foundation known as the Collegiate School.

By the Act of Uniformity of 1662, all clergymen, university teachers, schoolmasters and tutors were obliged to assert their assent to everything in the Prayer Book. As a result, some two thousand Puritan clergy were expelled from their livings: at the same time, private Dissenting Academies began to spring up throughout the country. Then in 1746 John Wesley founded Kingswood School, near Bristol, as a boarding school where young Dissenters were to be trained for the ministry. Other Nonconformist schools followed: Mill Hill dates back to 1807, and its foundation was followed by that of Caterham, Silcoates, Taunton and Tettenhall. Then came Bishop's Stortford, where in 1850 the Rev. W. A. Hurndall, minister of what was then known as the Independent Church in Water Lane, approached the Rev. F. W. Rhodes (father of Cecil Rhodes), who had recently been appointed vicar of St Michael's Church, with a view to securing his co-operation in the establishment of a non-sectarian Proprietary School [1] in the town. The idea was at first received politely by the new vicar; and by agreement with him Mr Hurndall proceeded to call a meeting at Mr Rhodes's house, of which one of those present, Mr J. G. Nash, left the following account amongst his papers: 'At a meeting held at Mr Rhodes's, vicar of Bishop's Stortford, Feb. 13th 1850, at ¼ past 3: present, Mrs Rhodes, Mr Rhodes (in bed), Mr Hurndall, Mr Hodson and self: Mr Rhodes stated that he did not favour the Proprietary School, to prove which he said that Mr Hurndall called upon him, and that his observation to Mrs Rhodes was 'what a bore!': that he returned Mr H.'s call in a few days, and as the school was mentioned by Mr H., he (Mr R.) said that he could not undertake to assist, but wished the affair God's speed,

[1] A Proprietary School was a school run by a group of owners acting as a registered company and known as 'the Proprietary'.

meaning to be polite: but that he differed was evident from his quoting *The Times* newspaper and Dr Turton's pamphlet, and from his returning to explain that he could not assist but wished it God's speed. Mr Hurndall then stated that from what he could recall of Mr Rhodes's manner and conversation, he decidedly was not averse but would consider of it; but that on his return to Mr H.'s house he rushed into the drawing-room, saying that he did not wish Mr H. to misunderstand him, that he could not become one of the Counsel [*sic*], but that he wished it God's speed. Some time after which, Mr H. wrote him a note requesting him to attend at Mr Mulligan's, which note Mr R. never answered. This statement was made subject to frequent interruptions from Mr Rhodes, who contradicted having mentioned the word Counsel, which Mr H. affirmed to be the case.'

We can well understand, in view of the feeling at that time between the Established Church and Dissent, the horror that Mr Rhodes must have felt at this attempt, brought upon him by his wish to be polite, at involving him in the establishment of a school in association with Nonconformists. It may well have been this emotion that inspired him a few months later to give up his comfortable vicarage and establish in it what he called the High School. This was claimed to be a revival of the old Bishop's Stortford Grammar School, which was founded in the sixteenth century (1579) but had been closed in 1770. Meanwhile the Rhodes family moved to a house in South Street, nearly a mile from St Michael's, called Thorleybourne; and here Cecil Rhodes and most of his ten brothers and sisters were born. (It was not until 1873, when the High School moved into new buildings in the Hadham Road, that the vicarage reverted to its proper use.) After varying fortunes the High School, which later functioned again under its old name of the Grammar School, finally ceased to exist, shortly after the death of its last headmaster, Mr J. Bruce Payne, in 1930.

Another instance of the tension between Church and Chapel in the mid-nineteenth century may be mentioned here. Cecil Rhodes's half-sister, Louisa Rhodes (*d.* 1923), told Basil Williams, the author of a biography of Cecil Rhodes published by Constable in 1921, that once when her brother was on his way to Sunday School, some 'old Dissenting ladies wearing long black veils' stopped him and tried to persuade him to go to the 'Dissenting place'. Just how he declined the invitation was not stated; but that he convinced the ladies of the unseemliness of making such advances may be inferred from Louisa's recollection that this occurrence, when related at Thorleybourne, caused huge delight to Cecil's brothers and sisters! For the Nonconformists were numerous and influential in Stortford, and the 'Dissenting place' was the large and imposing Congregational Church, with manse adjoining, in Water Lane.

It is plain that, in spite of the rebuff from Mr Rhodes, the Nonconformists of Bishop's Stortford were not to be dissuaded from their educational project; for in 1850 [1] the bye-laws of the first Proprietary School were promulgated, in which it was laid down that the Headmaster must be an Anglican and the Second Master a Dissenter. It is interesting to note even at this early date the definitely non-sectarian nature of the school from which in a sense the present School may be said to be descended: we shall see that the Nonconformist Grammar School under Alliott, and still more Bishop's Stortford College under Young and his successors, has always maintained this non-sectarian tradition. It seems that the first school was established in the Manse (demolished in 1966), opposite the Independent Church in Water Lane, under the Rev. G. F. Simpson. In 1852 the School was moved to the present site off the Hadham Road, while the new Headmaster, Mr J. Bell, apparently lived in Terrace House, Rye Street, of which we shall have more to say in a later chapter. The School now became known as the Collegiate School,[2] and it was the buildings of this School which were to be taken over by the Nonconformist Grammar School sixteen years later.

No doubt the High School, founded or rather resurrected by Mr Rhodes, would attract most of the boys from the Anglican families in the district: conversely, most of the Dissenters would send their sons to the new foundation. This would account for the fact, mentioned below, that so many of the shareholders of the Collegiate School were members of the Independent Church.

Meanwhile Nonconformists in East Anglia had been considering the possibility of establishing a public school in that region with a definitely evangelical and Nonconformist atmosphere. As early as 1863, at a meeting in Ipswich, it was resolved 'that it was highly desirable that a Dissenters' Proprietary School for the Eastern Counties should be established, and that a meeting for the purpose of originating such an institution should be convened by a circular to be issued forthwith'. In November 1865 Mr Edward Grimwade of Ipswich, helped by Mr Arthur Jones, a local journalist, and Mr Robert Pearce, a solicitor (later Sir Robert Pearce M.P., famous for his advocacy of Daylight

[1] We follow here the account written by N. P. Wood.

[2] The most distinguished alumnus of the Collegiate School was A. S. Wilkins, who became Professor of Classics at Victoria University and then at Owen's College, Manchester.

Saving), issued a circular signed by thirteen leading East Anglian Nonconformists, convening a meeting to be held at the London Coffee House on 9th May 1866. This meeting resolved 'that, having had its attention directed to the great importance of establishing a Public School for the Eastern Counties in which Evangelical Nonconformists might secure for their boys an effective and Christian education, on terms that should not be beyond the reach of the middle class generally, it sympathized very heartily with the suggestions that had been offered by Mr S. Morley M.P., Mr John Crossley and Mr Grimwade, and formed a committee for the purpose of collecting information on the subject'. It was at the first meeting of this committee, held on 29th May 1866, that the Rev. W. Cuthbertson, the Independent minister at Bishop's Stortford, reported unofficially that the Bishop's Stortford Collegiate School was in the hands of a Proprietary holding two hundred shares, all of which save nineteen were held by members of his congregation, and that it would therefore be possible to treat with the committee of that school, with a view to an amalgamation or transfer.

The next step was the appointment of the Rev. W. Cuthbertson and Mr Thomas Isaac of Maldon to meet the Committee of the Collegiate School; and on 18th June they reported the willingness of the Proprietary to negotiate. Steps were taken to form a small company for educational purposes in the eastern counties (Norfolk, Suffolk, Hertfordshire and Essex), and for the acquisition and enlargement of the Bishop's Stortford school, to be managed upon strictly Nonconformist principles. The terms arranged were embodied in an instrument dated 7th February 1867, and were accepted by the Proprietary at a meeting in Bishop's Stortford on 5th March 1867. By subsequent negotiation the land adjoining the school was purchased from the five gentlemen who had bought it for the use of the Collegiate School, and as one of the terms of its acquisition the Johns Scholarship [1] was established, thus perpetuating the name of the original owner of the land, Mr E. B. Johns.

The Company was duly incorporated on 31st May 1867 under the name of the East of England Nonconformist Schools Association Ltd, and the shares were subscribed with great readiness throughout the eastern counties. In the meantime the school was carried on under the headmastership of Mr Joseph Bell, who had been for some years headmaster of the Collegiate School; but in October 1867 Mr Bell resigned this position to take up a post in Yorkshire. The Directors thereupon issued advertisements, and in due course the committee to whom the selection of a short list from the many applicants had been entrusted

[1] Tenable for three years by a boy who is a native of Bishop's Stortford.

submitted three names to the Directors. These three gentlemen were interviewed by the Directors at a meeting in London, and on 25th February 1868, upon a ballot, the Rev. Richard Alliott, a B.A. of Trinity College, Cambridge, was unanimously elected, to commence his duties on 1st September 1868: subsequently it was arranged that, as there were only a small number of boys, the School would carry on under Mr Esam (who had been Vice-Principal of the Collegiate School) at Terrace House, Rye Street, until Easter, after which Mr Alliott would take over. Meanwhile presumably the necessary enlargement of the Collegiate School buildings off the Hadham Road was put in hand. The formal inauguration of the new school was put off until the September term.

Mr Alliott, then aged twenty-nine, was the Congregational minister at Knutsford in Cheshire, and had had no previous experience as a schoolmaster. His father, the Rev. William Alliott, was pastor of Howard Chapel, Bedford, and tutor in classics and mathematics to the Congregational Theological College in Bedford. Educated at Bedford Grammar School, Richard Alliott won an exhibition tenable for three years at Trinity College, Cambridge, where he graduated in 1858. He had been head of the school in classics at Bedford, but his undergraduate career at Cambridge was handicapped by illness, and he missed one or two terms on this account. This prevented him from doing himself full justice in his degree examination; but later the energy of his nature overcame the hindrances of his earlier ill health.

From Cambridge he gained a Dr Williams Scholarship to the Lancashire Independent College in Manchester, where he studied theology from 1859 to 1863. In the latter year he began a very successful ministry in Cheshire at the Congregational Church of Knutsford (the 'Cranford' of Mrs Gaskell's novel).

No doubt Alliott's more remote ancestry appealed to the group of earnest Nonconformists who were the first Directors of the new School. His great-grandfather, the Rev. Richard Alliott, had been pastor of Vicar Lane Church, Coventry; his grandfather, also named Richard, had been pastor of Castle Gate Meeting, Nottingham; and an uncle, Dr Richard Alliott, after pastorates in Nottingham and London, had been in succession Principal of Western College, Plymouth, of Cheshunt College and of Springhill College, Birmingham.

It was agreed by the Directors that the boys should wear an academic cap with white [1] tassel, and that the highest class should be allowed to wear a gown; also that the bedrooms of the new School 'should be so

[1] The colour of the tassels seems to have been changed to blue during the eighties.

fitted up that each boy should be private'. Exactly what degree of privacy was envisaged is not clear, but considerable enlargement of the existing buildings was found necessary. The Collegiate School had occupied the northern part of the present School House, including what was till 1965 the Headmaster's house, with a corresponding gabled wing to the south, which appears to have been a chapel and was surmounted by a cupola. The style was Victorian Gothic, with an abundance of stone mullions. The architect who was employed to make the alterations, Mr Jasper Cowell, replaced the chapel by the present School House buildings, comprising a schoolroom and dining-hall. (The former came to be known after the 1914–1918 war as the S.H. Common Room: it is now the Senior Common Room, and the former dining-hall is the Junior Common Room.) He left the northern part of the buildings more or less intact: thus the northern part of the present School House block is recognizably the old Collegiate School, while the southern part, dating from 1868, was built in a style to harmonize with it.

The alterations cost some £3,250, and provided accommodation for about one hundred boarders. At the same time the drive was constructed, giving access to the School from the main Hadham Road, in addition to the entrance in Maze Green Road (or 'The Lane' as it was still called as late as the 1920's), which had been the only entrance to the Collegiate School.

Incidentally it may be of interest to note that from the seventeenth century Maze Green Road had been known as Pest House Lane: the field where Grimwade House, Alliott House and R.P.H. now stand is marked on a tithe-map of 1829 as Pest House Pasture. No doubt there was hereabouts some kind of lazar-house which in times of plague was used as an isolation hospital (several local outbreaks of the plague are mentioned in the Parish Records of St Michael's Church). The same map marks the field just west of Colman Field as Maze Green Field, and this name has superseded that of Pest House Lane for the road leading from the School to the playing-fields.

The Nonconformist Grammar School was formally inaugurated on 23rd September 1868. The Rev. T. Binney, minister of the King's Weigh House, London, and a former chairman of the Congregational Union, said in his inaugural address that they were opening not a mere day school nor a small private boarding school, but a public school, one which it was hoped would one day be filled by large numbers of boys. After the ceremony the company, some two hundred in number, repaired to the topmost dormitory which had been converted into a dining-hall for the occasion, and 'partook of a cold collation'. After the meal the Rev. W. Cuthbertson, in proposing the health of the new School, said that for many months his life and thoughts had been mainly occupied with this School. Those who had worked for its foundation wished not only to take a public part in the great question of higher education, but also to benefit a special class, namely the ministers of the Eastern Counties. They saw, painful though it was to mention, that in a great many instances parents who were by nature and feeling ladies and gentlemen and were expected to maintain a fair social position, were in fact unable, without outside help, to give their children anything higher than what would now be called a primary school education. The idea of sending them to a boarding school, except with the help of some friend, was impossible. For such boys he advocated the founding of special scholarships, and suggested that the sons of ministers might be admitted at half the normal fees in the proportion of one to ten of those paying full fees. He therefore appealed to his friends in the ministry to tell their friends that their children would get a thorough education at Bishop's Stortford, where it was intended to make the School a 'Nonconformist Rugby'. He added that if it had not been for Mr Edward Grimwade, the first chairman of Directors, the School would never have been founded.

After the toast of H.M. the Queen had been drunk, and then that of the chairman, Mr Binney, the latter proposed 'prosperity to the School'. In his reply the Rev. W. Cuthbertson read a letter of good wishes from the Rev. Dr George Smith, the honorary secretary of Mill Hill School; after which he proposed the health of the Rev. Richard Alliott and Mr Esam. Mr Alliott, responding to the toast, said that as a pupil of a public school and an alumnus of the University of Cambridge, it had always been his feeling, ever since he began to think about the position of Nonconformists in this country, that the real way in which to carry on their fight was by cultivating the best boys and sending them on to the higher seats of learning, there to show the country that they were as good as the rest of the world. And then, as a matter of course, all bitterness having passed away, when they and their brethren in the Church of England got to know one another, there would be that glorious state of religious and political liberty and friendship so much to be desired. In his opinion, Nonconformity did not for one moment mean sectarianism. While they protested against the sectarianism prevailing in many public schools, they must take care lest any should exist on their own part. He rejoiced that some of their boys were sons of Church of England parents, and hoped that their number might be very much multiplied. All they desired was to take that which was the foundation of the belief of every body of Christians and teach the gospel of Christ in all its simplicity. A great many hard words had been said against the Classics—and no wonder; for some people had come to think that the whole scheme of education in past years had been wrong, and that a new way must be introduced if they were to realize what men might be. His own opinion, however, was that the classical was the best education for turning a boy into a man and qualifying him to act in all circumstances. Whilst making use of English grammar, French and German were also essential to the very idea of a grammar school—to the teaching of grammar and the analysis and philosophy of language. Taking these with Latin and Greek, they had the most philosophical grammar to be found, which would help them to understand their own English language; reading and writing were of course the first things in a lad's educational growth, and history too was a very important branch of study.

This was a public school, and Mr Binney had referred to some of the objections that were raised against schools of that class. He himself, while at Cambridge, found that the men most easily led astray were men who had not been at a public school: the real, solid, substantial morality of the university lay with the Rugby men and with those coming from public schools where there was a good tone of morality in the school itself.

It has been thought advisable to quote extensively from the report of Mr Alliott's speech on this, his first public appearance at Stortford, as it throws some light on the ideals and ambitions with which he entered upon his thirty-one years as the Headmaster and the virtual founder of the School. He could be described as a militant Nonconformist, but it must be remembered that he lived in a period when all Nonconformists worthy of the name were militant. He had been the only Nonconformist at Bedford Grammar School amongst a hundred boys, and at Cambridge had been one of a very small minority of Nonconformist undergraduates. But he had many friends amongst members of the Church of England, and, for all his Nonconformity and radicalism, he was essentially a broad-minded man. It must also be remembered that it was not until three years after the foundation of the School that, in 1871, Gladstone's first government passed the Act of Parliament which abolished the disabilities under which Nonconformists laboured at Oxford and Cambridge.

A prospectus inserted in the *Bishop's Stortford Advertiser* in the early days of the new school reads as follows: 'The distinctive object of this School is to provide a liberal and at the same time religious education. The general course of instruction embraces the Classics and Mathematics; the ordinary studies of an English education; and the French and German languages. Three exhibitions of £15 per annum, tenable for two years, are awarded to boys who, before the age of sixteen, have taken a first class in the non-Gremial [i.e. external] examinations at the University of Cambridge. It is intended also to found an Exhibition of £20 per annum, tenable for two years by a pupil proceeding to the University of Cambridge.

'The domestic arrangements are very complete and under the care of an efficient matron. The situation is most healthy, there is a large playground, and the pupils are regularly drilled.

'For every ten boarders one pupil, being the son of a Dissenting Minister labouring in the Eastern Counties, is by the appointment of the Directors received at half fees. Every pupil must be nominated by a shareholder of the Company.' The fees were, for boarders, thirty-five to forty-five guineas per annum, according to the pupil's age, and for day pupils, eight to twelve guineas: a notice was added to the effect that the fees for boarders would not be increased during their stay at the School.

2. Richard Alliott and the N.G.S.: 1868–1899

THERE is a regrettable lack of information about the first eighteen years of the N.G.S. (1868–86). The minutes of the meetings of Directors, together with a great mass of documents connected with the early years of the School, were stored in the London office of Sir Robert Pearce M.P., who had been the first Secretary of the Board, and were totally destroyed with that office by enemy action during the war of 1939–1945. There was no school magazine until May 1886; but from that date we have a continuous record of the life of the School, first under the title of the *N.G.S.* ('being the journal of Past and Present Members of the Nonconformist Grammar School, Bishop's Stortford') and, after March 1902, under that of the *Stortfordian*.

The School numbers grew in the first five years from 40 (17 boarders and 23 day boys) to 103, and by 1877 they were 131. In the latter part of Alliott's time and during the first years of the present century they tended to decline; but from 1910 they increased rapidly, reaching 279 by 1919.[1] For the first year or two there was an additional boarding house under Mr Esam: this was in the house of the former headmaster of the Collegiate School, opposite the Wheatsheaf in Rye Street. It is not clear why this extra house was needed, as the school was at first by no means full; but it was presumably acquired with the rest of the Collegiate School buildings, and was no doubt useful while the Hadham Road buildings were being enlarged. (After 1869 this house became the East of England Nonconformist Girls' School, under the same directorate as the N.G.S.; but before long that school was moved to other premises.)

In 1875 certain additions costing some £2,390 were made to the old premises. The north wing of the School House was extended by the

[1] The exact figures were: 1910—135; 1912—155; 1914—197; 1916—216; 1918—240; 1919—279. (After the first year, boarders always outnumbered day boys.) See also p. 196 for later figures.

building of new kitchens, and of the 'E' dormitory on the floor above the present needle-room: there were now 118 boarders, so that a fifth dormitory was an imperative necessity. (The 'E' dormitory later became the School House 'infirmary' or sick-room.) Also the so-called Racquet Court block was built adjacent to the School House, comprising three classrooms (one serving also as a library), the 'old' laboratory (later the School House changing-room, and now housing the showers and hot baths), a masters' common room and six boys' studies; together with a 'tuck-shop', consisting simply of a couple of cupboards from which monitors served out tuck over their shoulders to the surging crowds of waiting boys. Finally, a foot-racquets court was built on the south side of the new block. This is the block which now houses the Headmaster's study, the administrative offices and the School House changing-room extension. At the same time the old Box Room, a large wooden structure (now the Art Room), was erected in its first position, which was opposite the schoolroom on the south side of the playground, at the north-east corner of what is now called 'Middle Green'. According to another account, however, it was bought from the Commissioners of the Great Exhibition in Hyde Park after 1851. If that be true, it must have been purchased by the Collegiate School when it moved to the present school site in 1852; in which case its original position may or may not have been that indicated here. The Box Room was the only gymnasium the School had until the Leo Price Gymnasium was built in 1957; and from 1883 it also housed the Carpenter's Shop, which was largely fitted up by the boys themselves. It was indeed used for many purposes: throughout Alliott's time, for instance, the Prize Day luncheon was always held in the Box Room. It was also at times used as a recreation room, and was often called the Play Room. In 1894 the Box Room was moved farther west to its second position, opposite the (later) New Classroom Block. Meanwhile in 1883 an Infirmary was formed from a house on the north-east border of the school grounds, later to become Elgar House: it was referred to as 'The Hospital'.

In 1888 the Cinder Track round the Old Field (now called Lower Green) was completed, having evidently taken some years to make, owing chiefly to a shortage of cinders! The ashes from the school fires, augmented by the gift of an occasional load from some friend of the School, had not been enough to finish the task, but in this year an anonymous donor provided all the ashes that were required, and load after load was brought up to the School. The boys, under the watchful eye of Mark Matthews, the gardener (known as 'Jumbo'), did most of the work themselves, excavating and removing the earth, filling in with clinker and cinders, ramming them down and rolling the track. Thanks to the free cinders and free labour, the only cost involved was that of cartage: this was considerable, and at the end of the summer term two concerts were given in the schoolroom, to which friends of the School were invited, a small charge being made for tickets in order to defray this inevitable expense. 'When completed', reported the *N.G.S.*, 'it will be a great improvement on the ordinary grass course, and will be at all times a delightful promenade.' Later generations may remember it more poignantly as an instrument of punishment, when they were sentenced for some misdemeanour to 'twenty tracks'.

In 1889 the School was presented with the sundial (on the south side of School House), by C. P. Bartholomew, an Old Boy of the School: this has additional interest in that it was the work of his own hands. It was on this occasion that a distinguished visitor is said to have produced the time-honoured translation of the motto on the sundial *Soli Deo Gloria*, 'Glory be to the sun-god'! And indeed this mistranslation almost seemed to be countenanced by the *N.G.S.*, which always bore on its cover the words of the motto encircled by what would heraldically be called a 'sun-in-splendour'.

The last addition to the buildings during Alliott's headmastership was the indoor swimming-bath, built in 1895. The opening of the new bath on 9th April 1895 was a great day in the history of the School. It was preceded by athletic sports in the school grounds and aquatic sports in the bath, followed by a water-polo match. The company then adjourned to the schoolroom, where Sir Walter Gilbey performed the opening ceremony. It is believed that at this time only one other school in the country had an indoor heated swimming-bath.

The new bath, which cost something in the region of £5,000, was an immense addition to the athletic life and amenities of the School. Before it was built, swimming was possible only in the summer term, in a part of the River Stort near the cattle-market that had been railed off as a town swimming-pool: here such things as broken glass bottles would be found at times on the muddy bottom, with grave danger to the bathers' feet. Now, with a heated bath under cover, it was possible to bathe the whole year round, and the swimming standard of the boys improved greatly as a result.

In Alliott's time Association Football only was played, the Rugby game not being introduced until F. S. Young's headmastership. But in the very early days a curious game appears to have been popular, with very few rules, that was something of a hybrid between the two codes. An article by an anonymous O.S. written in 1886 gives some interesting details which he himself got from one who was at the

School from 1868 to 1871. There were no matches during those early days, except some very fierce encounters between Boarders and Day Boys, in which the latter generally came off second-best. Sides were chosen, and the ball started by 'huge kicks', followed up immediately by both sides in a heap, like a pack of wolves. Set places in the field were undreamed of, go-as-you-please being the order of the day: charging was of course freely indulged in, and carrying the ball was also allowed, though the carrier might be hacked *ad lib.* by his opponents. The ball might be fisted to any extent, and if it was fairly caught the catcher was allowed a 'free place kick' on the spot.

From 1871 to 1876 there is singularly little evidence available, though there is no doubt that there was a 'fifteen' during those years, and that matches were played; but against whom and with what result is not known. The writer records that on two occasions in 1877 he 'kept goal for the fifteen', and refers to 'the painful record of the only Rugby match the School ever undertook', against the Leys School, Cambridge. In 1878 the team still numbered fifteen, and definite places had been allotted to two backs and one half-back, the forwards still pursuing the old go-as-you-please policy. 'In one match at Ware, finding that the opposing team were in some doubt whether we were going to play according to Rugby or Association rules, we naturally decided on the latter, though we had to be content with a Rugby ball. The result was a victory for the School by one goal to nil, after a close and somewhat amusing game.'

These early peculiarities of Stortford football are not surprising when one remembers that long after 1823 (the date when 'William Webb Ellis, with a fine disregard for the rules of the game, first picked up the ball and ran with it', thus instituting the distinctive feature of Rugby football), it was still customary at Rugby School, as we read in *Tom Brown's Schooldays*, to play with very large sides—as many as fifty or more; it was only with the formation of the Rugby Union in 1871 that the modern rules were drawn up and imposed on all playing the game.[1]

By 1886 it is plain that the School had settled down to orthodox Association Football: it is mentioned then as an innovation that 'we have played three half-backs during this season'. But in the meanwhile, as early as 1879, the new 'passing' style of play had been introduced in a match against Saffron Walden; it was taken up and practised ardently, to such effect that in the following season the school team's record was:

[1] Rugger teams were originally composed of 22 players, then 20, and were finally stabilized at 15 in the 1876–7 season. It was not until 1890 that the present division of the team into 8 forwards and 7 backs was officially adopted.

matches played 13, won 11, drawn 2, lost 0; goals for 36, goals against 6. The captain of this remarkable team was W. B. Hayward, afterwards headmaster of the School for the Sons of Missionaries, Blackheath:[1] it was during his captaincy that school colours were first instituted for football. All matches at this time were still played on Old Field: indeed, the 'New' Field (now Middle and Upper Greens) was not levelled until 1896–7.[2]

In cricket the appointment of Sam Clarke as cricket 'pro' in 1886 had led to great improvements in the standard of play. Sam was the pro at the famous Rickling Green Cricket Club, one of the oldest in the country: himself an All England player, he was evidently an excellent coach. He soon became as much of a school 'character' as Mark Matthews, with his continual exhortation to 'keep them shoulders open!' Before his time Joe Silcock, the pro at the Stortford town club, had helped to coach the N.G.S. as well. And when Sam Clarke left he was succeeded by J. Jones, who had followed Silcock as pro at the town club.

The summer of 1890 saw the beginning of what has since become an outstanding feature of Stortford cricket, the organization of the first 'Past and Present' matches by C. D. Whittaker. It was originally intended to arrange an Old Stortfordians' cricket tour, but owing to the difficulty of raising a full team of O.S., members of the school team were invited to join. The first match was arranged for Whit-Tuesday, in order to secure the help of the Old Boys who had come down to play the annual match against the School on the Monday: the Past and Present played a strong eleven from the Stortford town club. On 23rd July, the day after Prize Day, a similar fixture was arranged against Moor Hall, away: and another away match on the following day against Sheerness town club, where R. H. Brightman O.S. was the leading spirit.

Meanwhile in 1880 a handful of Old Stortfordians had met in Cheapside under the chairmanship of H. M. Livens and established the Old Stortfordians' Club: meetings were to be held monthly, and the subscription was fixed at the modest sum of half a crown a year. A. E. Turberville was appointed honorary secretary—an office which he held and magnified for so many years thereafter; and in due course the Rev. R. Alliott became president, remaining in office until his death in 1899. The early efforts of the Club were far from adventurous, and for some time to come the meetings were confined to discussions of such time-

[1] The S.S.M. moved from Blackheath to Eltham in 1912, and is now known as Eltham College.

[2] The first *cricket* match recorded as played on New Field was in 1903.

honoured subjects of youthful contention as Darwinism, the Theatre, or the Habit of Smoking. With the arrival of the Donnison brothers, music began to play a welcome part at the Club meetings; and finally came the annual dinners, which were first held at the King's Head Tavern in Fenchurch Street.

Incidentally it was A. E. Turberville who in 1888 was the leading spirit in enlisting a number of other Old Stortfordians to establish a series of evening classes at Vere Street Board School, near Covent Garden. In spite of the provision of compulsory elementary education a few years before, it was felt that many elementary school children soon lapsed into complete illiteracy; and this movement was an attempt to provide, for children in the more poverty-stricken districts of London, further education in a form that it was hoped would be attractive. From a progress report in the following year it is clear that certain difficulties were encountered: '... perhaps there are half a dozen quiet and orderly boys among the attendants at Vere Street, but for the most part they are dirty, rough, and very ill-behaved; though there is a marked improvement in manners and discipline since the opening, which is very encouraging'.

Unfortunately, before this work had gone on for a full two years it was brought to a stop, as the Vere Street schoolroom was no longer available. But it inspired an interest in philanthropic work which the School has maintained ever since. For instance, in 1893 Dr W. S. Colman O.S. appealed in the *N.G.S.* for help in a case of great poverty and hardship in connection with his work at the Children's Hospital at Great Ormond Street. Later, in F. S. Young's time, came the School's close connection with the Claremont Central Mission: the expeditions organized by H. L. Price to the depressed mining areas in South Wales and elsewhere in the thirties: and, more recently, the encouragement by P. W. Rowe of various types of social service locally.

It was about this time (1891) that the 'A' and 'B' dormitories were fitted with fire-escapes, there having previously been apparently no precautions against fire in the School House. When the fire-alarm was sounded the first boys had to make their perilous way down the vertical canvas tube by holding out their elbows and knees, much as a rock climber descends a 'chimney': they would then hold out the escape tube at an angle to facilitate the descent of the other boys. On one occasion at a later date, the canvas of one of the tubes split and a boy fell to the ground from a considerable height: fortunately no serious injury was sustained, but in future fire-drill practices boys were told to remove their boots before descending, lest some protruding nail should split the canvas again.

In 1886, as has been mentioned, the first number of the *N.G.S.* appeared: the magazine would seem to have been edited at first by Alliott himself, assisted by C. D. Whittaker, who later took over the whole burden of production. In an article in this first number headed 'Notes on Work', we find a reference to a revival of interest in shorthand (shown by the verbatim reports made of Sunday sermons in the Congregational Church!). The study of electricity and chemistry was increasing amongst the senior boys; and it is interesting to find that, already at this early date, the enthusiasm for natural history which has always been characteristic of the School was being encouraged by the offer from Richard Brightman O.S. of a prize for the best calendar for the month of June containing observations on the fauna and flora of the neighbourhood. In the account of the athletic sports of that year (1886) we find that a boy who was to become one of the greatest Stortfordian figures, F. S. Young, won the junior long jump and high jump. (He also competed in the bicycle race one and a half miles open handicap, but although he received 375 yards he was not placed!) An event that appeared for the first time this year was 'Dribbling the Football'. Later we find references in the *N.G.S.* to the award of a Good Conduct prize instituted by Alliott: the successful candidate was chosen by a vote of the whole School, presumably by a secret ballot. But this prize was abolished by F. S. Young soon after he became headmaster, on the very reasonable ground that it amounted to nothing but a popularity prize, and nearly always went to the boy who was most successful at cricket or football or some other form of athletics.

Some light is thrown on the academic life of the School in these early days by the annual reports issued to the shareholders of the East of England Nonconformist Schools Association. In the 1870 report we read that 'boys are given a general course of education which embraces instruction in Greek, Latin, French, German and English Languages, Writing, Arithmetic, Mathematics, Natural Philosophy, History and Geography. The fees are from 35 to 45 guineas, and the only extras are books and stationery 10*s* 6*d*, and washing, one guinea per term. At the close of the Summer term the whole School is examined by Gentlemen of ascertained Scholarship, and Prizes are awarded according to the merits of the pupils'. In 1873 we read of the institution of several valuable scholarships: in 1876 there are references to the new buildings of the previous year (also to 'a large Play Shed 80 ft long by 60 ft wide'—presumably the old Box Room already referred to). In this year the shareholders were, no doubt, pleased to learn that the number of boys had risen to 129, and that 'the Board again had the pleasure of recommending the declaration of a Dividend of £5 per

Growth of School House

The earliest stage, the Collegiate School in 1852: ground floor and one wing only of the future N.G.S. Headmaster's House.

The Collegiate School in 1860. The extra wing and storeys form the future N.G.S. Headmaster's House.

Another view, taken before 1860. The wing on the left of the 'Headmaster's House' can be seen to cover the area which in 1868 became the Dining Hall and 'C' Dormitory wing of School House. The white building on the right is Westfield House, later the Sanatorium, now Sutton House.

Taken about 1875. This shows not only School House and the Headmaster's House but also the old Box Room (later the Gym and now the Art Room) in its original position parallel to School House, and the Oak, rather more youthful looking than now.

REV. R. ALLIOTT, Headmaster 1868–1899.

F. S. YOUNG, Headmaster 1900–31.

SCHOOL HOUSE as from 1868.

1st XI CRICKET, 1890. Mark Matthews (groundsman), S. B. Gray, G. L. Moore, S. B. Watts, A. B. Edwards, F. H. Wilson, Sam Clarke (professional). *Sitting:* F. S. Young, H. R. Newport (Capt.), N. C. Goody. *In front:* G. B. Newport, S. E. Pamphilon, T. L. Partridge.

1st XI FOOTBALL, 1891–2. F. M. Kingdon, A. H. Windsor (Master), J. A. Alliott, A. H. Blandford (Master), S. E. Pamphilon. *Sitting:* R. J. Armes, F. H. Wilson (Capt.), G. B. Newport. *In front:* W. Moore, C. E. Deakin, R. L. Armes.

Mr C. D. Whittaker in the first Science Laboratory in 1892. This, later the School House Changing Room, is now occupied by the Showers.

Mr A. H. Blandford, 1892, in the classroom later kno as 'The Vestry' and now the Bursar's Office.

School House Dining Hall in 1892: taken from the dais looking towards the serving-hatch and the jam cupboard. This is now the Junior Common Room.

The Schoolroom (now the Senior Common Roon in 1892, looking towards what later became the Allic Memorial Library.

THE STAFF, 1894. F. M. Kingdon, F. R. Robert, F. Esslinger, A. H. Windsor, C. D. Whittaker. *Sitting:* R. Alliott, Mrs Spencer, W. Owen, Mrs Alliott, Mrs Schaeffer (the Matron). Mrs Spencer taught the piano.

THE ALLIOTT MEMORIAL LIBRARY. In 1933 this was enlarged, and the fireplace and bust of Mr Alliott were moved to the opposite end, opening up the present window.

THE FIRST PREPARATORY SCHOOL, Newbury House, Hadham Road. This photograph was taken just before demolition in 1967.

THE FIRST PREPARATORY SCHOOL GROUP, 1902. *Back row:* S. Kirkby, T. J. Mason, L. R. Harrison, C. Harrison, R. Dennis. *Next row:* P. W. Day, J. W. Strong, E. W. T. Cossar, S. G. Stephenson, E. L. Stephenson, E. G. Theed, S. A. Milbank. *Sitting and standing:* A. A. Pryer, S. L. Hocken, Mr E. W. Hurst, W. Edwards, G. J. Clarkson. *Front row:* R. D. Holland, H. E. Dodd, E. A. Dothie, G. W. Hocken, R. C. Williams.

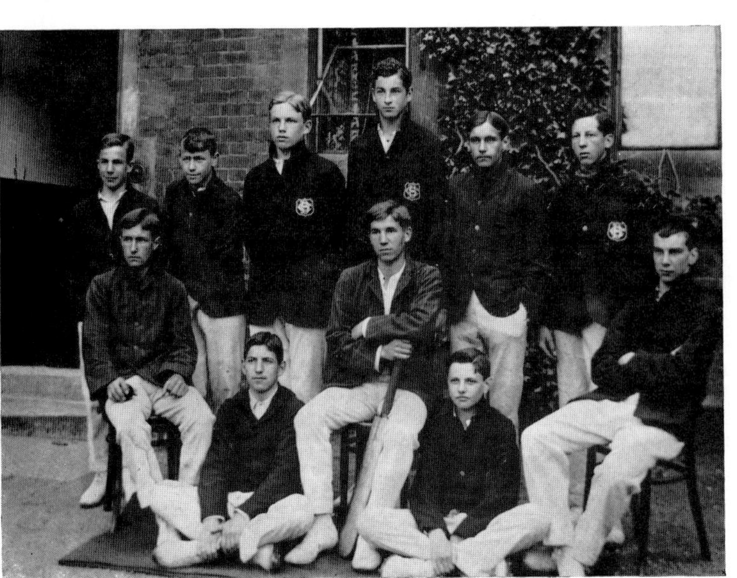

1st XI CRICKET, 1906. L. S. Palmer, N. M. Hadfield, E. A. Dudeney, D. V. Mirams, A. T. L. Grear, G. D. Read. *Sitting:* T. L. Owen, F. M. Cheshire (Capt.), W. Simpson. *On ground:* C. H. Edwards, A. Anderson.

THE MASTERS, 1903. C. S. Colman, R. L. S. Ager, F. B. Shawe, L. Moonen, F. G. M. Ogbourne, H. Kitchener. *Sitting:* F. M. Kingdon, E. W. Hurst, F. S. Young, C. Moser, A. W. Tristram.

THE MONITORS, 1903. F. M. Cheshire, H. S. Tee, C. Mellows, E. H. Colman, L. Radbourne, R. J. Stephenson. *Sitting:* W. G. Greig, J. Morley, Mr F. S. Young, O. A. Lee.

THE OLD RACQUETS COURT in use in 1892. The small building on the left, the Tuck-shop, formed, along with the buttress, the only side wall. The view of the sky beyond the Tuck-shop is a reminder that the Swimming Bath had not yet been built.

THE CHEMISTRY LAB, part of the new Science Laboratories, opened in 1901.

THE NEW FIELD. A 2nd XI game in progress, early 1900's.

cent. per annum for the past year'. And a new extra appears in the form of Pew Rent. Two years later the names of seven masters are given, in addition to the headmaster. In 1884 a personal appeal was circulated by the chairman, Mr Edward Grimwade, to pastors of Nonconformist Churches, urging them to bring the School to the notice of their congregations. 'We are continually meeting with the most ample and gratifying evidence', he writes, 'of the moral and Christian influence of the School, in the number of young men who received their education there and are now active and useful members of our churches.'

Mr Grimwade, as already mentioned, was chairman of the Board of Directors of the School from its foundation, and held that office till his death in 1886. He was succeeded as chairman by his son, Mr Edward W. Grimwade, J.P., of Croydon who continued to preside over the destinies of the School for many years. Another member of the Board for some time was Dr Henry Cribb, who was medical officer to the School from its foundation till his death in 1890. In spite of a busy general practice he was unremitting in his attendance at the School, where he was very popular with the boys. His portrait in oils (by Herbert Hampton O.S.) hung for many years on the wall of the School House dining-room, together with those of other friends and benefactors of the School, such as E. W. Grimwade, Senior, Mr Johns, Mr Nicholas and Mr Beldam; also one of an eminent Nonconformist divine who had no connection with the School whatever, but whose nobility of countenance was likely, in Mr Alliott's judgment, to have an edifying effect upon the boys. Incidentally other Old Stortfordians in addition to H. Hampton who were exhibiting at the Royal Academy about this time (1890 and the following years) were H. M. Livens, H. Trevor Haddon and J. R. K. Duff.

At the School the outstanding figure, next to Alliott himself, was C. D. Whittaker, who was on the staff from 1885 till 1899 and, particularly during the latter part of Alliott's headmastership, very largely ran the School. Of him, C. B. Young (brother of F. S. Young), who was at Stortford from 1894 to 1899 (and later, at Oxford, had the distinction of beating William Temple in competition for the Denyer and Johnson Theological Scholarship), writes as follows: 'Alliott was past his best when I was at Stortford, and the inner life of the school was mainly run by C. D. Whittaker: in my last years I believe he was the mainstay and prop of the School. At least it was Whittaker who counted most with us, and whom we got to know and rely on. Not even the monitors got really to know Alliott, and no one, monitor or master, dreamed of reporting things to him. But in spite of this, Whittaker was devoted to him: he followed him about the grounds like a faithful dog, often retreating with its tail between its legs when rebuked. Whittaker alone, as senior master, had a private bed-sitting room: here he used to ask senior monitors in and discuss with us boys' problems and behaviour while regaling us with fruit. I owe a very great deal to him for his kindness and instruction and his advice on ethical and religious matters.'

Another O.S., A. B. Day (1890–8), writes of him: 'Whittaker had no need to exert discipline—one look at him was enough for the toughest boy. He had a habit of flipping his hand at any adjacent surface and then sucking it: this was the explanation of his nick-name "Flip": he was also called "Flabby" in reference to his obesity.'

Finally, F. S. Young (1881–90) spoke thus of him at the prize-giving in 1899, on the occasion of Whittaker's appointment to the headmastership of Taunton School: 'For fifteen years he gave himself up to working for Stortford and everything connected with it. To say what he did for this school would be to enumerate everything a master could do and more. One thing, however, I should like to mention—the way in which he developed that harmony and affection between masters and boys which I have always thought characteristic of Stortford, as it should be of every school whose spirit is right: for only as masters and boys work with one heart can true training be given.' Whittaker, it may be added here, was headmaster of Taunton for twenty-three years, and indeed was best known to the general public for his splendid work in building up that school. On his retirement in 1922, he became president of the Baptist College, Bristol, where he remained for two years: he died in 1925.[1]

Meanwhile other staff came and went, but one figure was familiar to many generations of boys—that of Mrs Schaeffer, the matron, who came to the N.G.S. in 1873. She was a German widow from Heidelberg, and her sitting-room was full of pictures, ornaments and knick-knacks from Germany: here she used to give Sunday parties for groups of senior boys, at which she made earnest attempts to draw them out in conversation and encourage them in the minor social virtues, such as singing a solo in public. (Her daughter married an O.S., Dr Howard Champ, after whose comparatively early death Mrs Champ succeeded her mother in the office of Matron in School House, on the latter's retirement in 1902.) Mrs Schaeffer was an admirable matron, completely devoted to the School. Under her was Miss Winter, the needlewoman, who not only looked after the mending of the boys' clothes, but also nursed ill boys in the sick-room, which communicated with her

[1] A brass plate to the memory of C. D. Whittaker may be seen in the Memorial Hall, inscribed 'Huic domo valde amicus'.

own little parlour. It is worth noting that in 1898 Mrs Schaeffer had held her post for twenty-five years and Miss Winter hers for eighteen: while George Mitchell, the school butler, had been there for twenty-six years, and Mark Matthews, groundsman and gardener and general factotum, for over twenty. But of these two we shall have more to say later.

In 1888 we find Alliott forbidding bird's-nesting—on the ground apparently that a school of boys let loose upon the land would be an intolerable nuisance to farmers, rather than from any humane considerations; he felt that the faculty of observation could be equally well sharpened by an interest in botany, geology and not least meteorology. By the generosity of Mr Samuel Young of Harlow (father of F. S., G. H. and C. B. Young) the School was provided with all the instruments, duly certified at Kew, necessary for a meteorological station. These were housed in a wired-in enclosure on the edge of the Cinder Track, near the drive: it was known as 'The Meat Cage', and for many years it was the duty of the monitors, in rotation, to enter up the readings every day, to be read out at prayers. It was, however, removed in 1924.

In 1893 the Old Stortfordians' Club held a special social meeting to which all boys then at the School were invited, to mark the completion of Alliott's twenty-five years as headmaster. The Armfield's Hotel in South Place, Finsbury, the usual rendezvous of the Club's annual meeting in those days, was far too small for this occasion, and the gathering was held in the Memorial Hall, Farringdon Street. After Mr Grimwade had made a presentation, A. E. Turberville as secretary of the Club read the text of an illuminated address from the Old Boys, expressing their loyalty and affection for him, their appreciation of what he had done for the School, and their good wishes for his future happiness. Alliott's speech in reply revealed so much of his personality that it is worth recording some part of it. His life at Bishop's Stortford, he said, and the disappointment he had been to himself over and over again, had turned him from a light-hearted, careless man into a very sober-minded one indeed. He had reproached himself times out of mind for the little facility he had found in himself for working with other men and putting generous interpretations upon their words and deeds, and also for what he thought was the schoolmaster's great sin, that of impatience and injustice. Yet one could not admit that life had been altogether a failure when one encountered a gathering like the present one. He knew of nothing more precious in the world to schoolmasters than the esteem of young men who had been their pupils. No humbug could stand under the scrutiny of children, and any schoolmaster who tried to represent himself as something he was not might be certain that he would be found out and measured for what he was worth. It was a great thing if, after the measurement had come, respect remained: he thanked God for it, for it was an unspeakable possession.

In 1895 Alliott was successful in getting the N.G.S. registered by the Joint Boards of the Royal College of Physicians and the Royal College of Surgeons, as a recognized school for the study of chemistry and physics—an important event for boys wishing to enter the professions of medicine or dentistry.

There is no doubt that in Alliott's later years advancing age, the heavy strains of his office and a serious attack of typhoid fever in 1896 exaggerated his eccentricities and to some extent diminished his vigour. In the spring term of 1897, on his doctor's advice, he went with Mrs Alliott on a tour in South Africa, leaving Mr Whittaker in charge; but by the summer term he was back at his post. It was obvious during these last years that he was not a fit man; none the less his death in October 1899, at the age of sixty, came as a great shock to all connected with the School. It is difficult after the lapse of years to know how great a headmaster Richard Alliott was. Those who were his contemporaries at Cambridge and those who knew him in his prime spoke of his vivacity, his infectious high spirits, his wonderful drive. He was frank and outspoken, open as the day both in his likes and dislikes. Always easily moved to a white heat of indignation by anything that he regarded as mean or deceitful, he appears to have been unwilling to employ corporal punishment himself, but would enforce corporate responsibility by punishing the whole school for the misdeeds of one boy. But, while he was as much imbued as Thomas Arnold with the ideal of making boys into Christian gentlemen, he did not rely to the same extent as Arnold had done at Rugby on the co-operation of the sixth form or the monitors in maintaining a good tone in the school. Yet, by whatever methods he achieved it, he did succeed in securing a good moral atmosphere at Bishop's Stortford.

Such first-hand information as is available about his attributes as a headmaster inevitably comes mainly from those who only knew him in his later years. But C. D. Whittaker, who worked under him, as we have seen, in a close and intimate relationship until shortly before Alliott's death, wrote an obituary notice of him which is worth quoting here. 'When a man of the loftiest ideals and of unrivalled mental and physical strength, still in his prime but mellowed by experience, is devoting not the fair proportion of his power and vigour to the duties he has undertaken, but is rather daily sacrificing himself in his unwearied efforts to leave no wrong for a moment unrighted, and no ideal however lofty unstriven for, it is idle in the extreme to attempt to chronicle weeks and terms and years. He never for a moment all through his life's work paused to consider if a time had not come for the N.G.S. to rest satisfied with its laurels for a period. He never dreamed of sparing himself, and it was always an unsolved enigma to him that men could be found who could dream of sparing themselves. And so, as one looks back on the last fifteen years, one sees the smoke of constant battle for the right and hears the unceasing clash of arms fighting the good fight.'

C. S. Colman, who had been a boy under Alliott and for a short time had taught under him, wrote at the time of his death as follows: 'I remember very distinctly, only about a year ago, his sitting in his study and reading a letter which he had just received from a boy, thanking him for all that had been done for him while at school. "You have no idea", Mr Alliott said, "what a letter like that means to a headmaster. We scold and scold, for we have to scold; and perhaps one boy in twenty comes to know afterwards that we don't do it for scolding's sake, and would infinitely rather shut our eyes if it were not for the boy's own sake." But even as boys I think we realized the depth of his affection for us, and his sole desire to turn us out as honest workers and men who did right for its own sake, and not for fear of punishment or hope of reward. And we recognized also—none who knew him could ever fail to recognize—the absolute sincerity in every thought and deed, and the contempt for any shirking of a difficulty. He had become convinced that punishment of any kind for wrongdoing was a great mistake; for it seemed as it were to wipe out the wrong, whereas he felt that the only thing to be done was for the boy to acknowledge the error and fight for better things. Nothing in his view seemed small or insignificant, and tidiness in the schoolroom, thoroughness in play, and little points of orderliness were exalted in him by the dignity of the religion which entered into every part of his life. Only once in the last thirteen years of his headmastership was he compelled to expel a boy, and it grieved him sorely. As he said: "It is easy to run a school if you get rid of all the apparent failures, but a headmaster's business is to make them successes." And he never abandoned the attempt as hopeless.'

In these two obituaries one can sense the feeling of personal loss experienced by two very loyal disciples and colleagues; and under this emotion any weaknesses and foibles shown by the deceased were forgotten. To correct or rather to complete the picture, one must read what some of his Old Boys have written about him in lighter vein, as recorded in our next chapter. But meanwhile it is true to say, as his successor F. S. Young said of him: 'In the midst of his work he was cut off: he risked health, ease, everything, and laid down his life for the School he loved so well.'

3. Victorian Memories

It so happened that the end of the century, which marked the close of a period in our national history, was also an important turning point in the history of the School. It may therefore be of interest, before continuing the story of the School's development in the new century and under a new headmaster, to record at this point, by way of interlude, what a number of Old Boys of the School have jotted down when recalling memories of their Victorian schooldays.

One of the earliest Stortfordians was H. M. Livens, who came to the N.G.S. in 1869. (Later he became an artist of some distinction, whose work is to be found at the Tate Gallery and in other civic collections, both in England and abroad. He was a member of the International Society of Sculptors, Painters and Gravers.) Livens writes as follows of his schooldays: 'My father and mother brought me to the School, and as we drove up in the bus I caught sight of the two trees on the edge of the playing-field. The Oak and the Elm [1] have as much distinction almost as the School itself. Since that day the Elm has put on three score annual rings and mounts still: long may it live and magnify its place! It calls to mind a hard, bright winter's morning in my second term, with the snow deep on the ground. A common repugnance to being indoors that morning had possessed the whole school: we begged for a half-holiday in the snow, and got it on condition that we fought for it. Monster snowballs were soon being trundled over the field towards the Elm, around which they were built and shaped into walls: and so rose the snow fort, and within, piles of snowballs for ammunition. Then, under their respective captains, the opposing forces met in the joy of battle. Vigorous was the attack and stout the defence until, the ammunition of the defenders being spent, an armistice was called for reconditioning: the best part of this being the hot coffee sent out by good Mrs Brook, the Matron. Never was coffee more welcome—its

[1] See p. 101. Livens did not know the equally famous Walnut Tree, which, grown from a nut planted by Alliott in 1885, bore its first crop (two nuts) in 1896, amidst universal rejoicing, and is still in existence.

warmth and aroma come back once more. And so, change over to blows and shouting again.

'And then the Oak. I cannot stand under its wide-spreading branches without seeing the figure of a woman sitting beneath it—a large, reserved-looking woman in bonnet and shawl, with well-filled baskets of tuck before her. I take off my hat to Mrs Hardy ("Mother Hardy" she was to us), and I find myself munching one and then another of her delectable three-cornered puffs, crystalline, crumbling and warm from the oven.

'Richard Alliott, whom many of us learned to respect in terms of fear, nevertheless at first sight made an impression of kindliness on my mind which was never lost: his genial welcome to the smallest boy in the School, his rosy cheeks and rough hair won my heart.

'In the years that followed my half-holidays were a source of endless pleasure to me. We would go fishing in the river, finding caddis-worms in the mud and squeezing them out of their sheaths to bait our hooks: and then tramp back to school proud of our catch of sticklebacks and minnows. My imagination caught fire at their quaintness and beauty. Birchanger and Betts' Wood, too, were happy hunting-grounds: one's heart beat to a healthy tune when struggling up through the dense branches of a big fir tree to a sparrow-hawk's nest; when one found a shrike's "larder" on the blackthorn, or for the first time fingered the bronze eggs of a nightingale; or when by a lucky chance at a cricket match I was set to field just above a kingfisher's nest in the side of a brook. And what charm lay in the ingenious little nest of the golden crested wren, a creation of moss and down and cobweb hung on a fir branch, with its clutch of tiny, gold-besprinkled eggs.

'The bell used to ring us up at 6.30 a.m.—7.0 in winter; and it was a common occurrence for the whole school to turn out onto the landings shouting "Mitchell, no water!", for the supply for several years was defective. Assembled in the schoolroom with the door locked, all present answered "Adsum" to their names when called by the head boy. The hour's prep before breakfast was a dull, hungry, futile interval—it must long ago have disappeared from a more enlightened system. But the daily routine was of the grammar school type prevalent in those days, which seemed at pains to present to boys the dry side of education. What stuff that geography was, for instance! Marvellous that one's patriotism was not quenched outright at the fountain-head. Year in, year out, geography consisted of the repetition of columns of names of capes, rivers, countries, towns, and mountains. Happier hours were spent in learning good poetry, and I can remember many of the "pieces" I repeated in class. Towards the end of my schooldays we were allowed to nibble timidly at Shakespeare, like mice at cheese. The history of England was a delight, and what I learned before eleven has remained good ever since. Of science there was none: it was seven years after the opening of the School that a chemical "lab" was built and a classical scholar was set to amuse the upper forms by generating a few orthodox "stinks". My impression is that it was with the advent of Mr G. M. Hooker and Mr W. Field that mathematics began to get a grip, and Romans and even Greeks started rubbing their heavy eyes and wagging their dead tongues to a tune more alive than the rules of accidence and syntax!

'As might be expected, this drab system of education was not to be kept up to its stride without artificial stimulus. This took the form of impositions, which were distributed liberally in response to the irrepressible vices of talking and fooling: boys were told to stand out in the middle of the room or on the form. There they had to stay and write lines of prose, from fifty to five hundred or more. But the scribbling which this encouraged wrought havoc with the writing we had to practise in our copy-books: so in its place those arithmetical teasers known as "cubes" were introduced. They were heartily detested: and the riddle of the perfect imposition still proved evasive. So cubes came to be dropped in favour of drill: and Sergeant Cawdell was called in on a half-holiday to march the punishment squad up and down and round and round the playground for half-hours and hours as needed. In early days the cane too used to come to hand rather readily.

'As to games, in football we played soccer only, but with a team of fifteen. At matches the team wore blue velvet caps with gold button and tassel. Once or twice during the season the First XV challenged the whole school, seventy or eighty strong: it was a wild, cyclonic pandemonium, and the XV invariably won. Hockey was started one term, but as there were then no standard sticks, each boy hacked the biggest bludgeon he could find out of the hedge, and the game took on the features of a shindy: boys hobbled lame into school, with bruises and bandages about them. So hockey was vetoed from above. Of cricket in those days, I will only say that to be in the team to play a match at a distance was something to live for. We always drove to the field in a large wagonette drawn by four horses, usually greys, which were ridden by a couple of jockeys in white breeches and gaiters and Cambridge blue silk jackets and caps. Provided with long coaching-horns, we rallied the villages with musical blasts as we rattled through them, and set the horses and cattle galloping about the roadsides and fields.

'With no learned societies in the evenings to occupy our indoor leisure with experiment or discussion, with music or drama, we collected stamps and postcards, carved and polished cups and trinkets of coconut shell; and above all we played at knucklebones. This was a clever, agile game, played on the smooth surface of a blackboard with five lambs' knucklebones in a set: finger and eye were kept active by a great variety of manœuvres, as the pieces were picked up in order and tossed and caught in the air or swept up this way or that by the hand. But the game appears to have become extinct.[1]

'On the new boy's first night in the dormitory he was expected to sing a song, if not also to tell a tale. I well remember the musical effort of one small boy who has since risen to eminence in the public service:

> To market, to market to buy a fat hog:
> Home again, home again, jiggety jog,

which provoked rounds of applause and encores. If on the small side, the new boy might prove a convenient sample for tossing in a blanket. One thing he had to learn—that he must not snore: at the first symptom he would be violently shaken by his neighbour, and at the second offence his bed became the target for a concentration of slippers from all parts of the dormitory, which crashed against the wall over his head like bursting shells. Should he ever offend again by a single long-drawn, stertorous inhalation, a punitive squad crept from their beds, bolster in hand, and rained down upon him such a volley of blows that the snorer would rather lie awake till the dormitory master came up to bed than risk enduring it again.

'But the bolster is a weapon intended for nobler purposes: picture the scene with the gas lights turned up, a sentinel posted on the landing, the opposing forces with their captains ready on the open floor in the centre. At a signal the fight is joined: every boy finds his antagonist: round and round swing the bolsters: thud, thud, thud! they meet. Suddenly is heard the alarm "Cave! To your tents, O Israel!" There is a stampede of bare feet in all directions as the light is turned out. "What is all this noise about?" asks the stern figure standing in the doorway. But every boy is fast asleep, and the question remains unanswered.

'Suppers of contraband were shared with delight in the darkness, and included sardines, jam tarts and ginger beer. Or sloe gin . . . pocketsful of sloes were gathered from the blackthorn bushes, gashed and dropped into bottles, as much sugar as fruit added, and then gin, neat, up to the neck. The well-corked bottles were secretly stored in the play-boxes for their contents to mature. They did. The corks flew out not many days after, and the boxes on the shelves were dripping

[1] It was still being played some years after the last war.

with fiery spirits: but nobody was any the worse for it, as it all went down the gutter.

'It was perhaps a more rational inspiration that suggested the manufacture of blackberry jam. An empty nine-pound tin of the kind then used by Messrs Pink, the popular purveyors, was requisitioned for use as a preserving-pan. Filled to an inch of the brim with ripe, juicy fruit from the hedgerows, the vessel was suspended by a wire handle over the gas in the library: two boys standing on chairs held it patiently on a stick between them. It seemed to take a long time to come to the boil: but at last bubbles began to rise, when there was a cry of dismay—the whole cargo of spluttering jam was on the floor, and a ragged circle of crimson juice was spreading in all directions. The bottom of the pan had fallen out!

'At the end of term, peas were always to be seen in abundance, as they were ammunition for pea-shooters. These handy pocket weapons were carried by boys homeward-bound, to stimulate the activity of any biped or quadruped within range. Their disuse was due to an incident on the line: a sniper in the train, with greater skill than discretion, aimed a parting shot at a rubicund station-master on a wayside platform and hit him fairly in the face; so that he had to hold up the train while he let the passengers know what he thought about the outrage, and what the G.E.R. would think. And so they did: with the result that pea-shooters were no more to be seen in the hands of boys on the way home for the holidays.'

An Old Boy a few years junior to Livens writes of Alliott's desire always to hear the boys' side of any differences between them and the assistant masters. 'This led to the well-meant but, to my mind, demoralizing system of writing for Mr Alliott an account of any sin for which you had been entered in "The Book". The boy reported would take counsel with other scoundrels, and these worthies would concoct the most specious account their wits could supply. The results can be imagined: *suppressio veri* rapidly became a fine art. Let one example suffice in which, however, the naked truth could not be disguised. The two protagonists were a Mr Morley (who was very short-sighted) and one of the Sadd brothers. Mr Morley, as his nickname "Flaps" suggests, always wore a long frock-coat. One day Sadd, finding class work more than usually boring, amused himself by tying Mr Morley's coat-tails firmly behind the master's chair, which naturally, as the master rose, rose with him. Sadd, reported for this offence, was bidden to write his account of the incident. The offence was too flagrant and palpable to offer any chance of ingenious explanation, so Sadd wrote: "Dear Mr Alliott, I am sorry that it is quite true that I tied Mr Morley's tails behind his chair. All I can say is that I did it in a moment of abstraction—Your obedient pupil, Sadd." This letter, read out next morning to an amazed and slightly perplexed school, provided the text for one of the Old Man's most incisive "jaws".'

The Rev. J. W. Ewings, who was at school from 1875 to 1880, writes of the prominent school figures of those days. 'The School in my time was a small affair compared to what it is now. We had then only about 120–30 boys, and our buildings were limited to the School House and the Headmaster's house, the classrooms behind and the Box Room, just across the gravel playground. Easily first among the figures standing out in memory is that of the Headmaster, Richard Alliott. I seem to see him yet, coming into school with quick, firm step to take morning prayers; walking bare-headed about the playing-field; tending the roses in his garden; or linking his arm gently with some boy's, while he walked with him and talked to him. Another prominent figure in remembrance is that of Mrs Schaeffer. I can see her standing near the fire in the dining-room, presiding at the breakfast-table, noting the needs of any, and by a glance directing her maids. She had a gracious way of inviting now one, now another of the older boys to take tea with her on Sundays, and this was a privilege of which we were very proud. Her pretty sitting-room overlooking the quadrangle was the scene of some happy hours.

'Among the masters of that time many faces come back to me: Mr McIsaac, tall, warm-hearted Scotsman; Mr Legge, who taught me geography in the Cottage (afterwards the Hospital, and now known as Elgar House); M. Paul Rosselet, a fine runner as well as French teacher; and Herr Hermann Lutz, who taught me to swim in the old river-baths; not to speak of Sergeant Cawdell, the erect, imperious drill-master, or of Mr Willett the singing-master, who was also a great cricketer and who delighted us all by making 71 not out in an important match.

'One of the most unforgettable characters was Mitchell, the little serving-man. I remember him specially on bath nights, as he would confide to each boy his affectionate regard for him, accompanying his words with a gentle pinch of the skin of the neck; or on breaking-up nights, when in a high falsetto voice he would sing at the dining-room concert some rollicking song of the hour.

'Our football in those days was soccer, and our match ground Silver Leys. In Athletic Sports the hero was Furnivall, the England champion bicyclist (see pp. 30,31): I can still see the crowd on the cricket field as Furnivall mounted his high bicycle at scratch and set off to overhaul one by one the handicap riders. Cricket brings back some of my brightest Stortford memories: how we revered the first eleven! When they came home at night in a brake after a match at Waltham Abbey or the Leys School, with what eagerness we awaited the momentous news they brought, climbing the dormitory window-sills in night-shirts to learn the result! The summer term was my favourite, when we had cricket and fives and swimming, and sometimes long country walks; though the winter term ran it close when we had skating on Great Hallingbury Lake.'

P. S., who was at school in the eighties, wrote down his reminiscences in an article published in the *Stortfordian* of 1902: 'With a theme like that of the School, it is hard to know where to begin and where to leave off. Shall it be with the setting of the scene—the ivied red-brick buildings on the slope of a Hertfordshire hill, with the old oak tree and the elms and the larches, and the green fields all round, the rookery at the bottom of the playground, the rose garden by the drive, the wild grapes in the courtyard, the green lane running up by the side, the bats flitting round all the evening, and in the spring the nightingales in full song outside the study windows?[1] Do the bells of the village churches at Farnham and at Thorley and at Hallingbury still sound as sweetly on a Sunday afternoon, mingling with the tinkling of the sheep bells?

'One hears of many alterations, doubtless all for the better. Have you still got the Box Room, scene of yearly "cold collations" on Prize Days—not, alas! for the boys—and of many a football match with a tennis-ball for objective, and preferably Oxford and Cambridge for the sides? And the fives court—have you changed that? The writer seems to have played more cricket than fives on that court, with a hard india-rubber ball—one run into the shed, two if you hit the black wooden fence by the Box Room, and four (or was it six?) if you landed the ball on the grass by the oak tree. There were occasional hits (not occasional enough to suit the Headmaster) for "two-and-six", through the lower window of the schoolroom, until the authorities considerately placed wire-netting there, for the Old Man was always a sportsman.

'Of Mr Alliott himself I am not going to speak here; but it would ill befit a Stortfordian of the eighties to close without reference to those two indispensables, Mark Matthews and George Mitchell: Mark, the handyman, tiller of the ground and trundler of the wheelbarrow, good sportsman and cheerful companion. On occasion he indulged in cricket, and he yearly got up a team of his mates to meet and vanquish the local Total Abstinence Cricket Club, in which matches Mark, with a fine

[1] Nightingales still nested in 'the Lane' in the 1920's, and could be heard singing there as late as 1949.

scorn for abstinence, performed prodigies of valour with both bat and ball. And Mitchell, ever smiling, always clean and dapper, bearer of countless dinner plates, friend of master and boy alike: does he still venture undismayed "into the joys [*sic*] of death, into the mouth of hell" at the periodical concerts? If Mitchell appears at my next visit to Stortford, as he did at my last, ten years ago, all other changes will be forgiven.'

Of these two worthies we shall have more to say later, for they both had still many years of service to the School. Of Alliott, F. H. Maud, who was at school from 1885 to 1890, wrote as follows: 'I hardly know what to say of him. He was in many ways a fine man, but I feel on looking back that he was not an ideal schoolmaster: there was too real a tendency to something like cramming, and an apparent incapacity to realize the limits of a boy's powers of assimilating knowledge. On the other hand, and this is more important, Alliott was very keen on ethical standards. Two things stand out as symptomatic of those days. When I first went to school, the time between breakfast and morning chapel was taken up with reading the revisers' *Preface to the Revised New Testament*—a document possibly valuable to professional theologians, but to small boys rather heavy going. Later *Paradise Lost* and others of Milton's poems took the place of the *Preface*—a very real improvement. The other custom was that of taking notes of the sermon. This was universal: every boy had a "sermon notebook". I think this custom died out soon after the experiment of making the boys reconstruct the sermon from their notes: the results were not encouraging.

'Another activity was the "Parliament", divided into two parties, each led by a master—the Monarchists run by Mr Morgan and the Republicans run by Mr Stuart. This body met on one evening each week. The Old Boy hero of my day was Percy Furnivall, later surgeon at the London Hospital, but then better known as a cyclist on the old penny-farthing machine. He became amateur champion of England up to five miles; held for some years the record for the mile; and was, I believe, the first O.S. to achieve a place in *Whitaker's Almanack*.

'The later years of the nineteenth century were times of antagonism between Church and Chapel: in Stortford the fact that the N.G.S. and the (Church of England) Grammar School never met each other in games is an indication of the atmosphere. Alliott was a strongly Nonconformist Liberal. The School continued to be mainly Nonconformist, at least for a time, under F. S. Young; but the emphasis was changed.'

Incidentally Maud's memory played him false in one detail: for the School regularly played the Grammar School during the eighties in cricket (though not apparently in football); and A. B. Day, writing of the nineties, mentions that once, when the Grammar School was in the doldrums and the N.G.S. was due to play them that afternoon, Mr Alliott said after morning prayers: 'You must play your best, of course, but let Mr Shaw off as lightly as you can'; Mr Shaw, later Bishop of Birmingham, being then headmaster of the Grammar School.

Another contemporary of F. S. Young at school, the well-known novelist A. T. Sheppard,[1] wrote down many years later his memories and impressions of schooldays at Stortford. He too mentions Furnivall: '. . . At the time Percy Furnivall was much more a name to conjure with than that of Cecil Rhodes: at all events at the N.G.S. (Rhodes, of course, was at the High [Grammar] School). He was a nephew, I think, of Dr Furnivall, the great oarsman and Shakespearean scholar, and was the champion cyclist of his day. No school sports day was complete without Furnivall as competitor—and winner—against all comers in the Open Mile. Other Old Boys whom we regarded or were beginning to regard with veneration, unless I am anticipating their rise into prominence, were Holman Bentley, the pioneer missionary in the Congo; J. R. K. Duff, the artist; and Herbert Hampton, the famous portrait-sculptor.[2]

'But at the School itself the most conspicuous figure was Richard Alliott; a man indeed who could in no place and in no case have been inconspicuous. One remembers him in many different moods and attitudes. Perhaps he would be crossing the grass, bare-headed, his curly locks streaming in the breeze, with ever-faithful Mark Matthews behind him waiting to take instructions. Or again, he would be slippering the bare shoulders of any unlucky boy who dared to commit the heinous sin of washing in a bath instead of a basin. Or taking the Sixth in a corner of the dining-hall, when it was only necessary to learn the first line or two of ode or epic—he with rapturous eyes on the ceiling would do the rest. He was always impressive, always Olympian as, in some misdemeanour, he annihilated you with the thunderbolt: "*You*, the son of Christian parents!" Mr Alliott had many faults, many limitations, including a curious absence of any sense of proportion: but he had immense virtues.

[1] Author of *The Red Cravat*, *Running Horse Inn* and *Here Comes an Old Sailor*, etc. One of his short stories, *Abbotsferry* (published in *Argosy*, 1932), is recognizably written about Stortford.

[2] W. Holman Bentley was a member of the first group of missionaries (sent by the Baptist Missionary Society) to the Congo, where the tribesmen were still cannibals. He was also an outstanding scholar, and in 1905 Glasgow University conferred upon him an honorary Doctorate of Divinity.

J. R. K. Duff painted the portrait of F. S. Young that hangs in the Memorial Hall.

H. Hampton did the bronze bust of Dr Alliott in the School House Library: this was exhibited at the Royal Academy. He specialized in portrait busts of distinguished people, and also in designing medals.

'On Sundays we trooped down in our blue-tasselled mortar-boards to the Congregational Church, to hear the Rev. John Wood, whose "pulpit guns" we were expected to report afterwards: though I fear some of these have slipped my memory, as the mental strain of finding the places for Mrs Schaeffer in her huge brown German Bible was too exhausting for me to be equal to this fresh exertion. But then Mrs Schaeffer on occasion asked one to dinner afterwards. She had been brought up in the court of Württemberg, where her father held high office: her brother was, I think, Prime Minister to the Queen of the Sandwich Islands, and the latter's portrait and autograph stood in her room amongst her photos and the busts of eminent musicians and poets. No English matron could possibly have been kinder than Mrs Schaeffer.

'The N.G.S. seemed to have the knack of attracting "characters": another such was Miss Winter, the needlewoman: she wore blue glasses, and had been in the service of Dean Merivale, the historian, of whom she never tired of speaking. She was one of the (no doubt) few who did not anticipate F. S. Young's future eminence: "I cannot bear that boy," the little woman said to me excitedly on one occasion as he went out—probably after he had been asking for several clean collars in a week. As for Young himself, and C. S. Colman (who came with the reputation of knowing more about geometry than Euclid himself), and F. M. Kingdon, and others of my own contemporaries, they have their names written legibly enough in the chronicles of Bishop's Stortford.'

C. B. Young, whom we have already quoted, and A. B. Day were both at the N.G.S. in the nineties. 'To us boys', wrote the former, 'Alliott was very largely an enigma. From about 1893 onwards he was something of a crank, certainly an eccentric. Small things seemed to loom larger to him than greater. Coming in to take prayers one day he noticed a tiny scrap of paper on the floor: exclaiming "There is no worship in it; go to your classes!" he rushed out again without taking prayers. By then he did very little teaching, taking only a small sixth form in Classics. Indeed the gardens and grounds seemed to be his chief interests rather than school work. On Sunday afternoons all the boarders and the masters had to assemble while Alliott read out, very finely, passages of English poetry. In my time we heard thus all Milton's *Paradise Lost*, *Paradise Regained* and *Samson Agonistes*, and then much of Tennyson. But I fear that for most boys the whole thing resulted not in the arousing of interest in poetry, but in boredom.

'In my time a single block of buildings sufficed for teaching and for housing both boys and masters: an assistant master had a cubicle in each dormitory. The School Hall[1] was, especially in winter, the scene of various ploys—leap-frog, conkers, etc., and handicrafts such as the netting of hammocks. Silkworms too were kept and silk was spun from their cocoons. We played knucklebones: in the winter we roasted chestnuts. In the summer butterfly- and moth-hunting was an activity that C. S. Colman put us onto. We were left singularly free to pursue our own devices.

'As regards games, we only played Association Football and cricket, and practice games took place almost entirely in the school grounds: for matches, we had a ground at Silver Leys, on the Hadham Road, for football, and a pitch on the Stortford Town Cricket Club's ground for cricket. I fancy there was a tennis court at the bottom of the grounds, near the drive. In addition, there was the game of "Stortford fives", a game peculiar to the School because of the shape of the court (on the south side of the classrooms). There were three varieties of this game, as played by hand, by racquet or with the feet. For the first two, ordinary fives balls were used—in "foot-racquets" a tennis-ball was substituted, which required very skilful and accurate kicking. The court was merely a high brick wall—the end wall of the classrooms—with a narrow extension built out on either side at an oblique angle, and a cement floor. On the left was a much lower wall (actually the side wall of the tuck-shop) at right angles to the front wall, continued towards the back of the court by a retaining wall barely a foot high. It was an excellent game: unfortunately the building of the Memorial Hall after the First World War made the destruction of the old fives court inevitable.

'The standard of teaching in Alliott's time was academically pretty poor. There was one Classics master, L. W. P. Lewis (later to become headmaster of Bradford Grammar School), a very good scholar to whom the Classics were all in all. Whittaker's chief subject was mathematics, though he also took chemistry and physics: but the laboratories were very poor by present standards. For French and German Alliott appointed foreigners: there were Esslinger and Dr Ludwig Schellmann, Germans, followed by Tobler and Moser, Swiss [the latter of whom stayed on into F. S. Young's time and kept in touch with the School up to the time of his death]. Indeed, both of these men really identified themselves with the School and were much liked personally. Other subjects and the lower forms were to some extent taught by non-degree men: the best of these general-subject masters was A. H. Windsor, a minister's son who was universally liked or feared. C. S. Colman took on some Classics in my time and was first class.

[1] i.e. the Schoolroom.

'As optional subjects there were shorthand, drawing (though there was no special art master) and music: the piano was taught by a lady, Mrs Spencer, and the violin by Mr Moonen, a German Jew who smoked cigars and always reminded me of Svengali in Du Maurier's *Trilby*. The piano teacher did not convey any appreciation of music: there were endless scales and exercises, but I did learn to play some of Beethoven's sonatas.

'Alliott had a small organ in the School Hall, used sometimes at prayers. But there was no school chapel in my time, and indeed, apart from morning and evening prayers, no Sunday services in the School: all boarders alike were taken in a "crocodile" to the Congregational Chapel.' In this connection it may be noted that it was F. S. Young who first decided to hold the Sunday evening services at the School—a practice which was at first much deprecated by the local Congregationalist minister.

The above reference to Mr Moonen will remind many Old Stortfordians of the small wooden hut that was still standing, on the right of the footpath beyond 'the Mountain',[1] at least as late as the time of the 1914–1918 war. It was known as 'Moonen's Studio', and displayed a number of portraits and other photographs. Mr Moonen lived in a small cottage adjoining it, which has long since been pulled down, and seems to have started a business as a professional photographer.

C. B. Young does not mention John Farmer, who was Director of Music at Harrow School and later at Balliol College, Oxford (where he instituted the famous Balliol Concerts on Sunday evenings in term time). Farmer did not actually teach at the N.G.S., but in the nineties he used to visit the School to lecture on music, and also did a certain amount of examining. While at Balliol, Farmer brought out the famous song-book *Gaudeamus*, and it may well have been he who first introduced the book to Stortford. He had himself composed the musical setting of Robert Browning's lines which were later to become so familiar to generations of Stortfordians as the school song. *Heroes*, it is perhaps worth mentioning, is a part only of the Epilogue to *Ferishtah's Fancies*, written by Browning in Venice in 1883. (This poem purports to be a collection of Persian tales, but the stories are in fact entirely of Browning's own invention.)

A. B. Day was a contemporary of C. B. Young, but a day boy. 'The only thing approaching a school uniform', he writes, 'was that we all wore a dark blue peakless cap known as a Polo Cap, with a silver shield bearing the monogram N.G.S. This was, I think, replaced in my last years by a peaked blue cap with horizontal crimson stripes.

[1] See p. 44.

On Sundays a mortar-board with a dark blue tassel was worn. The First Eleven football team played in blue and crimson shirts. Being a day boy, I rarely visited the dormitories: somewhere upstairs was the Matron's room, where one paraded if unwell, and the needlewoman's room where I had to attend, in common with every other boy, on the first or second day of every term: the purpose of this visit being to enable Miss Winter to go through our hair with a very fine-toothed comb.

'The "pro" of the Town Cricket Club (Jones in my day) was engaged to do some coaching for the teams; but there was no attempt till quite at the end of my time to bring on any of the juniors in any sport. Equipment too was extremely poor, except for the teams: on one occasion a protest about the condition of the cricket balls, which were dangerous to use, brought the reply that there was no money in the sports fund, as it had been raided by Mr Alliott in order to send a donation to some missionary society!

'Athletics were hardly in the picture, and the Cinder Track round the Old Field was scarcely used. The "gym" was a wooden building situated on the far side of the gravelled playground south of the Schoolroom: I have heard that it was one of a batch brought from the site of the Exhibition held in Hyde Park.

'My first form-master was Mr Blandford, who later left to start a prep school in Broadstairs: he returned to Stortford during the 1914–1918 war. 'Blanny' was a gentleman, a disciplinarian and a good teacher: his class occupied the space beyond the partition in the Schoolroom: Class II was held one side or the other of the opposite or platform end of the room. Mr Alliott usually taught in a corner of the dining-hall: and there were four other classrooms.'

At this time the day boys, like the boarders, had desks for their books in the Schoolroom: during morning prayers they sat at their desks here, and then dispersed to the various classrooms. At the close of morning school all day boys, regardless of their ability to sing, had to attend a singing class under Mr Blandford: this was officially called a 'treble practice', and nominally no day boy was allowed to sing anything but treble! Mr Blandford taught F. S. Young in Alliott's time, and was later to serve under Young both in the Main School and later in the Prep. He did not finally retire until 1927.

'Of the rest of the staff', continued A. B. Day, 'I have written already about C. D. Whittaker:[1] three others stand out as really good—Mr Youngman, a most attractive personality who unfortunately left soon after I came in 1890; A. H. Windsor; and E. W. Hurst. The two latter were first-rate in every way. Of the procession of foreigners Dr Ludwig

[1] See p. 18.

Schellmann, a Ph.D. of Heidelberg, made his mark: he would talk to us about features of German life such as student duelling of which his description was so vivid and dramatic that one boy fainted!

'Mitchell, the handyman, was a natural comic, something like the early Charlie Chaplin. He could always be relied upon for an amusing turn at a concert, such as followed in the evening after the annual Old Boys' football match.

'For one period a week we all assembled in the hall for singing, which I fancy Mr Alliott himself took at one time—I have memories of him using a large tonic-sol-fa sheet and pointers (later it was taken by Mr Windsor).

'After about 1894 Mr Alliott became more and more liable to prolonged harangues about quite trivial matters; or he would indulge in short-lived crazes for this or that method or subject of study. Later, particularly after his severe illness in 1896 which seemed to exaggerate all his peculiarities, he became somewhat irritable, and the smallest peccadillo would be treated as a moral disgrace. But these tantrums were, without doubt, only the evidence of advancing senility, and give us but a caricature of the man in his prime.'

F. M. Kingdon was a boy at the N.G.S. from 1887 to 1894 and a contemporary therefore of A. B. Day, but a boarder. He wrote in the *O.S. Quarterly*, twenty years later, of his memories of being a monitor: '... "Ach, you moneetors, vat are you? You are nussing but von dunkey's skin stuffed with conceit!" Such was the opinion held of the monitors of my day in one quarter: fortunately it was not shared by Mr Alliott, as witness his final words one Saturday afternoon, closing an incident arising out of a School-in: "Now the monitors may go up to Silver Leys to see the town match, for they are the boys who have my confidence: the rest of you had better consider what you mean to do!"

'School-in was the principal feature of monitorial duty in those days. Twice a week on the average we had to ring the bell at twelve-thirty to discover the perpetrator of some misdemeanour or other. For the rest, we called the roll many times a day and with special zest on Sunday evenings before starting for chapel. We stayed in bed in the morning until prayer time, while lesser lights did morning prep; we claimed the right to remain in our studies until the last master locked up; we conveyed Mrs Schaeffer to chapel and dined with her afterwards; and we read newspapers at the dinner-table. No doubt we performed some useful functions also, such as lugging the rest of the dormitory out of bed in a gallant endeavour to get them all down in time for morning prep. But it is the privileges noted above which alone come back to one after the lapse of twenty years.'

Mr Kingdon's memories may be supplemented by those of another future Stortford master, N. P. Wood, who came to the N.G.S. as a boy in the year when Kingdon left. 'Discipline was rather slack,' he wrote, 'especially up at the top of the School. There was morning prep at 7 a.m. all the year round, but by an unwritten law monitors were allowed to stay in bed. Study boys were sent to bed at 9.45 p.m., but monitors were allowed to sit up till the master on duty called "All across":[1] as a consequence the dormitories were often left without monitors till as late as 11 p.m. Boys were often late for morning prep, and as a penalty they had to account for their sins on paper. I have seen the Head's desk at morning prayers covered with dozens of these letters. "Dear Sir," they would run, "I rose in good time this morning, and commenced to dress. Unfortunately, my collar-stud . . . etc. etc. Yours obediently, X. Y. Smith". Such letters would frequently be read out to the delighted School, and many a victim would be scarified with ridicule or abuse.

'Sundays were rather dull: sandwiched between breakfast and morning chapel came often enough a Milton or a Tennyson period for the whole School, when the Headmaster would read aloud to us: by common consent he read grandly, but I doubt if the younger boys enjoyed it. Followed a crocodile march, in senior and junior sections, to the Congregational Chapel. In the afternoon was a compulsory walk, led by the Head and Dr Whittaker; and in the evening, another visit to Water Lane.'

In this chapter we have quoted chiefly reminiscences of Stortfordian personalities and of the daily life of the N.G.S. in the latter part of Queen Victoria's reign. Let us end with a retrospect, visualized by N. P. Wood, of the appearance of the school buildings and grounds in those early days. 'Go back to 1852', he wrote, 'and imagine nearly everything nonexistent except the School House dining-room [now the Junior Common Room] and the Headmaster's wing—this will give some conception of the old Collegiate School. Neither Old Field [Lower Green] nor New Field [Middle and Upper Greens], neither drive nor pine trees existed then: just a small strip of land where the headmaster's garden [now the S.H. Housemaster's] flourishes, and a yard at the back—this was the School's territory then. Boys entered the premises, after strange fights with townees, through a five-barred gate in Maze Green Road. Mr Dillon had about thirty boarders at the School and Mr Bell, the Headmaster, took another

[1] At this time the boys' studies were across the courtyard, in the Racquet Court Block (now the administrative block).

dozen in a house in Rye Street opposite the 'Wheatsheaf'.[1] By 1868 the buildings included the present Schoolroom [now the S.H. Senior Common Room] and all that now constitutes the School House except the changing-rooms and the block on the north of the courtyard. Instead of this block there was a smaller group of rooms erected on the site of the old yard and the old classroom belonging to the Collegiate School. The whole block was remodelled, though not very extensively, in 1875: from the first it contained kitchen and servants' premises.

'How much land was acquired in 1868, and how it was laid out, I do not know; but I fancy that Old Field and the drive soon took their present shape, and that a line drawn across New Field from the top of the gravel (i.e. roughly from the present laboratories southwards) would represent the westward limit. In 1880 and 1881, however, the Governors bought up some cottages and adjoining land which seem to have stood near the foot of the drive; so my definition of our original boundaries must be left rather vague.'

[1] This boarding-house, under Mr Esam, was kept on by the N.G.S. for two years or so (1868–9).

4. F. S. Young: (1) 1900–1918

ALTHOUGH the death of Mr Alliott was soon followed by the appointment of Mr F. S. Young as his successor, it was inevitable that a term should pass before Mr Young was free to leave Mill Hill and take up his new duties at Stortford. In these difficult circumstances the Directors of the School appointed Professor E. W. Johnson, of Cheshunt Theological College, as temporary headmaster. Professor Johnson had not, as far as is known, had any previous experience as a schoolmaster, and no doubt theological students are more easily dealt with than schoolboys. He was a man of small stature, with a quiet voice that by no means inspired the young with awe: and during his period of office, which came to be known as the 'Interregnum', it cannot be said that he left any great mark on the School, nor indeed was it to be expected that he should do so in so short a time.

F. S. Young took over as headmaster in January 1900. His career as a boy in the School had been a brilliant one in every way. He had been a leader in both the intellectual and the moral life of the School, and by reason of his prowess in cricket and football he stood out above his contemporaries. He crowned his school career by winning an open scholarship in Natural Science at The Queen's College, Oxford, where he was joined a little later by his school contemporary Charles Stacy Colman, who was to be his lifelong friend and colleague. At Oxford Young continued his athletic activities, playing soccer for Queen's and rowing in the college boat.

After graduating in the Final Natural Science Schools at Oxford, F. S. Young became an assistant master at Mill Hill School, under the headmastership of that versatile man Dr, later Sir J. D. McClure. During his five years at Mill Hill Young achieved great popularity as a leader and as a distinguished athlete, and also obtained his cap for Middlesex at Rugby football. His coaching of cricket and football was of great benefit to Mill Hill: at the same time he usually managed to play in the Past and Present cricket matches at Stortford. (At Mill Hill the nickname by which he was known was 'Bunny' Young; the name never followed him to Stortford, though it was passed on to his younger brother, C. B. Young.)

The annual Prize Day had been postponed from the summer term of 1899 owing to an epidemic of mumps, and then was further postponed by Mr Alliott's death. It was finally held on 19th December of that year, when Mr Young came over from Mill Hill to distribute the prizes. In his speech he outlined his ideals for the School, stressing the equal importance of academic, moral and physical training: and he ended up as follows: 'These are the ideals of education I would set before you. For a school which gives him this training every boy feels a great love: each boy is anxious that his school should become great. This greatness you cannot *claim* for a school: it must *come*. A school will become great in two ways. First, by winning a character for truth: that no lie in word or deed, no deceit, nothing underhand shall have a place in the school—nothing that will not bear the light. And secondly, by winning a character for scholarship: every boy must value the school's renown for true, earnest, untiring work. If this universal love of work exists, the school can show its real power. Let us then strive in this way to make the School greater and ever greater.'

Endowed as he was with a magnificent physique and untiring energy, F. S. Young came back to Stortford absolutely dedicated to the School and seeing clearly what he intended to make of it. The strength of his character and his religious convictions soon impressed the School in a way that, perhaps, only those who were present during the early years of his headmastership can fully appreciate. He was always fair and just, but he saw to it from the first that the way of the malefactor should be hard: the change from the lax discipline of recent years to the atmosphere that he very speedily produced was remarkable. Alliott had often threatened boys with expulsion but hardly ever carried it out, and never used corporal punishment: Young did occasionally expel a boy, but only when he felt that a caning would not be effective. And the justice of the occasional caning was never called in question by public opinion in the School. From the first he was imbued with the ideal of Christian reunion; and whereas Alliott, in spite of his non-sectarian policy with regard to the School, had been nevertheless a somewhat militant Nonconformist, Young emphasized the points on which Nonconformists and Anglicans agreed, rather than their differences. As he grew older he found himself more in agreement with the Church of England, and indeed, after his retirement, took Anglican orders.

One of his first acts as headmaster was to persuade the Directors to change the name of the school: from the end of 1901 the Nonconformist Grammar School became Bishop's Stortford College—college rather than school, in order to avoid confusion with the Grammar School. Even so, mistakes continued to occur: in a letter to parents sent out in 1904 we read that 'several instances have occurred lately of confusion between the two schools at Bishop's Stortford. Parents have addressd their letters to the Headmaster of "The School" or "The Grammar School", Bishop's Stortford. They have thus received a prospectus from the grammar school, which has recently been reopened as The School, Bishop's Stortford; and on finding that the prospectus sets forth that school as conducted on Church of England principles, they have given up all thought of sending their sons'. The school magazine had also, of course, to change its name, and in 1902 the *N.G.S.* became the *Stortfordian.*

In that year also a new school shield of arms was devised by Mr Young, with the help of Mr C. Moser, the art master, and Mr H. G. Ibberson O.S., the School architect. In the old N.G.S. days, winners in the athletics sports were presented with medals on which was engraved a shield devised by Mr Alliott. This shield had the monogram N.G.S. in the first quarter, the hart of Hertfordshire in the second and third quarters and the school motto 'Soli Deo Gloria' in the fourth. Needless to say, no such shield is known to the authorities at the College of Arms. Nor was the new shield—the present one—ever officially 'granted' or registered by them (though they were said to have 'passed' it, whatever that may mean); indeed the thick gold dividing lines are not truly heraldic.[1] The hart and the 'seaxes' refer of course to these charges in the shields of Hertfordshire and Essex respectively; the open Bible was borrowed by Young from the arms of Oxford University; Alliott's 'Soli Deo Gloria' was retained as the motto.

The change of name was followed by a change in the constitution of the School. In November 1904 the shareholders[2] of the East of England Nonconformist School Association Ltd received a notice from the secretary as follows: 'I have the honour to report that since the 13th June 1904, the date of my last report, the liquidation of the Company has proceeded in due course. The assets of the Company have been handed over to the Bishop's Stortford College Association, and the liabilities have been assumed by the Association as from the 31st day of August, 1904.' E. W. Grimwade J.P., the chairman of the former Directorate and now chairman of the Governors, followed this up with a letter to parents: 'We have pleasure in stating that this school

[1] R. W. Hale O.S. points out that the division of a shield into equal upper and lower halves is uncommon in heraldry: in such cases the use of the word 'chief' seems a misnomer.

[2] One of these at the time was a boy (W. Simpson) still at the school, who therefore nominally had the right to be called a governor!

is no longer under the control of a private commercial company, but has been converted into a Public Endowed School. The new constitution has been completed, and everything is ready for carrying forward its object and making use of the generosity of former Shareholders and other friends of Nonconformity. Special representatives of the Baptist, Congregational and Presbyterian bodies have been placed on the Governing Council. The object of this change is that the School may be able to compete with the large public schools of England, which have all been aided very greatly by endowments. By this reconstitution endowments can be asked for, and subscribers will know that they are giving towards an object which is solely educational in aim, and that in no way can their contributions be used for profit-earning purposes.' In December the statutory first general meeting of the Incorporated Bishop's Stortford College Association was announced, to be held on 'Tuesday the 20th December instant, at 2 o'clock, at the Office of the Association, 116, Fore St, London, E.C., and if necessary by adjournment at the Cripplegate Institute, Golden Lane, at the same day and hour, to transact the business of the Association as required by Statute'.

Young's methods in controlling the discipline of the School were partly inspired by the ideas of Arnold of Rugby, but perhaps more by the example of Thring of Uppingham. He did not follow Arnold in delegating disciplinary powers to the sixth form as such, but to the monitors whom he chose personally, and who might or might not be in the sixth (though they usually were). Later, as the School grew, and other Houses were added, the original monitors became school prefects, and the housemasters appointed a lesser hierarchy in the form of house monitors. Compulsory fagging was never allowed, but a system of voluntary fagging in the studies, each of which was occupied by two senior boys, was introduced and on the whole worked very well. But this seems to have come to an end during the early years of the 1914–1918 war.

The outstanding feature of Young's headmastership was the influence he soon came to exert over both masters and boys by his strength of will, untiring energy and complete devotion to the highest ideals. His sermons in the school services on Sunday evenings did not reach a great height of eloquence, and were sometimes regarded as dull: though his transparent honesty seldom failed to impress. Rather it was in his scripture classes with the sixth form that boys came to realize most clearly his deep regard for truth and his firm belief—in which, however, there was no trace of obscurantism or 'fundamentalism'—in the Christian values.

Among the minor changes that Young introduced was the abolition of the custom, usual in Alliott's time, of playing masters in the school football and cricket teams. More important, in 1903 he introduced rugger, and by 1911 he had substituted Rugby for Association football as the School's chief winter game, though soccer continued to be played in the spring term until 1921. Himself a distinguished Rugby player, Young was enthusiastic in coaching the school rugger sides.

It is interesting to note the schools whose names occur on the football (soccer) and cricket fixtures lists of the N.G.S. and of B.S.C. in its early days. In the eighties the N.G.S. played football against the Friends' School, Saffron Walden; Newport Grammar School; St Catherine's School, Broxbourne; and Cheshunt College (presumably the theological college). Amongst the clubs played we find the intriguing name of 'The Old Salways'. In cricket, the same schools were played and also Theobald's School, Waltham Cross; the High School (Grammar School) Bishop's Stortford; and (but not until 1890) Mill Hill School. In the early 1900's, Harlow College, St Edmund's, Ware and the High School, Bishop's Stortford were added to the football fixtures; and Regent's Park College, Harlow College, Saffron Walden Grammar School and the School for the Sons of Missionaries, Eltham to the cricket list. Amongst local cricket clubs played were the Rickling Ramblers, whose club with its ground on Rickling Green is one of the oldest in the country. By this time the names of St Catherine's School, Broxbourne, and Theobald's School, Waltham Cross no longer appear in either fixture list.

In 1901 new laboratories were built to the west of the 1875 block, where room was thus made for an extra classroom: and the old 'D' dormitory in the School House was converted into six new studies and a masters' common-room. It was probably at the same time that the room to the right of the S.H. entrance, which had originally been the boot-room, with hand-basins round the walls, and, later, the music-room, was converted into the Headmaster's study. In the following year a bronze bust of Richard Alliott, executed by the sculptor Herbert Hampton O.S., was placed in the Alliott Memorial Library at the west end of the schoolroom, which was partitioned off as a reading-room. The bust was unveiled by Dr A. M. Fairbairn, Principal of Mansfield College, Oxford. In the same year the teaching staff of the School was greatly strengthened by the appointment of C. S. Colman, an Old Boy of the School who, after a brilliant academic career at Oxford, had taken up journalism, but found this work little to his taste; he was therefore glad to accept Young's invitation to return to Stortford and here he remained for the rest of his life. In spite of a severe physical deformity, due to a tubercular disease of the spine contracted in childhood, he entered into the life of the School with the greatest zest. It would be fair to say that, next to F. S. Young himself, Colman contributed more to the building up of the School than any other man, though Stortford has never lacked lifelong and wholehearted devotees. 'Chips', as he was always known, had a wit peculiarly his own, somewhat acidulated at times, but never unkindly. His lively mind and his remarkable range of interests made him a most stimulating influence on the boys. An enthusiastic lepidopterist, he inspired numerous boys with a love of 'bug-hunting', and many will recall the pleasure of going round with him treacling for moths in the school grounds. He was devoted to the Norfolk Broads, where he kept a yacht for use in the holidays, inviting successive parties of boys to accompany him. He was also a keen and knowledgeable botanist. Incidentally he was the youngest of five Stortfordian brothers.

In March 1902 a further addition to the School was made in the shape of a preparatory department. For some years a preparatory school had been conducted by a Miss Mumford at Newbury House, on the Hadham Road, and on her retirement the premises were secured by the School. Mr E. W. Hurst, then the senior assistant master at B.S.C., was placed in charge of this new department, which was to receive boys between the ages of eight and twelve years: he was assisted by Miss Good, who was later to become Mrs F. S. Young. 'The Prep' opened with eight boarders and eight day boys, the Matron being Mrs Tilsley. For several years the Prep had to play games, as a contemporary wrote at the time, 'amongst the hills and dales of the Mountain', that being the name by which the rising ground at the south-east corner of the school grounds was known.[1] It was not till 1910 that a pitch was allotted to the Prep on Upper Field.

In the summer term of 1902 the day boys, now numbering twenty or more as compared with about one hundred boarders, first began to be organised on House lines, their first housemaster being Mr H. Kitchener. He did not stay long, however, and the following year F. M. Kingdon, an Old Boy of the N.G.S., became housemaster of the Day Boys, a position which he held for the next ten years. In 1904 a small Day Boy room (the brick building still to be seen near the Lodge) was built as the Day Boys' first headquarters, remaining as such until 1920. (Later it became the Natural History Museum, and later still a music-room; with a short period in the Second World War when it served as the armoury and stores-room of the Cadet Force.)

[1] This name was still in use in the 1920's, but is quite unknown to later generations of Stortfordians.

Meanwhile a challenge shield had been presented by the masters in 1902, to be competed for by S.H. 'A', S.H. 'B' and the Day Boys: it was to be held for football in the Michaelmas term, for athletics in the spring and for cricket in the summer. It was in this year that J. Jones, the cricket pro who had been at the School for thirteen years, left for a few years; only to return, however, as groundsman in 1907. He remained at B.S.C. for another thirteen years until 1920, when he was succeeded by J. E. Nichols.

The numbers in the School had by now risen to 130, and further accommodation was required. In 1902 Mr Young announced that music-rooms had been built 'so constructed that every boy might only be an infliction on himself!'. These were the rooms later known as Purcell House, on the site of the later Sixth Form Library (now the Council Chamber). And in the summer of 1903 Mr R. L. Ager rented Westfield Lodge, in the Hadham Road, which was opened as a boarding house in the Michaelmas term of that year, with Mr Ager as housemaster. Mr Ager, himself an old Rugbeian, contributed greatly to the life of the School until in 1906 he left to become Headmaster of Tettenhall College, Wolverhampton. In its first term the new boarding house had only four boys, but it filled up very rapidly. On Mr Ager's departure, Westfield Lodge was taken over by Mr F. B. ('Becker') Shawe and until he retired in 1919 the House was known as Shawe's.

In 1904 Mr Young appointed as mathematics master F. S. Sutton, who had been educated at Bristol Grammar School and had won a mathematical scholarship to University College, Oxford. Here he had not only taken a First in his Finals, but had played both soccer and cricket for his college. 'Bobby' Sutton gave himself unsparingly to his work. He played also an energetic part on the soccer field, but it was in cricket especially that the School felt the impact of his arrival. For some thirty years he bowled and coached at the nets with tireless energy, being a prominent member of the Stortford town team, as well as of successive Past and Present teams.[1]

In the following year A. G. Tidmarsh, the second Old Boy of the N.G.S. to be appointed by Mr Young, returned to the School as a master. Mr F. G. M. Ogbourne, who for some three years had been a visiting master teaching music, had retired (Stortfordians may still know him at least by name, for it was he who set to music the two hymns, written by C. S. Colman, which are still sung on the first and last Sundays of every term); and Tidmarsh was appointed in his place, the first full-time resident music master the School had employed. The

[1] Incidentally it was in 1905 that the Past and Present made their record score of 376 for 4 wickets, against Rickling Green.

possessor of a magnificent baritone voice, 'Tid' could have made a career for himself on the concert platform, but preferred to devote his life to Stortford. It would be hard to exaggerate what he did for the teaching and appreciation of music in the School. But perhaps his greatest gift to the School was his sense of humour: he possessed to a remarkable degree the power of radiating gaiety, and had a genius for friendship, as many generations of Stortfordians know well.

His arrival on the staff was marked by an experiment which developed eventually into one of the most characteristic of Stortford's holiday-time activities. The School's long association with the Norfolk coast began in a small way in the summer of 1905, when a party of Old Boys and present boys spent a week's holiday in a cottage at Hempstead called 'Sea View': this holiday was so successful that it was repeated on a larger scale in the following year, at Beach Farm, Hempstead, the cottage not being large enough to accommodate the increased numbers. In 1907 N. P. Wood, who had been a boy at Stortford in the last years of Alliott's headmastership, returned as a master and became, with Tid, one of the prime movers in running these parties. The 'Norfolk Stortfordians', as the parties were called, began to arrange cricket fixtures—against Martham, or the Royal Naval Hospital at Yarmouth, or Honing Hall. Later they transferred to more permanent quarters at the neighbouring village of Happisburgh, or Hasbro', as it is now usually spelt. But of this we shall have more to say later.

Meanwhile at Stortford the field known as Preston Leys ('Upper Field' as it was called for many years) was acquired by the School in 1906, owing to the initiative and foresight of C. S. Colman, after whom it is now named. A good deal of levelling was necessary in the centre of the field: the cost of this and of the erection in 1907 of what later came to be known as the Old Pavilion was defrayed by a fund collected by Colman from a score or so of friends of B.S.C., themselves mostly Old Stortfordians. For the last sixty years these magnificent playing-fields, rather than the 'Old' and the 'New' Fields down by the School, have been the scene of our various athletic activities.

To these we may now return. We have referred already to sporadic experiments, from the late seventies onwards, in playing an early form of rugger, and to F. S. Young's decision in 1911 to substitute rugger for soccer as the School's chief winter game. Commenting on this at that time Nevil Wood wrote: 'It seems a curious irony of fate that this decision should have been made in the very year in which G. D. Read has appeared for the Cambridge XI and A. E. J. McLean has played in the Freshmen's Match at Oxford. It is also quite clear that Stortford is more likely to gain in reputation by playing soccer rather than by rugger. But there are indications that rugger has come to stay, though we have not yet tried the experiment of devoting a whole term to rugger. From 1903 to 1907 we were content with two fixtures a year, always with scratch sides: since 1908, however, we have had a much longer list, including two regular club fixtures. In 1909 Rugby colours were first awarded; and in 1910 the Old Boys' Rugger Club was formed.'

This latter event took place towards the end of that year, when the Old Stortfordians' Rugby Football Club was started with a membership of about fifty players; its first match being played on 17th December against Molesey (lost 5–0). The captain was F. M. Cheshire, and the secretary and treasurer H. R. Hadfield. In the 1911–12 season 17 matches were played, of which 13 were won, and in 1912–13 the number of fixtures rose to 26, of which 24 were won: and in the same year an 'A' XV was fielded. Evidently the club had got off to a good start.

This seems a suitable place for a retrospect of our record as a soccer school: we again quote Nevil Wood. 'It was in 1879 that we began to play real soccer with eleven men on each side, and our results were very good. The early eighties were great days: between 1880 and 1882 we played thirty-two matches and only lost one (the *Football Annual* for 1880 records the fact that ours was the heaviest public school team of the year).[1] In 1882 an Old Stortfordian Association Football Club was formed, with fixtures against Clapton, the Foxes and St Bartholomew's Hospital: but it was short-lived. The later eighties were not so good, except for a really brilliant season in 1889–90. In the nineties our best season was that of 1896–7, when out of 18 matches we won 13 and lost 5, scoring 96 goals to our opponents' 30: this was the season in which we piled up our record score of 22 goals to nil against the Royal Masonic School. Since the turn of the century we have won 48, drawn 14 and lost only 3, until last year's disastrous season.'

As a pendant to Nevil's account of the School's soccer record, we may recall here a famous match played in 1910, unique in the sporting history of the School, when the Stephenson family, consisting of Alderman James Stephenson and his nine sons (of whom seven were O.S. and the other two were still at school) challenged the School First XI at soccer and, scorning the offer of a substitute eleventh man, beat them 8–1. (At a water-polo match later in the day they were not so successful, the School winning 5–0.)

In March 1909 a new block comprising five classrooms and a masters'

[1] See above, pp. 13–14, for particulars of that year.

common room, with cloisters outside, was built to the west of the laboratory, adjoining the music-rooms. This building cost only £1,850 —a sharp reminder of the depreciation of the pound sterling that has since come about as a result of two world wars. (It was intended that this new block should in course of time be completed as a quadrangle, of which it would have been the northern side: but this plan was later abandoned.) As a result of these extensions, accommodation was found in the old (1875) classroom block for the School's first Natural History Museum (upstairs, where now the School House changing-room is), and below it (in what is now the Bursar's office) for a music-room. At the same time the room on the ground floor, which had been first a laboratory and then a classroom, became the School House changing-room (now the showers); and the previous changing-room (now the visitors' changing-room) was divided, to provide a photographers' dark-room and a bicycle shed.

It was in 1909 also that Mr Young's work was recognized by his election as a member of the Headmasters' Conference, a body which is limited to 200 schools and indeed at that time included only 105. And the following year he was invited to apply for the headmastership of Giggleswick School in Yorkshire; but he declined the invitation. In his speech on Prize Day, 1910, he referred to this, in words that are perhaps characteristic of the man. 'I suppose', he said, 'that any man would sooner carry out a work which he himself had initiated than build upon someone else's foundation; and I personally would derive far greater satisfaction and pleasure from being able to carry through the work here than from going to another school, however well-equipped and whatever its reputation.' And so he stayed on: and indeed the large entry of new boys to the College as it approached its jubilee, and the successes won by Old Boys at the universities, gave the brightest promise for the future of the school.

The next step in carrying out his programme was the transference of the Preparatory School from the Hadham Road to larger and permanent quarters at Grimwade House, completed in 1912 on the western side of the school grounds overlooking the New Field (which now came to be regularly used for the Prep cricket matches). The new building had dormitory accommodation for twenty-eight boarders and classrooms for forty (i.e. including twelve day boys): the age for going up to the Main School remained at twelve years. The opening ceremony was conducted by Sir John Barker on Prize Day of that year: 'Nigger' Hurst, as he had come to be called, continued to run the Preparatory School at Grimwade House.

In 1912 the School lost two members of the staff in the persons of

ESTFIELD LODGE, opened in 1903.

ıe first Westfield Lodge group, 1904. *Standing:* F. H. Cooke, D. A. Legg, H. Holtom, W. W. Holtom, H. L. Garnham. *Sitting:* Mr R. L. S. Ager, A. Wherry, A. H. Mellows.

DAY BOY HOUSE, 1906. *Back row:* P. W. Day, B. C. Cox, R. D. Holland, A. A. Pryer, Hedley Wright, A. P. Cook, S. A. Milbank. *Sitting:* P. F. Leah, L. W. Myers, Mr F. M. Kingdon, C. H. Edwards, E. U. Laurie. *In front:* W. Edwards, C. H. Barker, P. W. Robarts.

THE ORCHESTRA, 1908. *Back row:* H. E. Sears, F. W. Martin, A. H. Brunwin, J. T. Lean. *Second ro* N. A. Turner-Smith, S. C. Shillingford, B. M. Cloutman, J. H. Abraham, E. L. Stephenson, A. L. Anthon W. H. Bevan, C. C. Sennitt, Mr F. B. Shawe. *Sitting:* A. R. Kelsey, G. D. Read, Mr A. G. Tidmarsh, N. Shillingford, O. C. Carter.

THE CHOIR, 1911. *Back row:* U. A. Stephenson, R. D. Reid, W. W. Brown, F. Rhodes, G. A. Dunlop, A. J Sizer, A. L. Jones. *Second row:* G. E. Morgan, C. Dunham, A. L. Taylor, R. E. Griggs, W. R. Bion, G. D Martins, R. B. Viccars, S. B. Collett, C. V. Palmer, K. T. Boardman, W. H. Bevan, J. H. Davies. *Sitting:* G. A Rendle, G. P. Brown, L. A. Day, A. H. Mellows, Mr A. G. Tidmarsh, W. E. Palmer, M. Brown, J. T. Lean E. G. Nickalls. *On ground:* J. E. Shillingford, A. N. Dupont, T. E. Wall, S. O. Garnham.

F. M. Kingdon, Master 1899–1935.

C. S. Colman, Master 1902–36. (*top right*)

F. S. Sutton, Master 1904–49.

N. P. Wood, Master 1907–26. (*bottom right*)

A. G. Tidmarsh, Master 1905–44.

TWO INTERIORS OF THE RACQUETS COURT BLOCK, 191

Mr Moser teaching the Fifth Form in the room now the Headmaster's office. Names from the left: J. A. Morgand, A. I. Rae, H. L. Thurgood, G. L. W. Rowe (father of the present Headmaster), A. H. G. Sad J. G. S. Lee.

Mr R. G. Kelland teaching the Upper Third in the room immediately below the classroom shown above. Nam in rows from the left from the front: A. Itter, T. C. Butcher, L. Lawn; A. M. Davies, W. M. Hampton, J. F Doggart, F. A. R. Rand, G. M. Dyer, S. R. Mardon; W. H. Hogg, S. F. Cowell, F. H. Salmon, J. A. Matthew S. O. Garnham, R. H. James; J. C. Hunter, E. N. Carruthers, S. V. Evans, E. C. Wilson, A. F. Norman, T. E Wall.

A NEW CLASSROOM INTERIOR, 1913. Mr F. B. Shawe teaching the Fourth Form German Set Names in rows from the left from the front: A. N. Dupont; S. R. Mardon, E. N. Carruthers; S. F. Cowell F. A. R. Rand, R. K. Duchesne, E. A. Reavell, H. J. Harvey; A. F. Norman, J. A. Matthews, T. E. Wall H. W. Smith.

THE NEW CLASSROOM BLOCK, as built in 1909, with the Music Practice Rooms (Purcell House) adjoining on the right.

1914. Mr Colman teaching in his classroom, now Room 6. Against the wall are J. H. R. Sturgess-Wells, A. E. Blaxill, L. E. Bird. *Next row:* J. M. Tilsley, J. D. Butcher, R. W. Glendinning, G. G. Carruthers. *Next row:* H. Norris, R. Slaney, L. Schmassmann, P. Harvey, C. W. Richards. *Next row:* (A 186) H. B. Boyten, R. Birnage, J. D. Lake, D. Rae. *Next row:* T. C. McIlroy, G. Featherby, W. E. H. Garner, J. E. Hamilton, T. S. Hamilton. *Row nearest window:* S. N. Salmon, E. L. Smith, L. R. Chisnall, H. C. Sturgess-Wells, S. J. Furze.

View taken between 1909 and 1913. On the left of School House is the Racquets Block; next the Laboratories with creeper-clad gable and farther to the left is the Box Room in its second position. Behind, the roof of the 'New Classrooms' can be seen.

GRIMWADE HOUSE, 1913.

PRIZE GIVING in the Schoolroom, 1913. The Guest of Honour was Mrs David Lloyd George, wife of the then Chancellor of the Exchequer.

Mr (later Sir) Robert Pearce speaking at the unveiling of the foundation stone of Alliott House on Prize Day 1913. Mrs Lloyd George is on the right in conversation with the Chairman of the Governing Council, Mr Grimwade, over whose head can be seen Mr Young. Obscuring the foundation stone is Sir John Barker, and next to Robert Pearce is the Architect, Mr H. G. Ibberson, O.S.

George Mitchell, School House Butler, 1872–1913.

Above right: Albert Carter, 1914–59. School House Butler and Tuckman.

Right: Sergeant Salmon, 1906–38. P.T. Instructor and School Porter.

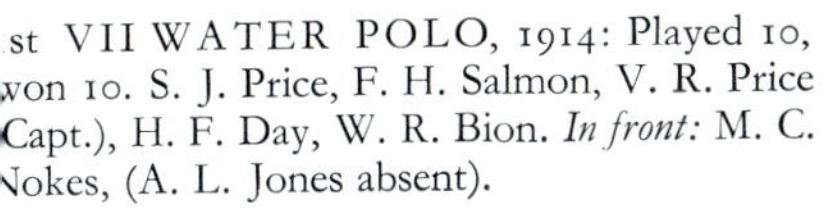

1st VII WATER POLO, 1914: Played 10, won 10. S. J. Price, F. H. Salmon, V. R. Price (Capt.), H. F. Day, W. R. Bion. *In front:* M. C. Nokes, (A. L. Jones absent).

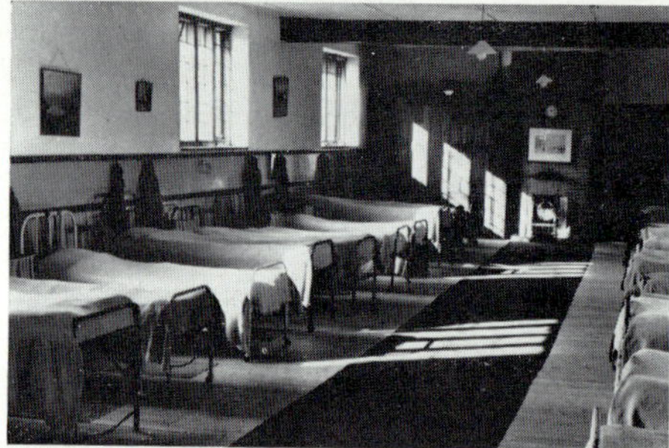

Above: The House in 1914.

Alliott House

Lower Dormitory, about 1950.

1915. *Raised back row:* J. H. R. Sturgess-Wells, R. E. Burr, F. G. Hogg, J. A. Smith, T. A. Rayner, R. E. Wheeler, A. L. Sanders. *Next row:* G. N. Herington, S. J. Rendell, S. N. Salmon, T. C. Zimmerman, C. S. C. Duchesne, F. L. Hamilton, W. H. Hogg, S. D. Herington, T. A. Davis, E. A. Reavell, J. M. Tilsley, L. E. Bird, R. W. Glendinning. *Sitting:* O. S. Huckett, Mr E. A. Knight, Mr C. S. Colman, R. J. Morton, A. D. James. *On ground:* G. W. Bitton (behind), R. C. Hamilton, H. C. Sturgess-Wells, T. A. M. Ionides, H. W. Duchesne, M. G. Ionides, D. St J. Sloane.

Mr Carl Moser and the School House Matron, Mrs Champ. The former had been for many years a much loved and respected master: not only in his teaching of French and German, but in his work in the gymnasium and the art-room he had made a great and beneficent contribution to the life of the school to which he had devoted so much of his own life. Throughout his long retirement at Altstatten in Switzerland he continued to show a lively interest in the affairs of the School, and many Old Stortfordians visited him in his lovely home among his native mountains. He died in 1962 at the age of ninety.

Mrs Champ had been matron at School House for ten years, having succeeded her mother Mrs Schaeffer, as we have seen, in 1902. She now left the school, and in 1913 married J. L. Glasscock, who was at that time the oldest Old Stortfordian, having been a pupil at the Collegiate School and then head boy of the N.G.S. when Alliott took over in 1868. By his death in 1929 perhaps the last personal link with the Collegiate School was broken.

In 1913 Mr Arthur Boardman retired from the position of local secretary to the Governors, a post he had held for fifty years: apart from his work in that capacity, Mr Boardman had given invaluable help to generations of editors of the *N.G.S.* and the *Stortfordian.* In the same year Mr Wood began his long association with the day boys, becoming Day Boy Housemaster, a position which he held continuously, apart from his years of army service during the first war, from 1913 to 1923.

It was in the summer term of this year that the Masters' Common Room in the New Classroom Block became a classroom (later known as the Sixth Form Library), and the masters transferred to a classroom in the old 1875 block (now the Headmaster's study).

In that year also a new publication first appeared, known as the *O.S. Quarterly*. This magazine owed its inception to the energy and enthusiasm of A. G. Tidmarsh, who not only was its first editor but himself contributed many interesting and highly original articles to its pages. The first few numbers especially contain articles and reminiscences by some of the older Old Stortfordians about their schooldays at the N.G.S. (some of which we have included in a previous chapter of this book) as well as discussions and correspondence about matters of Stortfordian interest. But to quote the Editorial in the first number of the *Quarterly*: 'The inspiration of all Stortfordian activity is keenness about the School; and the main purpose of the magazine must necessarily be to keep all Old Boys in touch with Stortfordian doings, and stimulate their interest in the School. Certainly there has never been a time when our pride in the place was more fully justified.' And so the *Quarterly* was from the first largely concerned with reporting the doings of individual Old Boys. During the 1914–1918 war years the magazine was not published: but it was revived after the war under the new name of the *Old Stortfordian*, and continued to appear thrice yearly from 1919 till 1938—a life span in all of a quarter of a century. Then war again supervened, and again the magazine ceased publication: and this time it failed to reappear after the cessation of hostilities.

Meanwhile changes in the aspect of the school grounds continued. In 1912 the Old Gymnasium (then still called the Box Room), with the Carpentry Hut at one end of it, was removed from its (second) site opposite the New Classroom Block to its present position in the south-east corner of the New Field ('Middle Green'), at the approach to the rising ground, known as we have said as the Mountain. This was followed in 1913 by the complete transformation of the area of waste land immediately to the west of the newly transplanted gymnasium, which had always been known as 'Gehenna'. By the inspiration and enterprise of Charles Mellows (who had returned to B.S.C. as a master the previous year), and the enthusiasm of a large number of boys, this area was reclaimed and converted into a series of rock gardens with a fishpond full of water-lilies, which for half a century provided much pleasure (and much toil) for a succession of amateur gardeners. The gardens were extended as the years went by: new pools and rockeries were added; and Chas brought home from his mountaineering holidays more and more Alpine plants. On a sunny afternoon in May, with fountains playing over some of the pools, and trout swimming amongst the white and yellow water-lilies, and the cherry tree in blossom above the miniature lawn, the rock gardens were indeed a beautiful sight. It is all the more sad that, after Chas's retirement, they gradually went to waste through lack of his inspiration and unremitting work: till in 1965 they were finally levelled and the site given over to other purposes.

In the spring term of 1914 Alliott House, a new boarding house that had been built immediately to the north of Grimwade House, was opened with thirty-four boys, under C. S. Colman as housemaster, with Mr E. A. Knight as his assistant housemaster. Mr Knight had joined the staff in 1909, and in the brief years before the 1914–1918 war had become one of the best-loved and most popular masters: he was killed in the war, and by his death Stortford suffered a grievous loss. Miss Slater joined Alliott House as its first matron. The House was formally opened in the following term by Mrs Alliott, the widow of Richard Alliott. In the same year Mr E. W. Hurst retired from the housemastership of Grimwade House owing to ill health, and was succeeded by the Rev. A. S. Le Mare.

It was during the decade before the war that Mr F. B. Shawe, who had played a leading part in introducing life-saving on his arrival at B.S.C. in 1902, laid the foundations of the School's prowess in water-polo. 'Present boys', he wrote later, 'have no idea of the difficulties that had to be overcome. Nobody had ever seen water-polo played; the game was not recognized by the authorities; and time for it had to be found as best we could. The only available time was before breakfast—and games were played in winter as well as summer (this was the heroic period of self-denial modified by "dog biscuits"). It was not till 1906 or 1907 that swimming generally, including water-polo, was officially recognized and taken over by the Games Committee: and later the time between the end of morning school and dinner was set aside for the game. The present standard of play is far higher than it used to be, and boys who take up the game now have much greater chances than those who in the early days had to find out everything for themselves. The small size of our Bath, however, does not give much opportunity for dribbling: this is one reason why ours is essentially a *passing* game.' One of the high lights of these early years was the defeat of Cambridge University in a water-polo match played in the River Cam in 1907, when the School won by one goal to nothing. With the return of Charles Mellows the School's prowess in the water improved still further, reaching its pre-war zenith in 1914, when under the captaincy of V. R. Price the results read: played 10, won 10; goals for 68, against 9.

In this pre-war decade the School developed a close connection with the Claremont Central Mission, in the Pentonville Road, Islington, where a number of Old Stortfordians had been working with the Boys' Brigade. It became the custom from 1908 onwards to invite boys down from the Mission to a 'camp' in the school grounds during the first week of the summer holidays. And each winter term A. G. Tidmarsh used to take the school choir up to Islington to give an annual concert at the Mission, preceded by a generous tea for the performers. This Mission work was indeed a continuation of the tradition of social service initiated, as we have already recounted, by a group of Old Boys of the N.G.S. twenty years before. 'Claremont', as the summer camps were called for short, was revived during the inter-war years, but was discontinued after 1939.

During the summer term of 1914 a number of amateur wireless-telegraphy enthusiasts at Stortford succeeded in constructing a piece of apparatus that could both receive and transmit wireless messages. A mast was erected on the roof of the Bath, and from it an aerial wire was carried with some difficulty to the school 'tower': wires were connected up and brought down through a glass tube into the Operators' Room, somewhere in School House: and soon the 5 p.m. weather report from Paris was being received. The following day the ten o'clock time signal from Paris was received as well as signals from Ireland (Clifden), Lincolnshire (Cleethorpes) and Cornwall (Poldhu); and at 8 p.m. the weather report came through from the Eiffel Tower. Then a mast (actually a rugger post) was erected on Upper Field, and the following afternoon the first message was transmitted from it to School House (an urgent query: 'Is the tuck-shop open?'). Within a short time the operators could transmit over a 15-mile radius and receive from 1,200 miles.

But these early triumphs of Stortfordian scientists were to be short-lived. On the last day of that summer term Austria declared war on Serbia. During the subsequent few days of uncertainty the Past and Present cricket was held as usual at the beginning of the holidays, and as usual the Claremont boys occupied the School grounds. Then Germany invaded Belgium and Luxembourg: the new wireless transmitter, by order of the authorities, was dismantled: we were at war.

When the School reassembled in September 1914, a good deal of confusion was caused by the use that various military formations encamped in the neighbourhood were making of the school premises. Units of the North Staffordshire Territorials were in occupation of the schoolroom and library; the gymnasium and some of the classrooms were being used as dormitories; and a miniature rifle range had been constructed in the swimming-bath, which was also used as a large-scale wash-house where relays of Territorials (of whom there were twenty thousand in Stortford and its immediate vicinity) performed their ablutions once a month. Swimming was therefore out of the question for the School throughout that term. But at the end of it, accommodation for the military having been provided elsewhere, the School took possession again. Fordham [1] no longer toiled at pushing desks around: packs and rifles disappeared from the floors and 'quaint military jests' (we quote from the *Stortfordian*) from the blackboards.

Meanwhile, the School grounds were used for drilling, both by the Special Constables and by the Volunteer Corps. The former included several masters: the latter, raised by Mr Kingdon, had in its ranks the Headmaster, Mr Shawe, and Jones, the school groundsman and professional. At the same time other masters were leaving to enter H.M. Forces. Mr Tidmarsh had indeed already joined up before term opened (he was released from the army a year later owing to ill health

[1] Fordham was at that time responsible for cleaning the classrooms.

and returned to B.S.C. towards the end of 1915): Mr Mellows left before Christmas 1914: in 1916 Mr Knight joined up, being replaced in Alliott's by Mr A. D. Hayward, who had joined the staff in 1914; and in 1917 Mr Wood and Mr Hayward both went to the war.

Fortunately it was not considered necessary to evacuate the School and, after the period of mobilization, staff and boys began to settle down to the conditions of war time. A Cadet Corps approximately one hundred strong was formed, of which Mr Kingdon was C.O. with the rank of captain; and a Boy Scout troop for the younger boys was run by another master, Mr E. C. Corelli, who had joined the staff at the beginning of the war. Black-out regulations were at first somewhat vague: lights were ordered to be concealed 'as far as possible' between 5.30 p.m. and 7.30 a.m. Later, as a result of the Zeppelin raids, stricter regulations were enforced, and boys struggled each day with blinds and improvised black-out screens made from rugs and curtains. In 1916 the Daylight Saving Bill became law: this bill, promulgated by an M.P. of the name of Willett, was steered through Parliament after the latter's death by Sir Robert Pearce who, as we have seen, was and had been for many years the secretary of the Governing Council of B.S.C. The advantages of Daylight Saving, especially in war time, soon came to be universally recognized.[1]

Changes of staff were inevitably frequent in war time, masters often staying for only a year or even a term. Two of these should be mentioned, for both left their mark on the School. S. H. Moore was a successful French teacher, whose skill won for B.S.C. the award of the Sèvres vase (now in the Library) presented by the then President of the French Republic for proficiency in French language and literature. After three years Mr Moore left to become headmaster of Silcoates School, Wakefield, a post which he held with distinction for the next twenty-five years. Another temporary master who will be remembered by those who were at school during the First World War was R. B. Graham, a Quaker and a somewhat militant pacifist: he was a first-rate teacher, as well as being a distinguished mountaineer. He eventually became headmaster of Bradford Grammar School. Other masters who came during the war but stayed longer were W. M. Ingram, who in 1916 took over the Prep from Mr Le Mare, and E. W. Edmunds, J. T. Daughton and J. D. Craig, all of whom came in 1917.

In that year Waytefield was opened as a new boarding house under Mr and Mrs Sutton, though only half the house in the Hadham Road was taken over at this time. 'Hazeldene', the Suttons' house in The Lane, now became the Sanatorium: here Jones, the cricket pro, was

[1] Daylight Saving was in fact tried out at B.S.C. before it was tried nationally.

installed, and Mrs Jones acted as matron. The Sanatorium had previously functioned, as we have seen, in a small house to the east of the Old Field known as the 'Hospital': this house was now taken over for additional music-rooms, and was named Elgar House. The Bursar's office, which had previously been in a room behind the School House kitchens (once the Matron's sitting-room) now shared Elgar House with the practising musicians; now also the old music-rooms at the end of the 1909 classroom block were named Purcell House. In 1918, No. 68 Hadham Road was opened as a temporary boarding house, in the charge of Mr and Mrs Craig.

As the war dragged on the School showed a laudable enthusiasm for helping the country to make good the shortage of labour caused by the demands of the armed forces. From the first a piece of land by Grimwade House had been dug up to make a vegetable plot, and by 1917 the gardening squads, under the supervision of Sergeant Salmon,[1] had two and a half acres under cultivation: volunteers were excused from football sides to help in this work. On most afternoons of the week a squad, composed at first of members of the Cadet Corps, marched off to Mr Stacey's farm to help in various agricultural jobs: later all boys over fifteen were organized in five squads, each in charge of a master, and extended their activities to Mr Prime's and Mr Cox's farms. The wages thus earned were given to charitable objects—perhaps to soothe the feelings of the cricketers, who complained that *they* didn't get fourpence an hour for playing cricket, nor extra 'agricultural' rations for tea! (The ordinary bread ration was now nine half-slices a day.) In addition to these agricultural squads, a party of boys in the charge of a member of the staff spent Sunday mornings at Featherby's munition works, helping to pack the shells manufactured during the previous week.

All these activities interfered a good deal with the Cadet Corps, which could muster only two-thirds of its full strength at parades: but it carried on, encouraged by the donation of a shooting trophy, competed for each year: and a team of four from the corps was entered for the Schools' Shooting Competition organized by the Society of Miniature Rifle Clubs.

This is not the place to list the names of the Old Stortfordians who served in the war. They are recorded, with many portraits, in a War Memorial Booklet published in 1920 by the Headmaster and Nevil Wood. The preface to this book ends with the following words: 'May the outward eyes of those who read this record, now and in the days to

[1] Sergeant Salmon was the P.T. and Gym instructor.

come when the war is ancient history, pierce beneath the bare statistics and behold the vision of the spirit of heroism and self-sacrifice which is contained within; and then behold the same spirit reflected more and more in the life and work of the School that sent them forth.'

In no one was that spirit reflected more typically than in E. A. Knight, who as we have recorded was assistant housemaster to C. S. Colman at Alliott's before the war, and who was killed in 1917. If ever a master ran the danger of being worshipped for his games, it was Knight. Yet no man ever cared less for popularity: it was his real knowledge of games and his entirely unassuming manner that won him his unique position in the School. He would have been the first to protest against a blind worship of athletics: and had he been devoid of all athletic ability, we should have loved him none the less. He seemed to do all things well. A polished classical scholar, a conscientious teacher and an able musician, he filled the schoolmaster's part with rare distinction. Above all, he excelled in the fine art of friendship. All his varied gifts were at the disposal of others. His affection for the School continually grew, and he shared more and more completely in its life—during Claremont week, in the Past and Present matches, or at Hasbro'. His death was an irreparable loss to the School and to all who had worked or played with him at Stortford: and it is fitting that his name should be perpetuated on the doors of the Memorial Hall, which were given in his memory.

Already by the end of 1914 some 140 Old Boys had joined H.M. Forces, and eventually nearly six hundred Old Stortfordians served. Like all other schools, Bishop's Stortford had to mourn the loss of many of her most prominent Old Boys, fifty-five of whom lost their lives. The list of decorations won includes three awards of the D.S.O., one of the M.B.E., thirty of the M.C., two of the A.F.C., two of the D.C.M., five of the M.M. and two of the Meritorious Service Medal. In addition a C.M.G. and some eighteen foreign decorations (including three Légions d'Honneur, one Croix de Chevalier and seven Croix de Guerre) were awarded; thirty-two men were Mentioned in Dispatches; and one was Commended for Services.[1] Finally, in the very last week of the war the V.C. was awarded to Major Brett Cloutman (later His Honour Sir Brett Cloutman Q.C.): the Headmaster read out to the School the citation in the *Gazette* describing his gallant deed: 'For most conspicuous bravery on 6th November 1918, at Pont-sur-Sambre. Major Cloutman, after reconnoitring the river crossings, found the Quartes Bridge almost intact, but prepared for demolition. Leaving his party under cover, he went forward alone, swam across the river, and

[1] The *Jubilee Booklet* published in 1919 gives full details.

having cut the leads from the charges, returned the same way, despite the fact that the bridge and all the approaches thereto were swept by enemy shells and machine-gun fire at close range. Although the bridge was blown up later in the day by other means, the abutments remained intact.'

Let us end this chapter with a quotation from a letter written in France in 1918. The writer was Nevil Wood, who had left Stortford to join up in the previous year: but he spoke for many other Stortfordians: 'I have of course an intense yearning to get back, under splendid new conditions, to the only sort of life I'm really fitted for. It's worth fighting for, and if I actually have to live in Flanders mud for it, I shall be all the clearer as to my little motives. Not for imperialism, not for the financiers and journalists and militarists, but for the Stortford that has been and shall be again after the war; for the priceless memories of the past, and priceless hopes for the young life that shall take the place of lives "hidden in death's dateless night".'

5. Some School Characters

George Mitchell

'Old Mitchell', the School House butler, has already figured in these pages. He retired in 1913 and died a year later. Of him the *Stortfordian* had much to say.

'When in your warm bed in the "A" or the "B" you have wakened long before dawn in the small hours of some chill November morning, you will have wondered drowsily when that infernal bell was going to ring; and your ear may have caught patient steps, plodding through the wet up the lane. That was old Mitchell coming to begin another day's work. Entering the kitchens from the back, he proceeds in a foggy silence to light the gas and to assault the mountains of dirty earthenware.

'"Over forty years sir—quite over forty years sir" — that is all the definite information he can give you. Great and little events, quaint and distinguished personalities have all become mixed and fused in his memory. There are stories—incidents of Mr Alliott "and them days sir": and how "the bell got stuck one morning, sir, and I rang a lil hand-bell in each room, sir, and didn't I have to dodge the pillars just!". There is a distressing reminiscence of an inverted and indignant Mitchell in a soapy bath: or the adventure of the boy who looked as though he had been hanged ("it made my 'art gall"). And there were stories about the staff—"Why, sir, I knew Dr Whiddager, I did, when he was quite a *lil* boy" (you will observe the significance of the adjective) "and Mr Colman and Mr Kingdon and Mr Young and allonem. Why, I remember when Mr Young was here like it was only last week. I remember how. . ." and a low chuckle, tinged with appropriate respect, rounds off a reminiscence of unusual succulence. . . .

'Every Old Stortfordian, from whatever generation, has his own particular picture which any reference to "old Mike" projects onto the screen of memory. The writer has two: one is of a sunny, blithe old gentleman of rosy face and prominent habit, clad in a white apron and carrying a circular tin of carbide round the schoolroom to supply the gas bulbs (how that stuff did flare when you chucked it on the fire!): for background, the old gilt-piped organ and the three great episcopal chairs that stood at the east end. The other shows the same rosy gentleman with the same smile and courtesy, clad in official black with the most lovely buttons, proceeding leisurely towards the shutter and, after a protracted interview behind the service screen, returning with short, choppy steps to the high table, and a faintly pontifical touch in his control of the soup tureen.

'One could dwell on other aspects and qualities—his remorseless punctuality, his absolute reliability, his loyalty to the School; his affection for all boys, young and old, and the rare memory for faces. "Was you wanting anything, sir?": that is really the keynote, sounded over forty years.

'Stored away within his capacious memory were the deeds of all of us, from 1872 onwards; though his stories were somewhat imaginative, and his pictures a little composite. He had the soul of a happy child, would sing and dance like a child. Happy the man who does not worship speed! Mitchell set his own pace, gentle and dignified but never lazy, and kept it. You could not hurry him, could not worry him. He knew his duty and saw that it was done. Was there a general election? Then Mr Young should tell him how to vote. . . .

'After his retirement, Mitchell was often to be seen sauntering through the town, a bright-eyed old gentleman attended by some faithful hound, with a pleasant smile for all his many friends. He died in 1914 as a result of a street accident: a man who for more than forty years had been the symbol of faithful service to the School.'

Mark Matthews

Mark Matthews we have met before, far back in Alliott's days; and we shall meet him again after 1919. He was already an institution when F. S. Young took over the School. 'We possess in Mark Matthews', wrote the *Stortfordian* a few years after the turn of the century, 'one of the oldest institutions in the School, and also one of the most faithful and loyal supporters of all that is connected with Stortford. He first came here in 1877 as boot-boy, being then seventeen years of age, and after four years was promoted to be gardener and groundsman. When one thinks of Mark, one nearly always thinks of a mower as well. As any past cricket captain will tell you, he has always been ready to mow the field: Mark remembers getting up at five o'clock one Whit-Monday in order to run over it once more and get the pitch into perfect condition. He has always been a keen cricketer and a very good bowler. Regularly every year he used to captain the Groom Gardeners' team, which played the 2nd XI and sometimes beat them, too. He usually took most of the wickets, and he once made 60 runs.

'He was a great naturalist and weather-prophet: Mr Alliott, whenever in doubt about anything to do with nature or with the elements, used to consult Mark, who usually turned out to be right. No doubt he turned his knowledge to good effect in his own interests too: for he had the reputation of having in his earlier days been the most cunning and skilful poacher in Hertfordshire. He was very proud of his gun, and would show you his gun licence, signed with his mark—a cross; for, as he would tell you, he could neither read nor write.

'He possessed a very kind heart: when old Mitchell was busy or unwell, it was Mark who would ring the bell for him. He used to feed and generally look after the red squirrels which up till and after the First World War were such a feature of the school grounds. He was, too, immensely strong: surrounded by an admiring crowd of Lower Third worshippers, he would display his strength by bending thick rods of iron piping or lifting heavy weights.

'One of his great achievements was the Cinder Track: the boys did most of the digging and the carting of ashes, but it was Mark who showed them how to do it, giving a hand here, measuring out a length there, and in general organizing the whole operation. He is proud to belong to the School, and the School is proud of him.'

Orme

In 1903 the school horse, Orme, for so long a familiar figure in the school grounds, died, 'so aged', the *Stortfordian* said of him, 'that his teeth gave no clue whatever to his antiquity. For years he wrestled with roller, haycart and mowing machine, but latterly with failing strength. Now alas! he is gone'. His demise inspired a poem which is perhaps worth reprinting here:

The Death of Orme

And is he gone? And shall his form no more
Grace all unwillingly the greensward stretch?
All gaitered in his mighty leathern shoon
It was his wont to wander down the Drive
Pursued by guardians bawling, at whose head
Ran, swift and very terrible, that man
Whose deathless name still echoes round our walls,

Old Father Matthews. Hail, old wizened churl,
Bandy, but bright and beauteous as a bird!
Fond memory recalls his stalwart form,
Accompanied by panoply of pail
And eke the futile broom. Anon with these
Jove-like descended he, and toyed awhile
Athwart the schoolroom; conversation done
Retired behind his cloud of boots, and shunned
In hideous night the wholesome Day (and Martin).
To Orme let us return: with pathos ask
Where is our favourite now? Mayhap he be
In horrid Stygian shades, whinnying with anguish,
Goaded by fiery imps and awful sprites
To run a weary, never-ending race
Upon a Track of Cinders, strewn white-hot.
The thought is hard. . . . Down in our hearts we know
That he, our Orme, our second Pegasus,
Roams somewhere in the equine Paradise;
Nor works he any, save perchance it be
Or here or there to bear upon his back
A laughing horde of sporting Cherubim.
Thus to eternity we trust he moves,
All glistering-white, sleek and magnificent,
Through pastures luscious, blest, celestial.

A. G. T.

Sweep

Orme was followed to the grave two years later by Sweep, the Headmaster's dog. 'For something over four years'—we again quote the *Stortfordian*—'he owned the premises and attended meals, matches and all ceremonies where the boys appeared. To our belief, the greatest sorrow of his life was that he was never allowed to accompany them to chapel. Everywhere else he went with them: once a week, however, there was a strange ceremony to which the boys passed slowly and (more or less) silently, and from this mysterious function Sweep was turned remorselessly away. In all else he may claim to have known the place and its ways more intimately than any man or boy in it, and many of us besides the Headmaster will feel a sense of personal loss.'

Ad Canem Mortuum

Bring forth the sackcloth, cypress, doleful yew:
Strew funeral ashes: Sweep our dog is gone.
Sound mournful hautboys, decent pity make;

Let sad-voiced cantors wail, and to the sky
Let sickly incense fume, that we may 'suage
The wrath implacable of those Powers above
That make us so unspeakably bereft.
Scarce are our sodden cambrics dry, and scarce
The last groan hushed, the last tear dropped adown
The shuddering shirt-front; scarce a daisy blooms
Upon that other mound most lachrymose
That swells above the heroic equine form
So lately laid beneath it. . . . How could we know
That unsuspected in his luckless blood
Disease lay ambushed? And yet, so it seemed,
That mystic, dread affection of the joints
Which men call rheumatism gripped him fast . . .
And then the end—how sad, how meet for tears,
As soothing chymic vapours put him off
This weary mortal coil. Gently was laid
The corse so lately gimblesome and loved
Beneath a bank of blossoms ushering Spring.
His rest is nobly earned. Peace! Sirius shines.

A. G. T.

You and Me

Sing a Song of Stortford—not for those who know
The School to-day, but as it was forty years ago:
Thirty-six, at any rate (let's be precise)
Days of Sydney, Ramo and H. L. Price,
Palmers, Doggarts, Hamiltons; Colletts not a few;
Sinclairs, Smiths and Stephensons; and—Me and You.
(Scrubby little 'new bugs', You and Me,
Singing in the boot-room for our tea!)
Alliott's was new as well—red brick and raw:
Westfield Lodge across the road (shades of Becker Shawe!
Do you remember how, in winter, he'd delight us
Sitting on the radiator, quoting *Heraclitus*?)
Chips, of course, had Alliott's: always seems to me
One couldn't think of B. S. C. and not of C. S. C.
(Saw him only recently: looks just the same—he sat
Smoking, I swear, the same old pipe beneath the same old hat.)
Nevil Wood—'dear Thing'—famed for his sophistic
Ability to quote offhand any school statistic.
And, dominating all, School House, whence o'er the School was flung
The steadfast, single-minded sway of F. S. Young. . . .
'*Some* boy called Sheldrake "Bluebeard"! *Which* boy?... See me at one:
If boys call Sheldrake "Bluebeard" THE SCHOOL CANNOT GET ON!'

(Sheldrake? Used to take us for Carpentry—a weird
Old bird with steel-rimmed spectacles and massive beard.)
Tid and Chas were School House masters then. Do you recall
Tid astride his Levis two-stroke (ludicrously small
For him) careering wildly round New Field—and how, one day
Chas stuck a garden fork clean through his foot? We used to play
Racquets on the concrete court (the Mem. Hall stands there now)
And 'C' Side cricket on New Field. . . . D' you remember how
The kids from Grimwade watched us, creeping shyly through the hedge
To perch on those old benches like sparrows on a ledge?
Rugger sides on Upper Field: how the sunlight glowed
On autumn afternoons amidst the trees in Maze Green Road.
Maths. with Bobby Sutton (hasn't changed a bit:
Still the same elusive smile and faintly mordant wit);
'Tea-Co's' in the Schoolroom—'condenny' and sardines;
Camp coffee; biscuits; tins of 'pork and beans'.
Old Field hasn't altered much . . . shouldn't like to say
What I'd feel like after running sixteen tracks today!

Sing a Song of Stortford—as it still appears
Glimpsed between the 'cloud-rifts' after many years.
Next time you go down there, stroll across New Field
And see, as I did lately, the vision 'faint-revealed',
As the brave new buildings fade from out the scene
Of Stortford as we left it in nineteen-seventeen.

ANON

6. F. S. Young: (2) 1918–1931

THE Armistice in November 1918 coincided with the outbreak at B.S.C. of what was popularly known as Spanish influenza. The epidemic struck, as happened elsewhere, with great suddenness, seventy cases occurring in less than three days (though that was by no means the total number of casualties), and the School had to be closed for three weeks. School House suffered worst: nearly sixty of its members were stricken, and the 'B' and 'C' dormitories had to be converted into sick-rooms. Trained nurses were almost impossible to obtain, and had it not been for the timely help of masters' wives, local parents and other friends the School House would have been in dire straits. The 'out-houses' (the collective name by which Houses other than School House were then still called) had in most cases been able to send their boys home before the infection spread too far; but not a single House was immune, and most of those who went home succumbed there. A number of those who were nursed at school were taken by masters in small groups to convalesce, at Yarmouth and elsewhere.

Meanwhile 23rd September 1918 had marked the Jubilee of the School's foundation; but the war was still on, and in the circumstances the celebrations had to be postponed until 1919. By the spring term of that year Mr Wood, Mr Mellows and Mr Hayward had been demobilized and had returned to the staff. Mr Wood had married, during the war, Miss Clara Tidmarsh, A.G.T.'s sister: and now Mr and Mrs Wood took over 'No. 68' (Hadham Road) from Mr and Mrs Craig. In August Mr Tidmarsh married Miss Gladys Palmer, herself a member of a Stortfordian family; they settled in Wynch Cottage, and Mr Mellows became Senior Housemaster at School House in Tid's place. In the meanwhile Mr Shawe had left after a serious breakdown at the beginning of the summer term, and was succeeded at Westfield Lodge ('Shawe's') by Mr and Mrs Craig. In that term also Dr J. Young was appointed as the school medical officer.

The autumn term of 1919 saw the School at length returning to the normal routine of peace time: the shifts and improvisations of the war years were becoming a thing of the past. Numbers were increasing, and this necessitated more staff: there were no less than seven new masters in the September term, only three of whom, however, were to stay at Stortford for any length of time. These were N. Monk-Jones, who joined Charles Mellows in School House as assistant housemaster, R. E. Pond and Rev. C. H. Stearn. At the end of the year a prominent Stortfordian figure, Mr F. M. Kingdon, who had been Bursar for the last six years, left the staff: together with Mr E. C. Corelli he started a prep school in Southport. But Mr Kingdon subsequently returned to Stortford, and we shall have more to say of him later. His place as Bursar was taken by another Old Stortfordian and father of Stortfordians, Mr E. C. Duchesne, who came to us from the Working Men's College, London, of which he had been secretary. Mr E. C. Corelli had acted as Day Boy housemaster during N. P. Wood's absence, had been in charge of the library and had been a very successful scoutmaster.

It was at this time that Dr O. O. Brooksbank, who had come during the war to help with the music, first brought out the School Calendar, which was combined with the Class Lists—a purely routine but none the less invaluable publication which has appeared terminally ever since.

It was about 1920 that the Governors opened negotiations with the Board of Education as a result of which B.S.C. became what was called a Direct Grant school: of this we shall have more to say later. Meanwhile in that year the Governing Council lost two of its most prominent members. Mr E. W. Grimwade, who had replaced his father as chairman of the N.G.S. thirty-three years previously, now retired, and was succeeded by Mr Watson Slack, himself an Old Boy of the School. At the same time the secretary to the Governors, Sir Robert Pearce, retired after no less than fifty-two years in that office. Indeed, he had held it from the foundation of the School, in which he had played an important part, embodying in its constitution the ideals of its founding fathers, and carrying into execution the plans which they tentatively outlined. It would be difficult to exaggerate the debt the School owes to his devoted work.

In spite of all these changes, continuity with the pre-war traditions built up by F. S. Young was ensured by the nucleus of devoted staff who had helped him to establish them in the halcyon years before 1914; though the School inevitably lost something of the family spirit which pervaded the smaller and more closely knit community of pre-war days. After the war not only was the School larger (numbers in 1919 were nearly three hundred—more than double what they were in 1910), but whereas before the war most of the boys had the same Nonconformist home background and many were actually sons of the manse, they now tended to be drawn from very much wider social circles.

Stortford was, by this time, beginning to make a name for itself among the smaller public schools of England: and Mr Young, who was personally becoming an influential member of the Headmasters' Conference, set himself so to organize the School that it might be able to meet the greater demands of education in the post-war world. It is difficult for those who are too young to remember the 1914–1918 war to realize what a complete break with the past that war represented in the history of the country and indeed of Europe generally: the whole political and social climate was different, and this was inevitably reflected in the world of education. New methods of teaching the more traditional subjects and a greater emphasis on the scientific side of the curriculum were observable at Stortford as elsewhere, while at the same time the importance of the artistic as opposed to the purely academic approach began to be appreciated. Stortford had in fact always encouraged various out-of-school activities such as music and painting, as well as gardening and, more especially, natural history; and during the period between the wars we shall find a steady and quite remarkable expansion of hobby activities of all kinds.

It was during this period too that Charles Mellows was able to build up the School's swimming on the foundations laid by F. B. Shawe. Charles, like his brother Arthur, had won his half-blue for swimming at Oxford before the war: now his experience and enthusiasm were devoted to improving still further the standard of the School's swimming and water-polo. In 1920 B.S.C. entered a team for the Bath Club Invitation Race, taking third place: three years later the Stortford team, consisting of F. J. M. Dent (captain), T. K. Collett and G. A. Redhouse, for the first time won the Bath Cup. The School's reputation stood high too in the universities. At Oxford W. R. Bion, S. D. Herington, M. C. Nokes and H. L. Price, and at Cambridge T. S. Hamilton, R. Barrett and G. H. Day[1] all won their half-blues, the latter captaining the team; so that, for two successive years, of the fourteen players in the 'varsity water-polo match no less than seven were Old Stortfordians. Indeed throughout the twenties Old Stortfordians regularly figured in the university water-polo matches.

An interesting game, recalling the Stephenson family's soccer match referred to in an earlier chapter, appeared in the swimming fixture list of 1925. In that year the seven Collett brothers played the School at

[1] G. H. Day under the *nom de plume* of Peter Quince wrote a novel *Left-handed Doctor*, in which reference is made to music at B.S.C. under A. G. Tidmarsh, who, however, appears under a pseudonym. The book is dedicated to the memory of A.G.T.

water-polo, and defeated them by four goals to nil: though it should be pointed out that the School was without its captain, D. B. Collett, who had defected to the family team!

At the same time our reputation at cricket was growing. C. H. Titchmarsh had indeed played for Hertfordshire before the war: now, in 1922, he was with the M.C.C. team that toured Australia and New Zealand. C. B. Fordham too was playing for Hertfordshire. At Oxford V. R. Price captained the university side, for which H. L. Price also played several times. At Cambridge A. G. Doggart won his blue, and J. H. Doggart captained one of the trial sides.

A. G. Doggart also won his blue for soccer at Cambridge, and played regularly for the Corinthians and the Casuals: and he represented England not only in the amateur international side, but once in the full England XI. A. N. Dupont, who had been in the same school side as Doggart, also played for the Casuals.

At rugger both Prices won their blues at Oxford, and W. R. Bion also played regularly for the university, though he missed the 'varsity match through injury. A. G. Doggart (occasionally; the claims of soccer being given priority) and P. O. Davies, once or twice, played for Cambridge. These and others figured prominently in Hospitals, Club and County rugger. H. L. Price played for England for several seasons. He also won his hockey half-blue (as it then was) at Oxford and then his England cap, thus becoming a double international; indeed on one Saturday during the 1921–2 season he was asked to play for England *v.* Scotland at rugger and also at hockey: he chose to play the former.

Finally in athletics M. C. Nokes [1] won his blue at Oxford for Throwing the Hammer, and S. D. Herington his half-blue for cross-country running. D. G. White, having narrowly failed to win the Mile for B.S.C. in the Public Schools Sports, went on to distinguish himself on the track at Oxford, winning the Mile and the Half-mile in the Oxford University Sports: he was awarded his athletics blue, and became secretary of the O.U.A.C. In the inter-'varsity relays he found himself running against F. B. Arnold, who also won the Mile in the Cambridge University Sports.

During these post-war years the growth of the School led to numerous extensions and additions, both to the buildings and to the playing-fields. In 1919 an army hut was purchased to serve as a temporary assembly hall, the numbers being now too great to be accommodated in the old Schoolroom in School House, which from this time became simply the School House Common Room. A site for the Hut was cleared on the Old Field near the Mountain: this unfortunately

[1] Later, in 1930, Nokes captained the English athletics team at the first Empire Games.

involved the sacrifice of a number of trees, chiefly elms, which were the haunt of the red squirrels. These charming animals abounded at that time in the school grounds, and could be watched from the School House disporting themselves in the trees that line the drive. But an epidemic disease destroyed them many years ago, and the far less attractive grey squirrels moved in to replace them.

The Hut, after an unfortunate setback owing to a sudden gale ('the wind blew, a door slammed—and it was no more', reported the *Stortfordian*), was completed in time to be used for a memorable Old Stortfordians' Dinner in June 1919. This was in a sense the Jubilee Dinner a year late, and it was a memorable occasion.[1] 'Seldom before had there been so large a gathering of Old Boys. Some of them had not seen the School for many years: many had not visited Stortford since the war, and these must have found many alterations since they were last here. There were some who had never seen Alliott House; comparatively few had known Waytefield; hardly any knew of our latest acquisition—the Hut, or had seen its many-windowed walls stretching over the far side of the Old Field. Then, passing along the much-widened paths to the new classrooms, the visitors found the office full of fresh reminders of their schooldays—photographs of old friends, fixture cards of long-past matches, magazines telling of the School as they had known it. But in spite of recent changes the School remained the same to them; and in the old favourites sung at the chantey held that evening in a marquee on the New Field, and in the old buildings which had now weathered their first fifty years, they found again the School which they had known of old.'

It was at this time that a Jubilee booklet was published, compiled by N. P. Wood. It contained a brief outline of the School's history, and included portraits of its first two headmasters, with photographs of the boarding houses and an architect's drawing of the projected new classroom quadrangle (which was in fact never completed): and the author appended a list of 'Prominent Stortford Figures', nearly all of whom he had known personally.

For the next three years the Hut was used for all school functions—for morning prayers, concerts, plays and similar occasions. After the building of the Memorial Hall the Hut was partitioned off into a music-room, an art-room and classrooms. Later these rooms were used partly as a general place of storage; but for many years now they have been given over to the activities of various hobbies.[2]

[1] We quote here from the *Stortfordian*.

[2] The Hut is scheduled for removal to make room for the Technical Centre metal workshop.

Later in the same year the accommodation at Waytefield was increased by throwing into one the boarding house and the semi-detached house next door that had previously been occupied by Mr Blandford. At the same time classroom accommodation was increased by temporarily installing two forms in Westgrove House,[1] the house opposite the entrance to the school drive, owned by Mr Young. In 1920 a new hut was erected near Elgar House for the Day Boys, whose numbers had risen to fifty or more, and the old Day Boy room became the Natural History Museum. In the same year the new dining-hall was built at Grimwade House: this released the old dining-room for use as the Shell classroom, and it continued as such for many years. It is now a play-room, only occasionally used for classes. Main School boarding accommodation was also increased by the opening of a small house in Bell's Hill, called 'The Chimes'. This was run by R. E. Pond as a temporary waiting-house and could take eight boys: previously 'overflow' boys had been parked out in twos and threes with various masters. Meanwhile the rugger pitches taken over on Silver Leys,[2] on the Hadham Road, before the war, continued to be used until the 'thirties. In 1922 a new tuck-shop was put up between Elgar House and the new Day Boy House; for the diminutive building by the racquets court (which, as the *Stortfordian* put it, had room for no more than 'an irate tuckman and two small boys') had been demolished.

But the chief addition to the school buildings during the early post-war years was of course the Memorial Hall, built in memory of the Old Stortfordians who had lost their lives in the war: of which the foundation stone was laid, on Prize Day 1921, by Mr Watson Slack, as chairman of the Governing Council, and Alderman James Stephenson, representing the relatives of Old Boys who fell in the war. A year later, on 13th May 1922, the hall was formally opened by Sir Arthur Quiller-Couch. 'Visitors arriving up the drive on that day might have thought that they had strayed and lost their way, had it not been for Mark Matthews, who stood unalterable at the head of the drive, and for the Oak, which has been particularly glorious this year. No sign of the wide sweep of gravel, of the racquets court and the tuck-shop upon its edge: no view of Alliott House in the distance behind its rose garden, or of the terraces of New Field. Instead was a semicircular parapet and two steps up to a gravel grass-bordered walk, leading to

[1] Lessons in these classrooms used to be enlivened by inquisitive cows, as they were driven to market, thrusting their heads through the open windows; or by the strains of blind Tom Glasscock's barrel organ, which (having been duly bribed) he played persistently just outside the gate.

[2] Silver Leys had from time to time been used for games in Alliott's time.

the steps of an impressive building whose stone front shone white in the afternoon sun.'[1]

Speaking of the war generation, Sir Arthur said that men who had gone through all the horrors and dangers of war were already beginning to forget it: so be it. But it was not for those who were too old or too young to share their experience to forget it; it was for such to look at the war clearly, face to face, and estimate their sacrifice. 'We must always think of these our elder brothers as ever dwelling in this place.'

The architect was Clough Williams Ellis, who was faced with the task of designing an all-purposes building which, while being primarily a memorial to the Old Boys of the School who fell in the war, should serve as chapel, theatre and concert hall. Many details, such as the colour of the bricks, which do not harmonize (nor indeed were they intended to harmonize) with the surrounding school buildings, and the colour scheme of the blue lapis lazuli at the platform end of the interior, were the subject of much controversy.[2] But the architect maintained that many found inspiration in just such colourful settings; and the building has continued for forty-five years to fulfil its threefold function, though, since the erection of the Leo Price Gymnasium in 1957, the Dramatic Society's productions, and often concerts, have been transferred to that building.

Many of the internal furnishings of the Memorial Hall were presented by the members of the various School Houses: for example, the gilt wooden lectern, with its two-headed Imperial eagle, was given by the boys of Alliott House in 1923. This lectern is interesting in that it formerly belonged to the chapel of Canford Manor in Dorset (which was sold in that year and became Canford School). It is baroque in style and probably dates from the early nineteenth century. It is likely that it formed part of the collection of Lady Guest, who at one time owned the Manor and who was a connoisseur of *objets d'art*: at the time of its acquisition it was reputed to have come from Czarist Russia, but could equally well be the eagle of the Holy Roman Empire.

The year 1922 was certainly an important one for the School architecturally; not only was the Memorial Hall opened, but the foundations of Robert Pearce House were laid. In the following year 'R. P. H.' as it was called (or simply 'Pearce' for short) was opened under the housemastership of A. G. Tidmarsh. Owing to the illness of Sir Robert Pearce, after whom the House is named, the opening ceremony was performed on 16th May by Lady Pearce, who afterwards entertained the whole House to tea. It was indeed sad that Sir Robert did not live

[1] Report in the *Stortfordian.*

[2] The west end was remodelled in 1968. (See footnote p. 207.)

to see the building completed: he died a week or two after the House was opened.

In 1923 also was held a very successful bazaar, the proceeds of which were devoted to the completion of the interior fittings of the Memorial Hall. And in 1924 the spate of building, so far from abating, gathered head. A porter's lodge was built by the entrance gates, to be occupied by Sergeant Salmon and his family; at Grimwade House a hut classroom was put up, encroaching, alas, on the playground space of 'clink', and extensions were built on to the somewhat constricted living quarters of Mr and Mrs Ingram; most important of all, further classroom accommodation was provided in the Main School. This was done by building extensions at either end of the 1909 classroom block: at the west end four new classrooms were built, jutting out southwards at right angles to the main block, which thus became L-shaped: while at the east end the Purcell House music-rooms were pulled down and a Sixth Form Library was built in its place, with a classroom over. At the same time the Bursar's office was removed from Elgar House (which was now entirely taken over for music lessons and practice) and installed in the two ground-floor rooms of the old 1875 block. One of these was the famous, or perhaps we should say notorious, 'Vestry', beloved by generations of School House veterans who, being in the Remove, had not achieved the privilege of private studies accorded to the Sixth Form. The Masters' Common Room upstairs was transferred to its present position at the west end of the 1909 classroom block, where previously the Sixth Form Library had been: and the room thus vacated became the Headmaster's School Study, though he kept on his House Study in the School House. It was at this time also that the pathway to and from Alliott House was laid out, descending eastwards by a series of brick steps and terminating at the parapet just short of the science laboratories: the hedge and most of the elms that separated Grimwade House from New Field were removed, and the rose terrace was formed that has ever since been such a feature of the school grounds. Incidentally this meant that the Prep could no longer play their matches on New Field, though practice games were still played there: from now on all matches were played on Upper Field. Finally, it was in 1924 also that Westgrove House on the Hadham Road, where as we have seen two rooms on the ground floor had already been used as classrooms, was opened as a second waiting-house for boarders, housing another eight boys who were in the charge of Rev. C. H. Stearn and his wife. In the following year the 'out-house' changing-room at the west end of the indoor bath was enlarged, and a new elementary laboratory built over it.

We have outlined in this chapter so far the chief changes in the visual aspect of the school—its buildings and its grounds and playing-fields. But these were of course only the background setting for the personalities and the activities that make up the life of a school. We have mentioned the additions to the teaching staff at the end of the war: in 1921 Mr E. Pascal was appointed as chemistry master, and Mr Brendan Bracken (later Viscount Bracken) temporarily joined the Prep staff: the latter only stayed two terms, but left his mark none the less—he was later to make a name for himself as editor of the *Financial Times*, and then as Minister of Information in Churchill's wartime government. It was in 1921 also that A. T. Q. Bluett joined the staff as senior modern languages master: he stayed for some seven years, and helped both with the rugger and cricket of the School, as well as playing at both games for the town. At the same time Mr P. Carlaw came as carpentry instructor, a post he was to hold for the next forty-two years: so that by the time he retired 'Pip' had been a familiar figure to many generations of Stortfordians. In 1922 W. R. Bion O.S., to whose prowess at Oxford both in rugger and swimming we have already referred, returned to the staff to teach history and French: he also became chairman of the Games Committee and took over the running of the rugger from Charles Mellows. With a brilliant war record behind him, as well as his subsequent athletic skill, his strong personality made a deep impression on the boys he taught in the classroom or trained on the rugger field. (Masters as well as Old Boys still have somewhat rueful memories of Bion's spartan methods at those senior side rugger practices on Upper Field!) He also imbued many of his pupils with his own enthusiasms for literature and pictures: it was a great loss to the School when, after a couple of years, he decided to take up psycho-analysis and left to study medicine.

In 1924 Mr H. W. Sumsion, a Mus. B. of Durham, joined the music staff on the retirement of Dr Brooksbank: and at the same time an outstanding Stortford personality joined the modern languages staff, of which he was to be the energetic head for over forty years, in the person of W. J. Strachan, then just down from St Catharine's, Cambridge.

Meanwhile Mr Young himself had completed twenty-five years as Headmaster: during this time he had built up the School, which he had taken over when it was in very low water, and set it on a sound educational and financial basis. The occasion was marked, as had happened in the case of Mr Alliott in 1893, by a ceremony, again held in the Memorial Hall, Farringdon Street, London, at which a presentation was made to Mr and Mrs Young in the presence of a large number of masters, Old Boys, parents and members of the School. Mr C. S.

Colman, as treasurer of the presentation fund, recalled that, at the time of Mr Young's appointment, there were only about ninety boys in the School, the balance sheet was depressing, and the financial position critical; while from a material point of view, the best classroom they had was now regarded as an unsatisfactory boot-room (laughter). Mr Young's castles in the air, however, had since been built in solid bricks and mortar and stones. Mr Young, replying, expressed his and Mrs Young's thanks for the gifts, and went on to say that some fifteen hundred boys had passed through his hands, for whom he had acted 'as at once Prime Minister, Lord High Executioner (laughter), Priest, Solicitor and Estate Manager!' When he first came to Stortford he had put down on paper the ideas he had for the expansion of the School, and had placed the future buildings in much the same position as they now occupied: while he had also had in mind boarding houses stretching up Maze Green Road. And in a letter which he sent out a few days later to the Old Stortfordians and others who had contributed to the presentation, he added: 'What I should like to do in the few years of work which, I hope, I may be capable of giving to the School without injuring it, is to leave a school provided with all the most important and necessary buildings and equipment for a school of about 350 boys in the Main department'.

He was indeed able to make numerous improvements in the School's amenities during the last six years of his headmastership, though as was to be expected they were less spectacular than those of the years immediately after the war. (See sketch plan on front end-papers.)

By 1926 the new fives courts, south of Grimwade House gardens, were ready for use. In the same year Westfield House and its beautiful garden, between the Lane and Hadham Road, were acquired by the School as a sanatorium, replacing the old 'san' up the Lane. This meant a rather shorter journey for anyone going 'aeger': the patient was transported in 'Black Maria', a curious vehicle—a sort of enclosed invalid chair—which remained in use till after the Second World War.

The Westfield House lawns were taken over by the staff: first for croquet (which had previously been played, chiefly by the more senior masters, on ground just east of Grimwade House, now built over by the extensions to the G. H. housemaster's private quarters), and later, when interest in this somewhat Edwardian form of recreation began to flag, for the more energetic game of tennis. Minor additions the same year were the new gate-posts at the entrance to the drive and the covered practice-wicket just south of the fives courts.

The year 1927 saw the erection of a second hut-classroom on the G. H. playground, and also the completion of the organ in the Memorial

Hall, which was inaugurated by a dedicatory service followed by a short organ recital. In the autumn of that year the field immediately east of Upper Field—part of the ground marked on a tithe map of 1829 as Windhill Field—was used for rugger for the first time, having been put down to grass the previous year. It was known at first as New Upper Field and later, when the field farther east of it was also taken over, as Middle Field.

In 1928 two new tennis courts were laid down between the covered wicket and the rock gardens: these were later (1935) replaced by hard courts. Tennis had previously been played at various places—on Old Field near the drive, on New Field, sometimes even on Upper Field. The Lawn Tennis Club was now put on an official footing and outside fixtures arranged.

Meanwhile work had been started on the open-air bath, owing to the initiative and energy of Charles Mellows, who organized squads of willing helpers to carry out the laborious job of digging out the preliminary excavations. Incidentally this involved the removal of the 'horse-trough', which stood in the field just beyond the present Art Hut. This was quite a local landmark, and the threat of a ducking in the horse-trough was used at times with good effect against the type of boy whose hubristic conduct was held to offend against the School's code of decent behaviour.

Such was the energy of Chas and his volunteer navvies that by 1928 the outdoor bath, as it was then called (it is now generally referred to as the outdoor swimming pool), was already in use, and it soon became, as it has ever since remained, one of the most appreciated amenities of Stortford life in the summer term. In 1929 the first part of what is known now as the Library Block of classrooms materialized (though as yet there was no library), on the site that Mr Young had long ago earmarked for that purpose. This was the ground floor only (with a 'temporary' flat roof, which in the event remained for more than thirty years) of the western end of the present Library Block, and was later taken over by the Prep. In the same year another successful bazaar enabled the Memorial Hall to be completed, the walls being now panelled and the final decorations added. Finally, in 1931, a small extension was added to the private house wing of Grimwade House.

During these last years of Mr Young's régime, the staff personnel underwent numerous changes. In 1925 Mr P. F. Horton came as art master, and though he only remained on the staff for five years, his robust personality, wide culture and immense enthusiasm left a permanent mark on the aesthetic side of the School's life. In 1926 Dr Barnes took over the directorship of music from Mr (now Dr) H. W.

Sumsion: the latter was shortly afterwards appointed organist at Worcester Cathedral and then at Gloucester Cathedral, where over a period of more than thirty years he has made a great name for himself, especially in connection with the Three Choirs Festivals.

But perhaps the chief loss to the School at this time was that occasioned by the appointment of Mr N. P. Wood in 1926 to be Headmaster of Eltham College. Nevil Wood was one of that devoted band of men who had helped F. S. Young to build up the School in the years before the 1914–1918 war. Himself an Old Stortfordian, he must have felt it a great wrench to leave the school for which he had such a deep affection. In a letter to the *Stortfordian* at this time, he wrote: 'I feel that I cannot write this letter without trying to express my deep sense of gratitude not only to the present School, but also to that curious ancestor of us all, the old N.G.S.; which, as I knew it, was on its last legs and destined, on the arrival of a new headmaster, to an honoured death, a decent burial and a marvellous resurrection. Decrepit though it then was, the old N.G.S. had for many of us a wonderful charm that evoked lasting gratitude and loyalty. . . . For me, the kindness that I experienced as a boy at school led me, perhaps mistakenly but I hope honestly, to see life in terms of Stortford, and to find in its progress and its success my greatest happiness.'

Perhaps this is the place to write of Nevil's life and work at B.S.C., for he lived only six more years after moving to Eltham: so that, apart from a couple of years at Yarmouth after leaving Cambridge, he spent his teaching life almost entirely at Stortford. With Tid, as we have seen, he founded the Hempstead and then Hasbro' holiday parties: he was Day Boy Housemaster from 1913 to 1923: president of the Old Stortfordians' Club in 1922; housemaster of the waiting-house at 68 Hadham Road from 1921 to 1926. But it was in his personal contacts that he made his greatest contributions to the life of the School. His friendships and correspondence with Stortfordians throughout his life must have been unique alike in quantity and quality. He saved and treasured every letter he received from Old Boys. In letters and conversation alike he was for ever planning how to preserve the ideals of the School and so to present them to everyone as to make them a real, vivid and spiritual force both in the lives of its members and in the outer world. To this end, as his many friends gratefully testify, no searching the archives of the past, no correspondence could be too heavy a task; no breakfast or tea-parties too numerous or hilarious; no tobacco parliaments round the fire talking Stortford 'shop' too long; no copying of scores, team lists, birth dates, athletic results, details of mark-books or committees too wearisome. The life of Stortford was to him a flaming altar; and to tend it, enlarge and protect it, and make sacrifices upon it was the prime object of his being. As a master he combined kindness and patience with great scrupulousness, devotion to his educational ideals, and unswerving loyalty to his headmaster and his colleagues. There is little to say of his headmastership of Eltham, where he was handicapped by increasing ill health which compelled him to resign in 1930; he returned to his beloved Stortford, where he died in 1932.

When writing of Nevil Wood, one thinks immediately of Ruth Searle, who was housekeeper to Nevil and to Mr Knight at 68 Hadham Road before the war. Her interest in the boys and their doings, her breezy comments on current situations and her unfailing kind-heartedness made her an ideal hostess. After her retirement to Rye Street she became almost an institution, and it was regarded by the older boys as quite an honour to be invited to her Sunday afternoon tea-parties; many were the quarts of tea and pounds of cake consumed in her little cottage parlour, where she once entertained no less than thirty old and present Stortfordians. She died the year after Nevil had left Stortford for Eltham: by her death many O.S. felt they had lost a remarkable personality and a loyal friend.

In 1927 J. T. Daughton, known to Stortfordians during his ten years on the staff as 'Fundy', left to become Headmaster of Brigg Grammar School in Lincolnshire. In addition to his work as geography master, during his last four years he had been Day Boy Housemaster. The geography teaching was now taken over by A. O. Ward, of University College, Oxford, who came to us from Taunton School (where he had taught under C. D. Whittaker); while the Rev. C. H. Stearn took over the Day Boy House. At the same time W. M. Ingram, who had been head of the Preparatory School and housemaster of Grimwade House since 1916, had to resign owing to ill health. He had built up the Prep from a nucleus of twelve boys into a well-organized, self-contained school of sixty pupils, and indeed tended to regard the Prep as a separate school, independent of the College; he coached his boys with an eye on the Common Entrance Examination and with a view to their entering other public schools as well as B.S.C., though the vast majority naturally went on to the College. He was a strict disciplinarian, and a keen cricketer who often played in 'Past and Present' cricket week. On leaving Stortford he retired from active work, though he continued to do coaching at his home in Walberswick for many years. He died in 1957.

Ingram was succeeded as head of the Prep and housemaster of Grimwade House by N. Monk-Jones, who had left School House on the occasion of his marriage the previous year. He had been for eight years form master of the Lower Sixth and latterly chairman of the Games Committee, as well as running the rugger since W. R. Bion's departure. He remained chairman of the Games Committee, but handed over the rugger to H. E. Wall, who at this time returned to B.S.C. as a master, joining Chas Mellows as assistant housemaster in School House. At the end of the year R. E. Pond left, returning as senior housemaster to Tettenhall College, where he had taught before the war. During his eight years at Stortford Pond had won the intimate confidence of a large number of boys, intellectuals and athletes alike, in a way that is granted to few schoolmasters. Many of his pupils will recall with gratitude long talks and discussions with him, in his bungalow up on the Hadham Road—on pictures and books, plays and music, as well as on the multifarious details and problems of a schoolboy's life. As a teacher, especially of German to the sixth forms, as a coach of junior teams in rugger and cricket, and as a producer of plays for the Dramatic Society, there was indeed, as the *Stortfordian* put it, 'no branch of our school life—scholastic, athletic or aesthetic—that Mr Pond did not touch'. And many of his colleagues were and are, as the present writer can testify, as much in his debt as were so many of his pupils. At the time of writing he is still living in happy retirement with his wife in their charming cottage in Herefordshire.

In the same year (1927) Mr Watson Slack retired from the chairmanship of the Governing Council: he was succeeded by Mr F. W. Grimwade, who was thus the third generation of that family to hold this office.

In 1928, by the death of A. E. Turberville, the Old Stortfordians' Club lost one of its founder members who, as past president and still more as honorary secretary for no less than thirty-nine years (1881–1920), had guided the Club's activities and encouraged its development. It was remarked of him that he was 'by profession an accountant and by occupation Secretary of the O.S.C.'; and the Club owes more to him than to anyone else in the course of its ninety-odd years' history. Shortly after his death an oak reading-stand for the Memorial Hall (not to be confused with the eagle lectern) was given to the School by the Old Boys in Turberville's memory. In this year also Dr John Young retired from the position of School Medical Officer, which he had held since 1917. Many O.S. will recall tea-parties at Dr Young's house in the Hadham Road. He took a keen interest in the School's activities, especially in the Cross Country Run, and maintained contact with the School till his death nearly twenty years later. He was succeeded by Dr R. P. Gammie.

In 1929 the Rev. C. H. Stearn left, after ten years on the staff, to become Professor of Classics at McMaster University, Toronto, a post he held until his retirement some thirty years later. He was succeeded as Day Boy housemaster by A. D. Hayward, the latter's place as assistant housemaster at Alliott's being taken by a Cambridge classics man, C. L. Howell-Thomas. In the same year F. D. Field-Hyde left to take up a post at Repton, after four years at Stortford during which, in addition to his modern language teaching, he had done a lot of rugger coaching and taken an active part in the School's musical activities. He was later to become Headmaster of Tettenhall College. His place was taken by Mr H. R. Spencer, who was not only a German specialist but contributed a lot to the dramatic activities of the School: he not only acted himself, but produced plays and, after the retirement of E. W. Edmunds, became president of the Dramatic Society until he left in 1938. Another new member joined the staff in the person of Mr R. W. Harre, who later became the first Careers Master at the School. He retired in 1936.

In the following year Mr E. C. Duchesne retired after ten years as bursar: a senior O.S. of whom F. S. Young said: 'He was a man of cheerful disposition and high spirits. I have never seen him anything else but cheerful, nor have I ever seen him lose his temper.' Even after his retirement E. C. D. retained his zest for living, being active in many town clubs and committees: he could still be met on Upper Field, wearing his faded Hampshire soccer blazer (as a young man he had captained the Hants and Dorset football team), and almost up to the last he retained an air of exuberant youthfulness. Later in the same year E. Pascal left, after nine years on the staff, to become Assistant Director of Education for Middlesex: as housemaster at 68 Hadham Road and later at Westgrove House, as a keen games coach, especially of rugger, and as the first president of the Science Society, he had contributed widely to the life of the School. It was in 1930 too that Percy Horton gave up the art mastership: we have already referred to the tonic influence he had on the artistic side of the School's life. Typical was his organization, with Mr Strachan's co-operation, of a school party to visit the exhibition of Flemish Art at Burlington House: in the twenties expeditions of this kind were by no means the routine outings they have become in the sixties, and were only allowed on the understanding that school work or 'preps' missed were made good. It was again as a result of his collaboration with Mr Strachan that a little booklet appeared, in aid of the Memorial Hall Bazaar in 1929, entitled *First Offence*, an attractive collection of poems and decorations, selected from school work produced largely in the lower forms, in English and drawing lessons during that year. 'He had a profound knowledge of art' (we quote the *Stortfordian*) 'and made the study of painting interesting and easy.' Horton subsequently made a name for himself both as a landscapist and as a portrait-painter: a one-man show which he held at the Ashmolean Museum at Oxford a few years ago illustrated the remarkable range of his work. He became Ruskin Professor of Drawing at Oxford, a post he held until his recent retirement. He was succeeded at B.S.C. by G. H. Rhoades, who was also an original artist who carried on the art teaching along the modern lines laid down by Horton: and the laborious and uninspired copying of plaster casts of so-called 'classical' sculpture or fragments of sculpture, which had lingered until the first war, was at long last a thing of the past.

Finally, it was in 1930 also that Jack Nichols, the popular groundsman and cricket pro, left to become coach to the Norfolk County Cricket Club: at the same time Mr Sutton gave up the running of the school cricket after more than twenty years, during which he had turned out many first-class cricketers. Nichols was succeeded by Harold Watson, who, conversely, left Norwich, where he had been the professional at the Norfolk County C.C., to come to Stortford.

During Mr Young's headmastership, the steady rise in the academic standards and achievements of the School was reflected in the increasing numbers of open scholarships and exhibitions at Oxford and Cambridge won by boys from the School. The Honours Board above the classroom staircase is headed by the name of F. S. Young himself, who in 1889 won a scholarship in natural science at Oxford (C. D. Whittaker had won an exhibition in mathematics at Cambridge as far back as 1883, though not straight from school). In 1891 C. S. Colman won a scholarship in classics at Oxford, a year after leaving school: and in 1899 C. B. Young, brother of F. S., did the same thing. But between 1905 and 1931 over thirty such successes are recorded, the majority due to C. S. C.'s teaching in classics, but a number also in history, mathematics and, in 1931, the first in modern languages.

In sport, various developments took place in the post-war decade. In 1922 soccer, which since before the war had been relegated to second place and only played in the spring term, was finally, to the regret of many, dropped altogether, though the annual matches against the O.S. were continued for a year or two more. It seems indeed regrettable that both games could not have continued to be played. But the general tendency to favour rugger was prevalent amongst public schools at the time, though of course there were and still are some notable exceptions: and it may well be that it would not have been possible to fit both codes satisfactorily into the year's athletic programme.

The new arrangement enabled the rugger house matches to be played off in the spring term; and in 1924 a system of league teams was organized for all boys not on senior side, and league games were played throughout the term. In cricket the 'Past and Present' week at the beginning of the summer holidays, first started as far back as 1890, was revived in 1919, and four years later for the first time all four Past and Present matches were won. In swimming, the School's success at the Bath Club in 1923 has already been mentioned: in that year also, for the first time, the water-polo House cup presented by Mr S. G. Cuff was competed for, and in the following year Mr and Mrs A. Reavell presented a House swimming cup. A third challenge cup was presented in 1927 by Mr H. R. Dent for a quarter-mile relay, in which eleven swimmers compete from each House.

The twenties were indeed to see Stortford's reputation as a swimming school at its height, our chief rivals in those days being St Paul's School and Dulwich College. After our initial success we won the Bath Cup no less than four times successively in 1926, 1927, 1929 and 1930. In the intervening year, 1928, the race was not swum at all: but that year is none the less important in the history of Stortford swimming, for it saw the establishment of the Old Stortfordians' Swimming Club. This was largely due to the enthusiasm and hard work of H. M. Wagstaff: he was the Club's first honorary secretary, a position which he held for more than twenty years. The Club got off to a good start: in water polo ten matches were won out of eighteen played, and in swimming the Club won the Old Public Schools Team Race—actually for the third time in succession, for even before the formation of the Club the O.S. had entered teams for this race. J. H. Morton swam for Ireland in the Taill-taen Games at Dublin: H. M. Wagstaff was invited to swim for England in the same Games, but was unable to accept. Two years later, however, he swam for England in the Empire and Commonwealth Games. The Club has produced a second international swimmer since then in D. J. Gray, who swam for England in 1939.

In athletics, a change was made in 1921 whereby the cross-country run for the Yeo Cup[1] finished downhill at the bottom of Sparrow's Meadow, thus cutting out that last exhausting grind up the school drive, with the risk of a dangerous collapse on the steps of School House. In the same year the hand- and foot-racquets tournaments, both of them, as we have seen, games peculiar to Stortford, were played for the last time, the court being obliterated shortly afterwards owing to the building of the Memorial Hall. Many generations of the older Old Boys will remember the popularity of these games, and the mad rush to get to the court first from the School House dining hall when lunch was over.

Shortly before the war A. R. Kelsey had distinguished himself as a gymnast at Cambridge, where he was captain of the University Gym-

[1] The Yeo Cup for cross-country running was presented in 1918 by Sir Alfred Yeo, the father and later grandfather of Stortfordians.

nasium Eight: in 1920 both P.T. and gymnastics at Stortford were encouraged by the House competition for a shield presented by Mr S. W. Pascall O.S. (Subsequently this was awarded for P.T. only, and the Garrould Cup was given for gym.) In the same year Mr R. J. Stirling, whose three sons were at Stortford, presented a boxing cup for annual competition. The boxing was run for some years by Sergeant Salmon, but was never generally popular, and the competition was dropped towards the end of Young's headmastership, though there have been short-lived revivals of boxing since, notably under Captain Mack in the fifties and sixties.

Meanwhile the post-war years saw an extension of the hobbies and various societies which have long been such a feature of school life at Stortford. Music flourished under Tidmarsh—choir 'colours' were instituted in 1922, and the Gramophone Society was founded in 1926. The Natural History Society, under the presidency of F. S. Young, continued to be exceedingly active. The rock gardens, under Charles Mellows' enthusiastic guidance, seemed almost yearly to show some new pond beneath a rocky eminence whose flowers would be reflected in it. Indeed the rock gardens at this time were a notable feature of the school grounds, attracting visits from many garden-lovers in the surrounding district and even from farther afield. In 1921 Mr Hayward started the Wireless Society at a time when even the B.B.C. was still in its infancy; and enthusiastic listeners were soon reporting the reception, on home-made sets with 'cat's whiskers' and earphones, of concerts tentatively broadcast from the Continent. By 1930 at least one boy was experimenting with television as well: in an early number of the magazine *Television* we read that 'Mr J. P. Shillingford of Bishop's Stortford College announces successful reception during the Christmas holidays. Mr Shillingford has surely set up a record for age' (he was still under sixteen years old).

It was at Christmas in 1920 that the Dramatic Society (though not yet officially organized as such) scored one of its great hits with *Mundus et Homo*, a play based on the Morality plays of the fifteenth century, specially written for the society by Mr E. W. Edmunds. Produced by Mr Tidmarsh, it was first put on in the old Assembly Hut: it was so successful that it was repeated in the following year, and again later in the Memorial Hall. Encouraged by this success to yet further enterprise, Mr Pond, greatly daring, assisted by Mr Monk-Jones, produced Aristophanes' *Frogs* in the original Greek—the first, and alas, the last time that such a feat was found possible, though later he put on the same author's *Birds* in an English translation. In 1926 Mr Edmunds followed up *Mundus et Homo* with a

1st XI FOOTBALL 1915. F. H. Salmon, L. F. Clark, C. E. Schnadhorst, W. R. Bion, M. C. Nokes. *Sitting:* W. V. A. Bracher, P. O. Davies, A. G. Doggart (Capt.), S. F. Prior, G. E. C. Hodges. *In front:* H. L. Price, K. W. Round.

SCOUTS TROOP 1915. *Back row:* J. E. Hamilton, F. W. Potts, H. J. Itter. *Next row.* W. R. Webb, G. W. Bitton, A. H. Jackson, A. D. Blaxill, D. D. Rae, G. G. Carruthers, J. S. Blomfield, D. G. Mirams, R. V. Goodliffe. *Front row:* R. A. Mirams, H. W. Duchesne, L. R. Chisnall, F. W. Lloyd, Mr E. C. Corelli, B. Blaxill, D. St J. Sloane, B. J. N. Tucker.

WESTFIELD LODGE 1915.
Back row: G. W. Sm
G. E. C. Hodges
J. E. Hamilton
R. B. Sykes
A. L. Taylor
N. K. Sanders
N. P. Atkinson
G. S. Sinclair
R. A. Sinclair
Sitting:
S. O. Garnham
C. W. Grose
Mr F. B. Shawe
Miss Shawe
C. G. McLachlan
A. Itter, A. J. Smith
Front: A. H. B. Daws
J. D. Butcher
L. R. Chisnall
H. J. Itter

1st XV 1920.
L. E. Lockhart
H. J. Wright
C. W. Hamilton
A. G. Hasler
W. M. White
L. F. Curtis
J. S. Blomfield
E. Vinson
Sitting: A. S. Hall
J. C. Collett
J. T. Clark (Capt.)
J. R. G. Barter
K. J. Collie
Front: R. H. Hill
J. B. Ashford
The Honours caps were presented by the O.S.R.U.F.C.

THE PREPARATORY SCHOOL 1921

Back: D. Knight, F. B. Goodliffe, W. E. Braybrooks, R. F. Jackson, V. Marriage, J. B. G. Smith, I. Davies, G Howells, K. M. Tate, C. M. Smith, F. K. Butler, D. G. Williams, J. H. Snelgrove, W. P. Hall, L. F. Hooper *Double row:* N. P. Stiles, L. J. Lawrence, J. M. Lukies, D. P. Lockhart, A. J. Birnage, J. C. Wilkerson, K. W Mawer, E. W. Harris, R. S. Bruce, J. P. Burls, F. H. Sutton, F. G. Rhodes, S. E. Shrive, W. E. Rhodes K. E. Hamilton, J. H. Stephenson, G. S. Vartan, A. J. Glegg, S. J. Houlden, M. Knowles, K. H. Houlden *Sitting:* J. W. Bramham, K. W. S. Flower, N. R. Callan, K. B. Pearce, Miss Blandford, Miss Parsons, Mr Ingram, Mr W. M. Ingram, Mr Bracken, Miss Campbell, A. S. Curry, H. A. Best. *Front:* T. D. Heaver, W. A Pritchard, R. F. Cornell, D. B. Pascall, S. J. Wilkin, J. A. Saward, T. J. Wood, B. J. Flower, G. O. Boardman L. J. Bacon, R. J. Johnston, W. E. Bruce.

THE LAST 1st XI FOOTBALL 1921. R. C. Southcott, D. E. de Rusett, W. M. White, G. M. Sharman, H. J. Wright. *Sitting:* C. Featherby, C. G. Godkin, J. C. Collett (Capt.), H. T. Seal, L. C. Sennitt.

CHOOL HOUSE 1920. *Back row:* R. E. Hawkins, J. P. Davies, F. Peltzer, C. J. Wood, N. S. Rook, G. Young, E. M. Stienon, L. C. Sennitt, F. C. H. Cornell, J. C. Collett, G. E. Kyffin, G. M. Sharman, P. Garner, R. C. Southcott, K. J. Collie, W. H. Robinson, H. B. Saward, L. F. Curtis. *Next row:* B. A. oulden, A. S. Hall, G. H. Peirce, C. J. Jackson, L. Stirling, H. A. Wilson, G. H. Clark, L. J. Bointon, W. Birnage, T. K. Collett, J. A. A. Paquot, R. H. M. McKechnie, R. F. Hughes, C. W. Dupont, J. Hartley-nith, E. W. Chidwick. *Next row:* A. S. Hatch, E. D. H. Renton, R. G. Rhodes, L. R. Glegg, A. C. Taylor, D. Kitching, J. G. Sainsbury, H. Stirling, J. K. Gale, H. W. S. Blewitt, R. R. Taylor, D. J. Cranswick, Larkins, J. L. Bonnar, D. M. Bruce, W. T. C. Jackson, C. C. Barry. *Standing on ground:* E. C. Comer, H. Rivers, C. D. Murray, B. Tilley, W. R. Brackett, F. M. Woollard, G. D. Dean, N. C. Coombs, M. N. nderson, H. V. Barter, C. W. Hamilton, S. H. Ormerod, A. W. Mann, V. M. Gibson, R. M. Sharman, W. O. Smith, R. G. B. Chadd, R. H. C. Archer, W. B. Millar. *Sitting:* J. S. Blomfield, T. C. James, R. H. mfrey, A. G. Hasler, A. H. Jackson, A. V. Leah, (B. Blaxill absent), Mr C. Mellows, Mr F. S. Young, N. Monk-Jones, (J. F. Attenborough absent), J. T. Clark, W. E. May, J. R. G. Barter, I. G. B. Garrould, B. Ashford, H. E. Wall. *In front:* B. Lawn, R. W. Brett, G. V. N. Chadd, D. N. Ryalls, N. A. Doggart, R. Braybrooks, S. E. Sturgess-Wells, A. L. Curry, G. A. Rowe, E. G. Hunt, A. H. Pringle, C. K. Dormer.

Waytefield 1917-38

WAYTEFIEI
1919

Standing: J. A. White, A. N. Todd, T. D. Stewart, J. R. Adams, K. K. Dean, C. R. Shoults, A. O. Rus C. A. Yeo, E. N. Davey, N. Bishop, G. W. Pritchard, W. M. Hartley, C. G. Godkin. *Sitting:* D. E. de Rus B. Scott, A. S. Thomas, Mr F. S. Sutton, E. S. Holtom, L. E. Lockhart, W. M. White, *In front:* H. C. Gol D. C. Pritchard, D. G. White, D. L. Jones, E. A. T. S. Alabone.

WAYTEFIELI
HOUSE XV 1

D. J. Young, J. E. Pritchard, V. D. Logue, L. R. Newton, D. F. Cock, A. J. S. Hodson, D. A. Greenhill, J. E. Lockhart, J. B. Douglas. *Sitting:* W. R. Lee, M. H. Farthing, H. S. Widgery, F. H. Sutton (Capt.), T. L. Rosser, W. R. Tanner, A. W. Claypole.

Jubilee Reunion 1919

S. CRICKET XI

Back row: R. J. Stephenson, P. H. Glasscock, N. P. Wood, H. L. Price, H. R. Hadfield, E. C. Duchesne, (?), W. A. Holland. *Front row:* J. Jones (umpire and groundsman), G. Dick Read, A. E. Turberville, A. G. Doggart, B. Blaxill (present boy, scorer), J. H. Doggart. The two spectators on right: C. H. Joscelyne and (?).

UNION GROUP: *Back row:* H. R. Hadfield, H. S. Tee, R. C. Williams, A. H. Mellows, L. C. Martin, 3. Kelsey, N. P. Wood, E. L. Smith. *2nd row:* L. F. Cocks, B. Bointon, H. B. Edwards, H. W. Smith, H. ɔhenson, T. D. Wheeler, N. A. Williams, A. T. K. Sykes, A. Itter, L. Whitaker, A. W. Winsor, W. E. H. ·ner, A. E. Blaxill, B. C. Dupont, L. A. Day. *3rd row:* T. C. McIlroy, W. Larkins, T. S. Hamilton, G. therby, C. H. H. Cowl, L. E. W. Smith, E. N. Edwards, J. L. Plumbridge, A. M. Davies, G. S. Sinclair, Davies, L. W. Myers, H. S. Collett, J. M. Fellows, E. J. L. Grear, R. Paterson. *4th row:* S. N. Salmon, G. D. rtins, H. C. Sturgess-Wells, B. H. Rhodes, R. A. Sinclair, H. F. Moon, A. J. Bailey, W. Barningham, J. H. nce, E. V. Payne, T. L. Davies, N. A. Turner-Smith, T. E. Wall, J. A. Smith. *Sitting:* C. Mellows, W. E. H. gane, H. E. Newsum, A. E. Turberville, F. S. Young, E. W. Grimwade (Chairman of Governing Council), W. Pascall, A. G. Tidmarsh, J. Watson Slack, C. S. Colman, J. J. Myers, R. J. Stephenson. *In front:* G. T. nn, P. O. Davies, S. F. Prior, J. E. Salmon, W. J. Wall, W. E. Palmer, G. A. Rendle.

THE HUT: used first for the O.S. Reunion Dinner 1919. The birch tree has grown to full size in the last fifty years.

THE SCHOOL HOUSE COMMON ROOM about 1920.

A DORMITORY about 1920.

B DORMITORY about 1920.

. Mellows, Master 1912–57.

Middle row)
. D. Hayward, Master 1915–56.

. D. Craig, Master 1917–47.

Bottom)
. Monk-Jones, Master 1919–58.

. J. Adams, Clerk to School 1920–56.

Staff going to Priz
Giving Marquee,
1921. Scaffolding
for Memorial Hall
in background.

Above: C. S. Colma
H. S. Tee (Govern
ing Council), F. S.
Sutton, R. E. Ponc
Below: E. C. Duches
(Bursar), E. W.
Edmunds, J. T.
Daughton, W. G.
Williams, Brendan
Bracken (later Lord
Bracken), N. Monk
Jones, A. G.
Tidmarsh.

.aboratories, Swimming Bath, Tuckshop and Racquet Court Block, School House and the Elm, 1920.

'his panorama is from vo consecutive photos ıken by J. K. Hare.

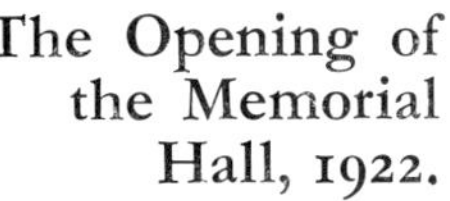

The Opening of the Memorial Hall, 1922.

THE CHOIR: J. H. Stephenson, L. F. Roper, D. J. Wilson, D. C. Williams, F. N. Salisbury, R. W. Brett, H. E. Wall, S. E. Sturgess-Wells, E. E. Hoe, J. H. Lankester, R. H. M. McKechnie, F. J. M. Dent, Mr A. G. Tidmarsh, J. T. Clark, R. E. Clark.

THE STAFF: C. Mellows, C. S. Colman, N. P. Wood, N. Monk-Jones, A. D. Hayward, A. R. Taylor, J. D. Craig, R. E. Pond, F. C. Ade, E. C. Duchesne (just visible), A. T. Q. Bluett, Sir Arthur Quiller-Couch, Guest of Honour, G. E. Whelpton, partly obscuring E. Pascal.

1922

The Memorial Hall

1960

The Roll of Honour

THE OPENING OF THE MEMORIAL HALL DOORS, 1922.

Extreme left, from top: W. R. C. Morton, I. Davies, A. J. Glegg. The Architect, Mr Clough Williams-Ellis, is on the left of the doors, Sir Arthur Quiller-Couch is at the doors and Sir Alfred Davies is next. J. Glyn-Jones and N. R. Callan are extreme right.

68 HADHAM ROAD, 1922
Back row: C. G. Boothroyd, D. A. Tansley, A. J. Glegg, L. J. Lawrence, H. A. Best, A. J. W. Birnage, J. W. Bramham. *Sitting:* J. C. Wilkerson, N. Bishop, Mr N. P. Wood, Mrs Wood, H. K. Lamplugh. *In front:* J. S. Padwick.

THE CHIMES, 1922
Back row: A. S. Collard, F. C. Rogers, K. W. S. Flower, O. W. Reynolds, A. T. Alderton. *Sitting:* L. J. Ayers, Mr R. E. Pond, E. W. Harris, I. Davies.

Taken about 1923. The Prep watching cricket on the 'New Field'. Note Purcell House, Tennis Court and the old Laboratories; also the sun-hats, a regular feature of the summer uniform.

An upstairs classroom in the Racquets Block, opposite the A Dormitory. Later the Headmaster's Secretary's Office, now the extension of the School House Changing Room.

One of the classrooms into which The Hut was divided after the Memorial Hall was built.

Gym with Sergeant Salmon

1922. *Back row:* R. R. Taylor, D. W. Maxey, D. C. Williams, M. N. Anderson, S. H. Ormerod *Standing:* C. C. Barry, L. C. Richards, E. C. Hardy, D. J. Wilson, R. B. Collard. *Kneeling:* S. J Colman, W. H. Kirby, F D. Goodliffe, F. W. Dave L. Stirling. *In front:* C. N. Lukies, F. N. Salisbury, C. K. Vartan.

Tableau, 1923. F. J. M. Dent is holding up the pair on the right, F. M. Woollard doing likewise on the parallel bars. The building, Elgar House, was once the School Sanatorium.

THE OLD GYM (now the Art Room) after the removal of the Carpentry Section. On the wall-bars, *from left:* R. F. A. Sharp, (?), K. W Wells, C. F. Berry, L. E. McLean. *At the ropes:* R. J. Dawson left, K. A. Cuff right. *With arms raised sideways:* M. E. V. Lane and J. H. Peters (*c.* 1934).

The Bath Club Cup

The first B.S.C. team to win, 1923: F. J. M. Dent, T. K. Collett, G. A. Redhouse. F. J. M. Dent, Esq. is now Chairman of our publishers and Sir Kingsley Collett Chairman of the Governing Council.

Swimming and Water Polo Team. 1929. *Back row:* J. L. Thompson, K. F. Wandless, B. Ingram, W. R. Lee, J. N. Starkey. *Sitting:* J. C. Newbold, S. J. Houlden (Capt.), A. C. Davies. *In front:* K. W. Banks, J. W. Edwards.

The most recent success, 1949: R. P. Collett, J. Groocock, J. M. Rae, D. E. Bromley. This was the third victory in succession.

Robert Pearce House, 1923

Back row: D. C. Bidwell, C. P. Weeden, C. F. Robinson, A. Comins, W. F. Roberson. *Second row:* G. W. Creighton, E. W. Hughes, A. R. Goodley, F. J. B. Harvey, W. Q. Connold, N. J. Dredge, D. B. Green, A. S. Curry, J. A. Bowes, G. W. Abbot, G. Davies, R. W. Hale, H. J. Morton, H. M. Wagstaff, A. B. King, H. W. Pumfrey. *Sitting:* A. B. Parker, J. R. Cuff, E. C. Arnold, G. C. Chamberlain, Mr W. R. Bion, Mr A. G. Tidmarsh, M. N. Anderson, T. K. Collett, J. W. Bond, T. Moffat. *In front:* T. W. Macdonald, N. B. Canning, G. Ashton, C. S. Clarke, K. M. Tate, (D. W. F. Starkey not present).

modern Morality play which he entitled *Lux Mundi*; of which the *Stortfordian*'s critic wrote: 'Here we felt that Stortford was striking out a line of its own—a production peculiar to itself and fit opportunity for a justifiable pride.' And in the following year, when Mr Pond produced the trial scene from Shaw's *St Joan*, the verdict was: 'This was the finest show we have seen from the school Dramatic Society.' In 1931 Mr Edmunds staged a successful revival of *Mundus et Homo*, with a musical setting provided by the then Director of Music, Dr A. F. Barnes.

During the early twenties a number of French plays were produced by Mr A. T. Q. Bluett, the senior French master: these were usually put on as part of the programme on Prize Day.

In 1927 Mr Strachan founded the Architectural Society, which over these forty years has gone from strength to strength: its annual exhibitions on Prize Day have produced a valuable series of photographs, drawings, paintings and models of all kinds of buildings of architectural or aesthetic interest in the surrounding countryside of Hertfordshire, Essex, Cambridgeshire and even farther afield.

The School has always encouraged holiday activities of various kinds: we have already mentioned the 'Norfolk Stortfordians' Club (later known as the Hasbro' Club). In the post-war years the summer holiday parties at Hasbro' became more popular than ever: and senior boys from the School were regularly invited to join these parties. Camping holidays were also organized at Bury, in Sussex, where Messrs Sutton, Hayward, Pond, Craig and Stearn all, at various times, ran most successful camps. Mr Hayward, as Scoutmaster, also organized scout camps and 'hiking' holidays for the 3rd and 7th Stortford Rovers: in 1931 he and Mr Ward took a party of scouts to the International Scout Chalet at Kandersteg in Switzerland. In the Preparatory School also, G. L. Coulson O.S. ran a troop of cubs for many years. F. S. Young himself, with Mr Mellows, took a series of climbing parties to the French or the Italian Alps. And for some eight successive years, beginning in 1926, two boys were chosen annually to attend the camps organized near New Romney, Kent, under the patronage of H.R.H. the Duke of York (later King George VI), at which some two hundred senior boys from public schools spent a week in camp with the same number of boys from factories and workshops. The Stortford representatives, at least, found these camps very well worth while as well as most enjoyable.

In 1927, when there was a total eclipse of the sun, the School closed down for a long week-end, enabling two parties of boys and masters to travel north to places from which it was hoped that they would be able to have good views of the eclipse. One party went to Southport, the other to Colwyn Bay; only the former had any luck, however, for at Colwyn Bay the eclipse was hidden by cloud. Both parties were kindly entertained by O.S. or by parents of boys in the School living in those areas.

The same year (to descend from the ethereal to the terrestrial sphere—we had almost said from the sublime to the ridiculous) saw the abolition of that peculiar Stortford institution, the 'bot-pad'. New masters joining the staff used to be surprised at first to see boys going from classroom to classroom carrying not only their books but also cushions of various sizes tucked under their arms: indeed the more sybaritic members of the School frequently brought to class, from their house studies, cushions of quite fantastic size. Apart from their legitimate function, these cushions made very effective missiles: and it may well have been this consideration, rather than any spartan tendency on the part of a Nonconformist headmaster, that induced Mr Young finally to prohibit their use. There were letters in the *Stortfordian* regretting and even protesting against the abolition of this long-standing custom: even parents wrote complaining of the increased wear and tear on their sons' trouser seats! Yet a compromise pad of regulation size, incorporating a compartment for carrying books, never found favour with the School and was soon given up. The following year saw the introduction of the first school 'uniform', consisting of open-neck shirt, blazer-type jacket and flannel trousers: this too was looked on rather askance by the senior boys and many Old Boys, who objected that 'we never dressed in that slovenly way in my time . . .'. Many different experiments have been tried in the matter of school dress since that time: this is indeed a perennial problem with which all schools are faced.

At the Preparatory School Mr E. J. Bland arrived on the staff in 1927, and for the next ten years his tall figure was to be a familiar sight in the classrooms and on the playing-fields: he was an enthusiastic if somewhat erratic games coach, and was especially helpful in his coaching of tennis both in the Prep and in the Main School. On his marriage in the following year his place as assistant housemaster in Grimwade House was taken by Mr J. C. Wheeldon, a keen chess player who during his seven years organized annually a series of highly successful chess tournaments among the day boys as well as the boarders. The same year saw the institution by Mr Monk-Jones of the league system at the Prep. All boys, whether boarders or day boys, were divided into four leagues (named Athens, Rome, Carthage and Sparta—the classical names in those days seemed natural enough) not only for games purposes but more generally; so that by any kind of excellence, in the classroom, on the playing-fields, in hobbies, private reading, artistic or musical achievement and so on, anybody could contribute, by the points he gained, to the success of his league. Thus in a sense the leagues corresponded to the Houses in the Main School. Mr Monk-Jones presented as the league trophy a copy in bronze of the famous figure of Victory that was found in Pompeii: the trophy (now known, we understand, as 'The Lady'), is presented at the end of each term to the winning league.

It was at this time that the first visit took place of a party of German schoolboys and staff from the Dorotheenstädtisches Realgymnasium in Berlin: they came towards the end of the summer term and were entertained by the School. The idea underlying Mr Young's invitation to them was to make a practical contribution towards better international understanding, in the spirit of the League of Nations Union, of which there was an active branch at the School. Trips to various places of interest were organized for the visitors, who also to some small extent took part in the games and even the classroom studies of the School; while in the summer evenings on Old Field enthusiastic Stortfordians could be seen learning from the Germans their game of handball, and rapidly acquiring no small skill at it. The experiment was regarded as successful enough to be repeated in 1929 and 1931; while in the intervening year the Headmaster and Mr Strachan accompanied a party of Stortford boys on a return visit to Berlin. One of the members of the last German party was a keen supporter of a rising politician who, he said, was going to restore the splendours of the German Reich, and whose name was Adolf Hitler. . . .

The year 1931 saw many changes at the School. In July Mr Colman retired from the housemastership of Alliott House, which he had held since it was first opened in 1914. The following term Mr Mellows, who had been running School House since his return to Stortford after the war, went to Alliott's, his place in School House being taken over by Mr Wall, who had already been there for four years as assistant housemaster. At the same time Mr Colman, who for so many years had run the athletic sports, now handed over this job to Mr Ward.

But the outstanding event of this eventful year was of course the retirement of F. S. Young after no less than thirty-two years as Headmaster. The year 1931 thus marks the end of an important period, perhaps the most important period, in the history of the School. (Indeed the public press would have it that it was the end of the School itself! This was due no doubt to the confusion caused by the closing down about this time of the old Grammar School in the Hadham Road; with the result that Mr Young, just before his retirement, received letters of condolence from as far away as Canada, the U.S.A. and India, as well as from friends of the School nearer home, regretting that B.S.C. should be forced to close down from lack of support!) At the presentation from the School to Mr and Mrs Young on 1st December 1931, speeches were made by the Head Boy, the chairman of the Governing Council, a member of the staff, a representative parent, and by the minister of Bishop's Stortford Congregational Church. Mr Young, in replying, looked forward to the School's future. Public schools, he said, were being severely criticized, but he saw no reason to fear that they were doomed. He felt sure the School would continue to flourish because of the personal relationships formed there from the earliest days of a boy's school life. That foundation of fellowship helped to build up a spirit of kindness, loyalty and goodwill which would bind the School together and hold it up.

The following day a record number of well over two hundred Old Boys attended the annual dinner of the Old Stortfordians' Club, at which they made their presentation to Mr Young. Mr C. S. Colman, as chairman of the Club, after outlining the Headmaster's achievements ('during his headmastership Mr Young has given, begged, borrowed or stolen no less than £70,000'!), went on to say that F. S. Young would be remembered even more for what he was than for what he had done. The first of his four great qualities was his optimism: he had always expected the best of every boy and every man, and steadfastly believed that in every boy there was a strong desire to make himself a better one. His second great quality had been his courage. When the School had been faced with very difficult situations, it was the Headmaster's courage that had inspired the Governing Council—a courage which in its turn was inspired by his absolute belief in his ideals. Thirdly, there was his honesty: the plain truth had always been more important to Mr Young than any dressed-up version to suit the occasion. And his fourth quality, the one that had probably impressed them all most, had been his absolute passion for fair play and justice in the countless problems which from time to time had arisen. In conclusion Mr Colman said: 'For once I will imitate the Headmaster and speak the literal, unexaggerated truth. For a faith that rarely wavered, for a hope that was rarely dimmed, for a charity that rarely failed, Stortford owes Mr Young a debt that will never be repaid and never be forgotten.'

The sketch-map on the front endpapers will give some idea of the steady growth of the School and its buildings during Mr Young's tenure of office. Talking to a friend shortly after his election as Headmaster, at a time when numbers at the school were down and the financial position was to say the least discouraging, Mr Young sketched out the possibilities of Stortford as he saw it in his mind's eye. To his listener it sounded a very pleasant fairy-tale—rather like the *Arabian Nights* and only wanting Aladdin's lamp to bring it into existence; but

Mr Young's faith had translated the dream into boys, bricks and mortar and land before he laid down his task.

On leaving Stortford Mr Young took Holy Orders. To those who knew his deep interest in theology and in all matters ecclesiastical this was hardly a surprise: it was the result of the steady development of his religious ideas, rather than of any break with his Nonconformist connections. After ordination he took a curacy at Church Stretton: unfortunately, to his great disappointment, ill health compelled him to retire after only a year's work in Shropshire. He returned to the south and took a house at Sawbridgeworth, within easy visiting distance for his former colleagues at B.S.C. and for his Old Boys. Here he was devotedly nursed by Mrs Young for two years, but his illness (paralysis agitans) became progressively worse, and he died in 1934.

We conclude with a last quotation from C. S. C.: 'There is no doubt that Mr Young's religious faith was the driving force of his work—his conviction that the labour was ordained of God. The school services were to him the centre of his work, and the compilation of the school service-book a labour of love. There was in him a passionate sincerity which dared not exaggerate and which cared nothing for the showy or the sensational:

> To my true King I offered, free from stain,
> Courage and Faith. . . .[1]

So long as the School exists, that faith and that courage will not have been in vain.'

[1] The quotation is from Macaulay, *A Jacobite's Epitaph.*

7. More Reminiscences

Claremont

O the great days in the distance enchanted,
Days of fresh air in the rain and the sun. . . .

To THOSE of us who experienced 'Claremont Week' the name recalls a carefree time: the first week of the summer holidays, with opportunities of enjoying, without formal restrictions, the amenities of the School and the companionship of friends in an atmosphere of light-hearted gaiety; the feeling of wellbeing heightened by the knowledge that we were giving a thrilling holiday to a group of poor boys from the Congregational Claremont Central Mission in Islington.

To a modern generation 'thrilling' may seem an overstatement; but Claremont Week, which was organized for thirty-two consecutive years, from 1908 to 1939, covered a time when, except for perhaps the last few years, many of the boys, sometimes all, would have no other holiday; more than that, Claremont Week was to most of them their first introduction to green fields and real country.

The first visit was of seven boys and a corporal of the 48th Boys' Brigade attached to the Claremont Mission. Within a few years the numbers were nearer thirty. When it ceased to be a Boys' Brigade camp, the boys were put on the train at Liverpool Street and became our entire responsibility on arrival.

And what an arrival it was! We 'orderlies', who, under Tid, were to be in charge, wearing a curious informal headgear consisting of a flowing silk kerchief, dashed down to the station with the Scouts' trek cart for our visitors' luggage, to be almost overwhelmed by the Claremonters, who burst from the train in a cheering mob, old hands renewing old friendships, new arrivals eager to make themselves noticed. The old hands were for racing to the school as soon as possible to see if the 'Punch Tree' (the Wellingtonia in the drive) was still so unbelievably punchable, or to be first in the swimming-bath. The indoor bath was one of their chief delights: many a Claremont boy learned to swim in that week, and their courage and enthusiasm in diving were astonishing. There was one boy of about ten who insisted on diving off the top board before he could swim: he dived obliquely so that he surfaced near the side, where anxious orderlies were waiting with outstretched arms to pull him out. He would perform this feat numerous times daily until he eventually learned to swim.

Meals, produced by the School House kitchen staff, were served in the open when possible, but frequently we had to resort to the School House dining-hall or common room because of bad weather. For a time the ingenious arrangement of a vast tarpaulin enabled us to have tables under cover in the School House courtyard. Sergeant Salmon was a great help in erecting this contraption. But the courtyard tended to be cold and gloomy, so after a year or two this was abandoned. Inevitably one remembers more the sunlit occasions, with three big School House dining-hall tables under the Oak, to which we transported from the kitchen serving-hatch vast tureens of stew or enormous dishes of rice pudding. (I wonder if Sandy Pearce recalls turning a huge milk pudding upside-down, thinking it was solid? I can still visualize his expression of dismay as the lot fell on the floor!)

The orderlies' first duty was to fill palliasses with straw. On these the Claremont boys used to sleep in the old gym. In the early days there was little formal organization of the 'camp', but when F. D. Field-Hyde took over the responsibility for it in 1928, he divided the thirty-six boys into six groups, each with an old hand as leader and each having an orderly to take a special interest in his group. The Claremonters slept in the gym arranged in these groups, and we took it in turns to sleep in pairs at the entrance in order to insist on peace and quiet at night and to prevent over-early rising. (A record of an earlier period refers to the Claremont Boys 'hurling sticks, stones, and other foreign matter into the Hut at 5 a.m., in a vain attempt to persuade a sleeping orderly to "take bathing"'.) This arrangement also reduced the opportunities of orchard raiding in the early morning. In this connection a story was current at the expense of that shrewd old character Mark Matthews, in the days of his retirement. Relying on the time-honoured practice he put in a claim for apples 'stolen', on what should have been the first morning of Claremont week. Unfortunately for him it happened that on this occasion the Claremont Boys for some reason had not yet arrived!

Sleeping in the Hut reminds me that in some of the earlier camps orderlies were left to their own devices as to where to sleep. There was one occasion when an unexpected midnight downpour surprised some optimistic orderlies who had settled down under the stars. With a natural homing instinct they sought refuge in the 'A' dormitory, much to the indignation of the School House Matron, the redoubtable Miss Dabb, who heard the noise and discovered mattresses and pillows being disturbed that had been tidily piled up for the holidays. In the midst of the confusion Sammy appeared in a long dressing-gown and drove us out with the typical gestures that those who knew him will recall. In later years the orderlies, when not on duty in the gym, slept in tents near by.

Weather permitting, most of the day was normally occupied in athletic pursuits, chiefly cricket, soccer and swimming. To those boys it was a delight to have a cricket bat or ball in their hands or a soccer ball at their feet, and informal games gave them much pleasure. In the late twenties and thirties, having adopted the group principle, we had competitions between the groups. After breakfast they tidied their sleeping quarters ready for inspection. Marks were given for neatness in folded blankets and personal smartness: rivalry in this competition was as keen as in those to determine the best group at cricket or soccer. But competitions were not run to the exclusion of more spontaneous games. A particularly popular item was an evening game of soccer, Claremont *v.* the Orderlies, in which the former sometimes overcame the latter by weight of numbers or in some cases by sheer skill.

But the weather did not always permit. The record of 1912 states 'the weather was not kind and there were frequent visits to the local cinemas'. In 1917 'the weather was atrociously bad and there were revels in the Schoolroom'. In 1918 'the weather was bad, though less formidable than last year'. Poor weather of course never damped the boys' ardour for the indoor bath. In later years, when they were becoming a little more prosperous, the tuck-shop was a popular spot. Climbing about on the beams in the gym attracted the more daring, the ladder those who preferred to be nearer the ground.

A visit to the cinema became an annual feature, though on occasions the exuberant cheering of our guests caused the management and the members of B.S.C. some embarrassment. On Bank Holidays, the flower show and fair on Silver Leys became a regular final outing. In the earlier days there are references each year to the very popular visits to Manuden, where Mr Burls and Miss Tyler entertained the party at 'Saucemeres', giving the Claremont boys a chance to see a 'real farm', and they were allowed to pick apples from a selected tree or trees in a 'real orchard'. They liked watching Past and Present cricket matches on Upper Field or on the town ground, taking a keen interest in those they recognized from previous visits or those they knew; for the orderlies provided a useful reserve for the Past and Present, and quite often one of them was invited to play.

Occasionally special stunts were devised to add to the fun. Some rather impromptu sports were graced one year by the presence of Lady Doorbarn Ward, who, tastefully overdressed, presented prizes with charm and a certain dignity, though it must be confessed that R. W. Glendinning's voice did not quite match the elegance of his appearance: some of the more astute Claremonters were not altogether convinced! In the thirties a visit to Hatfield Forest by double-decker bus became a usual outing. One year, for variety, an elaborate plan was worked out to discover who was responsible for the supposed theft of a cash-box: staff and Old Stortfordians' cars took groups of Claremont boys and orderlies to different points on the perimeter of the forest, where they found clues which led them to the villain of the piece, 'the man with a white beard'. I still have a vivid picture of 'Doc' Lloyd, wearing a Father Christmas beard, dashing for safety to Elgin Coppice, dropping the cash-box and getting over the high fence only just in time, with the pack of howling Claremont wolves at his heels!

Evening prayers were a normal proceeding, at which Mr Young sometimes came to help. Once the length of his prayer tried the patience of at least one of the young worshippers, who in a suitable pause interjected a vigorous 'Awmen!' Those who remember Sammy [1] will not be surprised to learn that this had not the slightest effect: imperturbably he continued to the predetermined end. On Sunday we had a short service: friends were called in sometimes to give an address: I particularly think of 'Pa' Duchesne and Stanley Tee.

To us, the orderlies and the members of staff who helped, the week had its exhausting side. Supervising cricket or football matches, taking bathing, which often involved teaching swimming, waiting at table and helping in various other ways taxed one's patience sorely at times: when quarrels took place, one had to display the combined virtues of Job and Solomon. All sorts of minor crises were liable to occur, but, as far as I can recall, no injuries worse than cuts, bruises and wasp stings were sustained. However, I once got a terrible fright: three small boys came dashing up the track from the gym, consternation on each face. I heard a piercingly desperate cry: 'Sir! Come quick! Harold Whip's belly's come out!' I raced down fully expecting to see the poor boy disembowelled: there he was, rolling in apparent agony, trying with a leather belt to hold in a tummy that, after too large a meal, seemed to have extended like a balloon! But he soon recovered. It was

[1] Mr Young was at first known in the School as the Guv'nor or the Guv, then as Sammy, and latterly as the Doff.

a great delight to have him call on me after the war: he had been wounded and lost an arm, but was cheerfully driving a lorry. The Whips incidentally were a large family, representatives of which came over a number of years. Other well-known characters were Joe Baker and George Skeggs.

The week could be exhausting, but there were periods of relaxation too: bathing, watching the Past and Present cricket and going down to Long's for their incomparable doughnuts, or to the Corner House for their ice-creams made with real cream.

All too soon the week was over. Luggage was piled into the trek cart and down to the station we hurried. Though glad to be free for our own holidays, we were sorry to see them go. The visit had genuinely endeared many of them to us, and vice versa. 'Goodbye! See you next year. . . .' The older ones dropped out, but we sometimes renewed acquaintance with a few of them at Claremont concerts in Islington. It was all rather ephemeral; but it was well worth doing, and it was fun.

H. E. W.

Bowling for Pops

One of the glamorous features of Whit-Mondays, before the 1914–1918 war, days that in memory were always sunny, was 'bowling for pops'. Half a dozen cricket nets were put up on the New Field, near where the Young Memorial Library now stands. At about 9 a.m. the members of the First Eleven took their turn at the wickets, and any boy in the school could elect to try and bowl them out. Instead of the usual bails, the great men put one penny on each stump: if bowled out, the batsman threw the pennies to the bowler, who proceeded as quickly as possible to the tuck-shop, where Mr Gook dispensed 'ginger-pop' and the various types of chocolates and sweets then in favour.

Unfortunately this old tradition came to an end early in the war, perhaps because the tuck-shop was closed. There was indeed a rumour (possibly quite untrue) that a puritanical parent had complained to the Headmaster that the game encouraged gambling!

R. J. N.

Figures of Speech

Slang, according to the *Shorter Oxford Dictionary*, means 'the special vocabulary used by any set of persons of a low and disreputable character'. A few years ago such a 'set of persons', calling themselves

The Antiques, were sitting round the fire at Hasbro', trying to recall the slang words and phrases used at B.S.C. in their day; and I think their reminiscences, augmented by contributions from others, may be worth recording here.

VOCABULARY OF STORTFORD SLANG, ETC.

Aeger, absent through illness.

Bags I!, I claim (occasionally corrupted to '*Hag I!*').

Becker (*later Becca*) *Shoes*, gym shoes marked with a B, reserved for use within the precincts of the bath.

Becker's Toe-nails, corruption of *Devil's Toe-nails* (q.v.).

Bloitch, weep, cry: hence noun *Bloitcher*.

Bot-pad, small cushion carried around by boys for use in class or in 'prep': frequently employed as missiles.

Bugs, *The*, name given to boys at the Grammar School (also known as the High School).

'*Cab to the station*,' same as '*It's Jackson's for you*' (q.v.).

Cave, warning cry when one in authority is approaching.

Condenny, sweetened condensed milk.

Devil's Toe-nails, a stage in the game of knuckle-bones.

Dosh-basket, dirty-linen basket.

Extra Meat, additional vitamins for breakfast, provided at the expense of one's parents.

Fain(*s*) *I!*, a disclaimer = 'I won't do it!'

Fainloss!, 'I call those present to witness that I reserve the right to return and claim this (chair, book, etc.)': much the same as '*Bags I!*'

Foci (verb), to aim at some position or status symbol in the school hierarchy.

Gehenna, name given to the waste ground where later the rock gardens were made; now covered by the 'Hard Surface'.

Gob Sunday, the last Sunday of term, when the boarders on their way to morning service in Water Lane used all to spit as they passed the Robin Hood public house.

Gravel-pit, the standard currant pudding.

Groitch (verb), to be selfish: (noun) a selfish person.

Herp (*also Hirp*, *Hurp*), navvy or workman: derived from a queer noise made from the back of the throat with teeth clenched, and supposed to represent the Essex accent.

Hoy (*also Hoi*), same as *Herp*; also used as adjective, e.g. hoy cap, etc.

Hunky, huge, unwieldy.

'*It's Jackson's for you*', a warning: '[be careful or] you will be expelled.'

Jacob, a frog.

Moonen's Studio, a small shed, used as a photographer's showroom, that stood by the footpath near the Convent School.

Mountain, The, name by which the rising ground to the east of the outdoor swimming-pool was known. A footpath used to cut diagonally across it, leading to Windhill.

Noitcher, same as *Herp* (q.v.).

Ock!, warning shout indicating that a place was already occupied.

Pawitch, porridge.

Pax, declaration of peace at the end of a fight, generally made by the loser in acknowledgment of defeat.

Pingle (verb), to pick and toy with food in a dainty way (local word).

Pod (for more usual '*pot*'), a protruding abdomen.

Pounce I!, same as '*Bags I!*'

Quis? . . . Ego!, 'Who wants this? . . . I do!'

Scuff, food illegally removed from table after meals (chiefly used at Grimwade House).

Sock (*also Cook's Sock*), boiled suet pudding, suet roll.

Spidge (adj.), smart, posh.

Stew, In a, 'in an overheated state or bad temper'; (verb), *to stew*, to work hard.

Sum (*in full 'Adsum'*), 'I am present': used in answering name at roll-call.

Swine-mixture, cocoa and sweet condensed milk mixed into a paste.

Swot, anyone who works hard (usually in a pejorative sense). The word is said to have originally meant a mathematician.

Tea-Co (*or Teaco*), group of boys who joined forces for the term to make tea, cocoa, etc. in the schoolroom, especially before afternoon school. (Derived from Tea Company, or according to others a portmanteau word for Tea-Cocoa.)

Tea-Pot, The, the cupboard in Mr Mellows's classroom in which offenders were liable to be incarcerated during his pleasure.

Tosser, potato.

Many of the above words, especially the Latin ones, were of course common to most schools in the last century. Some yet linger at B.S.C.: you may still hear shouts of 'Quis?' in the common-room, answered by a chorus of 'Ego's', or 'Cave' in the classrooms. (A grammatically purist Prep boy once tried to popularize 'cavete' in the interests of accurate scholarship, but without success.) Until recent years 'sum' was universally used at roll-calls, and is still so used in the Prep.

'Fain(s) I!' according to Partridge's *Dictionary of Slang* dates from the early nineteenth century: it is derived from to 'fend' (off), i.e. to reject:

its earliest form was 'fen' or 'fin'. This derivation may well apply also to 'fainloss'.

One word at least Stortford can claim as an original contribution to the English language: for in another slang dictionary, published in several volumes half a century ago or more, the word 'bloitch', meaning to cry, is said to be 'peculiar to the boys of Bishop's Stortford College, Herts'.

Other words in our list have a more specifically Stortfordian reference. 'Becker' was the name of Mr F. B. Shawe, who once ran the swimming here: hence the 'B' Shoes (B for Bath) were soon named after him. He was a man of quick temper, and this explains why knuckle-bone players, instead of speaking of 'Devil's Toe-nails', came to use the term 'Becker's Toe-nails', or simply 'Beckers'. This eventually became 'Eckers' or even 'Eckles'—a good example of the swiftly changing nature of school slang.

The word 'Dosh-basket' recalls a curious incident (not, however, connected with the word) in the School House 'press-room', where in 1929 no less than 532 handkerchiefs were found to have been abstracted from the clothes-baskets, over a period of several terms, by rats and stuffed under the floorboards. They were discovered during repairs to a leaking tap: some had belonged to boys who had left more than two years previously.

Gob Sunday was observed, presumably without the knowledge of Authority, up till the 1914–1918 war: the origin of this vulgar practice is unknown.

'Jackson' was the name of a local cab proprietor patronized by the School. A boy who had been expelled had been sent to the station in Jackson's cab: hence the expression, 'It's Jackson's for you'. (Others maintain that Jackson was a school gardener in the early days, and that the reference is to some form of punishment, by which a boy had to report to Jackson for weeding or some other fatigue duty.)

'Jacob', meaning 'frog', was reported in the *N.G.S.* as being often heard in the School during the early nineties: it was said to be commonly used in the East Anglian vernacular.

The derivation of 'spidge' is typically devious. It is said to be a corruption of 'spadger' or 'spadge', a common slang word for 'sparrow', and was the nickname of a boy [1] who owned a very smart racing-type bicycle. The owner's name was forthwith applied to his property, and later 'spidge' came to be used for anything smart in appearance.

'Tosser' was introduced apparently by one of the famous Stort-

[1] A. Handford.

fordian family of Stevensons who farmed in Lincolnshire: it seems probable that, like 'jacob', it was a word of East Anglian origin.

Most of the words listed above, though obviously not all, were probably in use before the turn of the century, and will already sound archaic to present boys. For many years now English speech, like the English way of life generally, has been increasingly subjected to American influences: and it may well be that future Stortfordians will, alas, use a slang more American than traditional as they stroll across what is already being referred to as the college Campus.

N. M. J.

Of Songs and Singers

CHANTEYS at B.S.C. have been of various kinds—school chanteys, house chanteys, choir chanteys (the latter slightly superior in style and content), but above all O.S. chanteys. As early as 1885 I read that, at a meeting of the Old Stortfordians' Club in London, the chairman 'inaugurated a new style of entertainment, calling upon those present to help themselves, by anyone doing anything that he thought might please the rest'. The example of the Old Boys (usually referred to in the pages of the *N.G.S.*, officially and in all seriousness, as 'Old Storts') was soon followed in the School, where the first 'Scratch Concert' was organized in 1887. 'We use the term "Scratch"', reports the *N.G.S.*, 'as it seems to be earning itself a place in the school vocabulary. At these concerts old favourites in the way of songs are preferred to novelties, and as many choruses as possible are included. All the masters help in some way or other: boys who have songs sing them, others get up pieces to recite: Mitchell takes his usual part with songs or recitations.' A year later boys and Old Boys joined in an end-of-term concert, organized to raise funds for the making of the Cinder Track: after the visitors had gone, 'the fellows, not yet satiated with music, joined for some half-hour in a kind of rough and ready concert, and then went off to bed'. (If Old Boys were all 'Old Storts', present boys were always 'the fellows'.) But though there must have been sing-songs throughout Alliott's time, they seem to have been only occasional.

It was not till 1905 that A. G. Tidmarsh signalized his arrival on the staff by organizing fortnightly 'chanteys' of the type that we have known ever since. He himself was the outstanding performer, and soon 'King Charles', 'The Two Grenadiers', 'My Old Shako' and other songs, first sung by Tid, became the common property, as it were, of performers at subsequent chanteys. Later he introduced 'One fish-ball' (sung to the tune of 'Sucking cider through a straw'). Bobby Sutton could be relied on for a rendering of

> 'Gi'e I pudden, gi'e I lots of pudden:
> I don't care what it's made on
> As long as it's a good 'un!'

And was it not Billy Williams and Arthur Mellows who, with Tid and Bobby, formed the original quartet who first gave us that old favourite, so often heard since, 'The Chafers' (zum, zum, zum. . . .)?

Shortly before the 1914–1918 war fortnightly House chanteys were instituted, for which Tid presented the Lyre Trophy: these seem to have been superseded during the war by competing choir teams, and the curious portmanteau-word 'queams' occurs in the *Stortfordian.*

In 1919 the O.S. chanteys started up again with a special Jubilee performance in a marquee put up near the Prep oak: and soon the old favourites were in full swing once more. But new talent too was forthcoming. Norman Williams would come over from Cambridge, to do fantastic things at the piano—playing 'The Policeman's Holiday' in the minor key, 'ragging' Dvořák's *Humoresque*, or combining it with 'Home, Sweet Home' as a ground-bass. And it must have been in the early twenties, or perhaps even before the war, that Chas Mellows brought the house down with his first performance (where did he get that rich Devonshire accent?) of 'Widdicombe Fair'. George Day sang ruefully of unrequited love—'Sweet Kitty Clover she bothers me so'; and by 1926 his brother Leonard is reported as giving 'his usual piece', the reference being, of course, to his famous rendering of 'The Charge of the Light Brigade' as performed by the Man with the Automatic Arm. (Later, John Kitching took it into his repertoire.) Norman Monk-Jones contributed 'The Great American Railway' (Patsy-ory-ary-ay): the tune caught on and was taken over by Haycroft Stirling for an original composition entitled 'Prunes and rice and Sunday stew'. And Max Dyer 'knocked 'em in the Old Kent Road', as did Sid Houlden later on. In 1925 the masters put on a chantey at which Walter Strachan assured us that 'Youth's a Season made for Joys', accompanying himself on the mandolin (no, not on his double-bass!), and Eric Pascal obliged with a ditty whose intriguing title was 'Mummy's Rummy Tummy'. But the high spot of the entertainment was a popular song of the day entitled 'The Ogo Pogo', rendered chorally with what the *Stortfordian* called 'linguistic variations'. These consisted of translations of the song into French, German, Italian, Greek and Arabic, the latter provided by Chas.

Before the first war the only place where a large audience could gather had been the old Schoolroom: now there was the Hut, which, however, was not much favoured for chanteys, the old gym being preferred. Later the 'Mem. Hall' was the usual venue. In the twenties too the pre-war practice of holding chanteys on fine Sunday evenings in the School House courtyard was revived during the summer terms. They were known as *soirées*: the courtyard would be decorated with Chinese lanterns, and the School House matron, Miss Dabb, would provide much-appreciated refreshments. The *Stortfordian* recalls in nostalgic vein the picturesque surroundings of these open-air chanteys: 'the sun sinking in a glorious sky, the cool breeze of evening, and the tuneful gurglings of the bath-waste all added to the beauty of the setting!'

Against that setting I remember Tid giving us once again (for it belonged, surely, to the pre-1914 period) 'In Poland stands an Inn', the refrain sung double-forte by the audience to the *staccato* tune of the Freshmen's Song in Brahms' *Academic Festival Overture*; and that gifted actor J. A. ('Muddy') Hall reciting one of his monologues—'The 11.59', was it, or perhaps 'The Ever-Open Door'.

At O.S. chanteys in the late twenties Stanley Collett would give us 'Heraclitus', or S. E. Sturgess-Wells delight us at the piano with another old favourite, 'I think of you, dear', whose 'sick' humour never failed to receive an encore. And there would be 'Gormy' Young or F. J. Ethiraj to improvise *ad lib.* on the piano with jazz rhythms of considerable technical brilliance.

At times the chantey programmes were varied by light sketches: such was a *tour de force* by Alec Clifton-Taylor, then a boy in the School House, entitled 'David Downham's Dilemma: a Daft Drama', in which every word throughout began with a D.

Shortly after Leo Price had become headmaster, a memorable entertainment was staged by the masters to the huge gratification of their audience. It was produced by 'Bim' Kingdon, who himself gave his highly dramatic recitation, another favourite from pre-war days, of Edgar Allan Poe's 'Tintinnabulation of the Bells'. The programme included two quartets, 'The Goslings' sung by Bobby, Tid, Walter Strachan and Norman Monk-Jones, and the ever-popular 'Chafers', in which Leo Price replaced N. M. J. Then followed 'Villikins and his Dinah' sung by Tid and mimed by Gerry Coulson and Mr and Mrs Bland (all from the Prep), and a short sketch 'A Little Fowl Play', in which (reported the *Stortfordian*) 'Mr Wall's business with the telephone was amazingly clever and caused howls of laughter'. The last item was The Policemen's March and Chorus from *The Pirates of Penzance* ('the singing was powerful, though it could hardly be described as tuneful or audible').

About this time the experiment was made of holding the O.S. chantey round the steps of the south door of the Memorial Hall: it was pleasant to recline on rugs or in deck-chairs on the New Field, but the songs did not come over well in the open air, and the experiment was not repeated.

The thirties brought new names to the O.S. chantey programmes: Clifford Newbold ('The Man on the Flying Trapeze'); Roger Collett and Malcolm Anderson ('Under the Spreading Chestnut Tree', with variations); the Dyke brothers, Tom (recitation, taken over from J. A. Hall, 'How we saved the Barge') and Bewsey ('The Darkies' Sunday School'). But of course the bright particular star of those years was John Glyn-Jones—irrepressible, indefatigable, indispensable. Perhaps his 'Old Russian Folk Sonk' was our first favourite; or was it 'The Hats', in which he treated us to an astonishingly adroit piece of miming, manipulating simultaneously an incredible number of hats.

After the Second World War the O.S. chanteys started up again. Arthur Evans himself thoroughly enjoyed them: he would often conduct from the platform, and his own contribution 'The Swazi Warrior' took on at once. Glyn-Jones still came down fairly regularly, adding 'Polly Perkins' to his inexhaustible repertory. Geoffrey Allen catered for the jazz fans at the piano (only now it was 'boogie-woogie'). I remember too a new kind of turn in which Richard Wheeler produced fantastic facial contortions as he mimed to the accompaniment of gramophone records; and 'Professor' Geoffrey Strachan parodying the Children's Hour programme on television; and John Ferguson producing brief but witty sketches with the minimum of rehearsal.

But there was a tendency for the 'Old Storts' to be replaced by 'the fellows' as chief performers at these chanteys. Individual turns and sketches by the prefects became usual. Then Freddy Harris, Bill Coucher, Oliver Hunt and Tim Herring formed a group, instrumental and vocal, which gave us some delightful renderings of English and even French folk-songs. Tim Herring, especially, popularized 'The Elephants on the Spider's Web', translated (? by himself) from an old French ditty. Chris Jones and Tom Hickling seized on the occasion of a change in the regulations about school dress to regale us with a highly topical song 'Old Suits, New Suits'. And we must not forget Ted Smith's solos on the double-bassoon.

The masters continued to do their bit, even rising on one occasion to a performance of Haydn's *Toy Symphony*. And, lest the staff should be thought to be growing too highbrow, Teddy Wall delighted highbrows and lowbrows alike with the story, related with musical illustrations at the piano, of 'The Village Organist'. This original art form ended with 'The Policeman's Holiday' in the minor key, woven into a remarkable contrapuntal pattern in which echoes of Chopin's *Dead March* alternated with snatches of the same composer's *Prelude* and Beethoven's *Moonlight Sonata*.

I have written chiefly of soloist performances: but a varying proportion of the items always consisted of songs from 'Gaudeamus' on which the audience, boys and Old Boys alike, could let themselves go. Favourites were 'Forty Years On', 'Ode to Tobacco', 'The Poacher', 'John Peel' and 'All Through the Night'.

During recent years the regular O.S. chanteys have lapsed. But for many Old Stortfordians the playing of those introductory bars of *Heroes*, with which the chanteys always ended, will still recall vivid memories of songs and singers first heard 'ten, twenty, thirty, forty, fifty years ago'.

N. M. J.

8. H. L. Price: 1932–1943

THE appointment of Mr H. L. Price as Mr Young's successor must have been an obvious choice for the Governors. For many years Leo Price had been an outstanding Stortford personality. As a boy at B.S.C. he was a brilliant athlete, and he rounded off his school career by winning an exhibition in mathematics at Corpus Christi College, Oxford. We have already mentioned his all-round athletic prowess at the university, and his later repute as a great international player both of rugger and hockey. On leaving Oxford he taught for a time at Uppingham, and then at Christ's Hospital under that outstanding headmaster W. H. (later Sir William) Fyfe. Now that he was returning to his old school as headmaster he had the great advantage of the goodwill of Governors, staff, boys and Old Boys alike.

Price was a Congregationalist, and from the first he set out to strengthen the Christian values, derived from a Nonconformist background, upon which his predecessor had built up the School. Unfortunately both for him and for Stortford, his achievement during his twelve years' headmastership was continually handicapped by lack of funds, due to the slump in the country's economy with which his term of office coincided. But there was a general feeling, none the less, that a new era in the School's history was opening, and a forward-looking spirit permeated staff and boys alike.

In spite of financial stringency, the second part of the so-called Classroom Block (now the Library Block) was built in 1932. This enabled the Preparatory School, whose numbers were steadily increasing, to take over the classrooms in the older part, which in turn made improvements possible in Grimwade House: here, what had been two separate classrooms were thrown into one large common-room, with a folding partition in place of the old dividing wall: at the same time, what had been the Shell classroom (and, before that, the dining-room) was partitioned off to form a recreation-room, with a passage outside it leading to the dining-room and kitchens. (The staff would have appreciated this change earlier, as it had been somewhat trying, to say the least, teaching in a classroom through which the houseman had to pass with his coal-scuttles and the housemaids with their dustpans and brushes). Meanwhile the Prep hut classrooms were moved, that of the old Form II to the west end of 'clink', where it became a changing-room with showers attached (and where it remained till 1963); that of Form I to a point near the fives courts, where it became the school Carpentry Hut.

In 1933 a house for the groundsman was built in Maze Green Road; and in the summer term of that year the New Pavilion on Upper Field was first used. This finely equipped modern pavilion, whose contemporary style of architecture contrasted sharply with the thatched roof of the old wooden pavilion, was generously presented by the Doggart family in memory of their father, A. R. Doggart, Esq., who had himself been an old and generous friend of B.S.C. The School had long outgrown the Old Pavilion, and the amenities of the new building have continued to be appreciated both by Stortfordians and by visiting teams from other schools and clubs. It was shortly after this that the row of poplars, the gift of Arthur Itter O.S., was planted between the gate of Upper Field and the New Pavilion.

In the following term the field east of the cinder-path leading from Maze Green Road to Sparrow's Meadow—the eastern part of the field marked on the 1829 tithe map as Windmill Hill—was taken over by the Preparatory School as their playing-field: a small wooden pavilion was built, and there were two rugger and two cricket pitches, and a short pitch for Mr Monk-Jones's 'tip-and-run' enthusiasts; also in the spring term, running tracks and long-jump pits for the Prep Athletics. (This field was ploughed up during the Second World War and sown for crops: after the war it continued to be farmed, and, partly no doubt owing to the School's acquisition of Cable Field, was not again used by the School until the autumn term of 1966, when rugger posts once again appeared on it).

The School was now magnificently provided with playing-fields. Gone were the days when matches were played down at the School, on Old or New Field: and even the rugger pitches rented at Silver Leys on the Hadham Road, though still kept on for a time after the war, tended to be less and less used, and were eventually given up.

Minor alterations were made in 1933 in the School House, where the House Library was increased in size and completely divided off from the common-room, and furnished more comfortably; and in the arrangements at the east end of the indoor swimming-bath, where showers and baths for use after games were installed in what had been the S.H. changing-room, while the old bicycle shed was converted into a separate changing-room for visitors. At the same time a new School

House changing-room was built above these ground-floor rooms, communicating with a gallery on its west side from which boys could watch when swimming sports or water-polo matches were in progress; so that it was no longer necessary to scramble onto the top of 'the boxes' (changing cubicles) to get a good view.

In 1935 the school grounds lost a familiar landmark by the disappearance ofthe famous elm tree outside School House. This magnificent tree had, alas, to be cut down, for it was seriously affected by the Dutch elm disease which was then prevalent, and was pronounced to be dangerous.

It was ironical that, just when the school buildings and playing-fields were thus being improved and extended, the actual numbers of the School, like those of all the smaller public schools throughout the country, were rapidly shrinking. Of this the most obvious outward sign was the closing down, at the end of the summer term of 1933, of Westfield Lodge. First opened, as we have seen, in 1903 under Mr R. L. Ager, it was taken over three years later by Mr F. B. Shawe, and in 1919 by Mr and Mrs J. D. Craig. Always a small house, it was for that reason seriously handicapped in games, though during its thirty years it turned out several Heads of School and Captains of Rugger. In the last two years of its existence Westfield Lodge, for the purposes of house matches, had been joined with Waytefield—not an altogether happy arrangement for either House. Mention may be made here of Arthur Itter, who was head of W. L. during the first war, and afterwards became a member of the Governing Council: it was through him that the School was enabled to acquire Westfield House (see p. 72), and he and his family have been generous benefactors of B.S.C. He died in his mid thirties in 1934.

Five years later Waytefield too was closed down: a sad occasion, marked by the attendance of over sixty old members of the House (including seven foundation members from 1917) at the last House Supper in July 1938. Waytefield had been running for just twenty-one years, during which time 'Bobby' Sutton was its sole housemaster and Mrs Sutton its only matron: and (we quote from the *Stortfordian*) 'he and Mrs Sutton looked after the House with such loving care that Waytefield had an atmosphere all its own, a unique individuality'. This was emphasized in the speeches at the House Supper just referred to (held in a marquee in the beautiful garden at Waytefield, which Mr Sutton had always so expertly tended): reference was made to Waytefield's athletic record—three Captains of Athletics, three Swimming Captains and four Captains of Cricket, the game for which Mr Sutton himself had done so much over so long a period. The proceedings ended on a lighter note when a comic ritual-ceremony was organized, and a 'funeral procession' marched from Waytefield over to the school grounds, escorting a grave-stone (it only disappeared when the rock gardens were levelled in 1965) inscribed: HIC IACET WAYTEFIELD.

Meanwhile a fitting memorial to a great headmaster had been erected in 1936, when the Francis Samuel Young Memorial Library was formally opened by Mrs Young. Joining the two newest classroom blocks on the New Field, it welded them into a single whole, as Young himself had planned. Professor N. H. Baynes said, in his address at the service which preceded the opening ceremony: 'In the place intended by him for a library stands the library building which is today to be dedicated. Built in his memory, it forms part of the legacy of his giving.'

The last major building that materialized in the period immediately prior to the Second World War was the well-appointed Manual Workshop which was built in the south-east corner of the school grounds opposite the Old Gymnasium. The workshop had in the old days functioned in the western end of the gymnasium, and more recently in the hut near the fives courts, which had been vacated by the Prep in 1932. The new building came into use in 1939; officially referred to as the Manual Workshop, it nevertheless took its old name with it, and is still known amongst boys and staff alike by the inappropriate name of 'the Carp Hut'.

So much then for the extension of the school buildings during Price's headmastership. Meanwhile numerous changes were taking place on the staff. In 1932 Dr W. V. Lloyd was appointed as senior chemistry master: the following year C. L. Howell-Thomas became assistant Day Boy housemaster. In that year also the school music suffered a severe loss by the death of Percy Green, a delightful personality and a most sensitive musician who for many years had taught the violin: he was succeeded as violin master by Mr F. W. Greenfield. The year 1935 saw the appointment of two men to the teaching staff who, though they did not stay long, both left their mark on the School in their several ways. One was A. L. Creed, who came as assistant housemaster to Robert Pearce House: he left four years later and is now headmaster of Kingswood School, Bath. The other was James Fisher, an outstanding biologist who specialized in ornithology; he only stayed a year at B.S.C., where he was assistant housemaster at Alliott's. Since then he has made a national and indeed worldwide reputation as a writer, lecturer and broadcaster on birds. In the same year T. C. Sims came to the Prep as assistant housemaster in Grimwade House. In 1936 arrived four young and energetic new masters, W. A. Jones (history), G. A. Goodban (classics), S. W. Woodward (modern languages) and

L. P. Madge (biology), who together supplied a valuable injection of youth into the Masters' Common Room. In that year C. L. Howell-Thomas left, to take up an appointment as housemaster at the newly founded Indian public school, the Doon School at Dehra Dun. In 1937 A. G. Tidmarsh retired from the housemastership of Robert Pearce House, moving back to Wynch Cottage next door: he was succeeded at R.P.H. by W. J. Strachan.

On the debit side the School, by the death in 1934 of the Rev. Frank Lenwood (a former secretary of the London Missionary Society) lost a very loyal friend, an old Rugbeian who, especially in the early days of Young's headmastership, had been a tower of strength both to Young personally and as a member for ten years of the Governing Council. In 1935 three senior members of the staff retired—F. M. Kingdon, E. W. Edmunds and the Director of Music, Dr A. F. Barnes. 'Bim', as Kingdon was known to generations of Stortfordians, was a boy at Stortford, and taught here for two years (1894–6) before going up to Cambridge. He returned to the staff in 1899, being housemaster in School House until his marriage in 1903: he then took over the housemastership of the Day Boys for ten years. From 1913 till 1919 he was Bursar. After a year's absence he returned once more to the teaching staff in 1920, and remained at Stortford until his retirement. Both as a boy and as a young master he was a prominent performer at soccer and cricket, as well as playing an energetic game of rugger. He showed the keenest interest in all the activities of the School, as well as in his mathematics teaching: at various times he helped with the magazine, the Games Committee, the Dramatic Society and, during the 1914–1918 war, the Cadet Corps, of which he was C.O. He frequently acted in school plays, as well as producing them: and was in great demand at school chanteys. He died, ten years after his retirement, in 1945.

E. W. Edmunds joined the staff in 1916. He was not only a biology specialist, but also taught English to several forms: indeed, during his teaching career he published a number of English textbooks, of which his *Historical Summary of English Literature*, a useful compilation for examinees in English, was perhaps the best known. He was for many years president of the Masters' Common Room. Like C. S. Colman, he was something of a 'polymath': and it was both instructive and entertaining to listen to Edmunds and C. S. C. pooling their intellectual resources, over a cup of tea in the M.C.R., in the effort, almost always successful, to solve the more recondite allusions in the clues of Torquemada's crossword puzzles. Like Kingdon, Edmunds too was interested in the drama: he was president of the Dramatic Society, and reference has already been made to the Morality Play *Mundus et Homo* which he wrote specially for the Dramatic Society. He was also in charge of the botanical section of the School Natural History Society. He remained a keen botanist to the last, and after his retirement became a founder-member of the local Natural History Society in Bishop's Stortford. He died in 1948.

Dr A. F. Barnes, during his nine years as Director of Music, composed a number of part songs and orchestral pieces which he tried out on the school choir and orchestra with success: more especially he wrote some fine hymn tunes, and these he included in the Supplement Hymn Book which he compiled in collaboration with F. S. Young, and which is still used at the school services on Sunday evenings. Dr Barnes' work was temporarily carried on by Charles Groves (who has since become widely known as a conductor): later in 1935 R. G. E. Oakley was appointed as the new Director of Music, a post which he held for more than twenty years.

In 1936 the Preparatory School suffered a great loss by the death, after an operation, of G. L. Coulson at the early age of thirty-seven. An O.S., he returned to Stortford in 1922, and for six years was assistant housemaster at Grimwade House. Here he was master in charge of cricket, and also played an active part in the coaching of all games and sports, as well as running a Scout troop and organizing numerous out-of-door activities. In 1928 he gave up his resident post to get married, but continued to devote all his spare time to the Prep. In that year he was appointed housemaster of the Prep Day Boys. His sympathetic understanding of small boys won him the respect and affection of many young Stortfordians, especially those who had newly arrived at school.

In the same year the School said goodbye to C. S. Colman, who finally retired in 1936 after thirty-four years on the staff. The part that C. S. C. played in the building up of the School in the early years of this century was second only to that played by F. S. Young. We have referred in an earlier chapter to his brilliant career at Oxford, where he took First Class Honours in both Classical Moderations and Modern History, and a Second in Greats. He spent some years in journalism, during which he was at various times editor of *Land and Water* and assistant editor of *The Sportsman's Year Book* and of *The Encyclopedia of Sport*: at the same time he was a free-lance journalist. During these years he gave a lot of his spare time to the Working Men's College, of which he acted as secretary.

From 1902, when he was appointed to the school staff, he helped F. S. Young in the adventurous, not to say risky, project of building up Bishop's Stortford into a modern public school, giving generously of his labour, his money and all the resources of a vivid and versatile personality. He was admirably fitted for his new position: in matters of policy he was a trusted adviser, with sound business instincts: as a schoolmaster he rarely punished or needed to punish, for his discipline was never questioned. He enjoyed general respect, and among his own pupils immense popularity: we quote from some of the tributes written by former pupils or colleagues that appeared in the *Stortfordian* at the time of his retirement. Charles Mellows wrote of him as follows: 'One of F. S. Young's early ambitions for the School was to win scholarships at the Universities. Colman made himself an unpaid coach out of school, as well as a master working full time in school hours. He was always willing to read with his pupils—during the holidays, in his own home, on his boat. And he very soon secured the entire confidence of his Sixth Form. There followed a regular succession of scholarships and exhibitions in Classics and History. He was a great teacher: so strong was his influence over his early Sixth Forms that he left his mark permanently on each of their members, and there are few who do not remember him with gratitude.

'He had a lively interest in sport of all sorts. He was himself a very keen fives player: in early days an interested crowd would often stand near the old tuck-shop (long before the Memorial Hall was built) to watch Colman and the Headmaster, each with a boy partner, engaging in great duels in the old and distinctively Stortford game. (Present boys and visitors, as they pass along the "Mem. Hall passage", are still puzzled to explain the black line on the bricks marking the old fives court.) At cricket, we have been for many years familiar with him not so much as a player, but as one of the School's kindly critics and loyal supporters. And did he not once, playing for the Masters, dismiss the whole school with his harmless-looking lobs? When a boy at school, he was a clever performer at soccer, playing at right-half for the XI; and for a time he played rugger when we changed over to that game. For many years he refereed Senior Side rugger: he ran the athletic sports, and for twenty years was a familiar figure, with pistol or with stop-watch, standing stoically amid the snow showers of Sports Day on Upper Field. The stop-watch was his constant friend, and not only on these occasions: for the sermons of visiting divines at Sunday evening services did not escape this ordeal. Colman himself was a strong believer in brevity in sermons: his own rather too occasional efforts endeared him to his congregations not less for this than for the directness and lucidity with which he always expressed himself.

'No sketch of him, however brief, would be complete without some reference to his activities as a gardener: but it would be impossible to include all his activities in the School. In his day he ran the school magazine: he organized Past and Present cricket teams: he was president of the Natural History Society and was himself a naturalist of no ordinary keenness: he was a pioneer in the architectural hobby, and a supporter of the Dramatic Society in its early days, for which he staged a magnificent production of *Macbeth*: magnificent, even if it was not Shakespeare. He founded the Carlyle Club, a literary society to the members of which he dispensed generous hospitality as he listened tolerantly and benevolently to "first offences".

'In the holidays, Colman would often spend his New Year at Wasdale Head, trudging up Great Gable or Esk Hause, and displaying a sure touch at billiard fives in the evenings. As a good fenman he was an expert skater in his day: once he took a party to Switzerland for a hectic ten days' ski-joring and cricket on the ice at Lac Champex. In its early days he was a frequent visitor to Church Farm at Hasbro': but his visits were generally brief, for the lure of the neighbouring Broads was too strong, and it was here that most of his holidays were spent. Some hundreds of Stortford boys must have shared with him at one time or another the pleasures of a trip on the *Moth*. I was talking once to a local yachtsman and, as we chatted, the *Moth* sailed by. My friend said reflectively: "I wonder who that little man is, who sails his boat better than anyone on the Broads?".'

Of Chips in the classroom J. H. Doggart, another former pupil, wrote: 'Someone is construing, or let us say spluttering, a series of unrelated Latin and English words in agonized alternation. A Latin word is vilely pronounced. No sound comes from Mr Colman, but his head tilts almost imperceptibly to one side. Then follows a real howler of a mistranslation. C. S. C. still awaits the interpretation of those booming hexameters. Silence falls. The boy looks up with a blush, to encounter C. S. C.'s impassive gaze—but no, not completely impassive, because his lips have begun to move in a slow succession of whimsical patterns. A quivering disturbance flutters across his shoulders. Slowly the quiver amplifies into a heaving, and Mr Colman openly rocks with laughter. Soon his mirth is communicated to the rest of the class, including the flounderer, unless that boy should happen to be a wretched sulk; but this last complication does not often arise, because C. S. C. being devoid of malice confines his raillery to those who appreciate its harmlessness.'

'During his nineteen years of retirement', wrote H. E. Wall, 'he still remained very much part of the School. I remember that he helped me with the chess hobby: as anyone who took him on at this game will know, playing him was always exciting! His interest in the work of the School, especially on the history side, his proof-reading for the *Stort-*

fordian, his watching of school games and house matches went on practically to the end.'

He died in 1955: the *Stortfordian* wrote of him as 'a man who, perhaps more than any, living or dead, was the incarnation of all that is best in what we mean by "Stortford"'.

In 1937 H. S. Evason left, after ten years on the staff as a teacher of modern languages, especially German. He had been assistant housemaster first of the Day Boy House and then of School House, where on Sunday evenings he ran the Goethe Club. He left B.S.C. to take charge of modern languages at Wellington College, Somerset.

In the following year a great Stortford character passed away in the person of Sergeant Salmon, known universally (from his oft-repeated injunction to 'Hile your Jints') as Sergeant Hile. He came to B.S.C. as part-time gymnastic instructor in 1906; after a few years he introduced fencing, and later still he organized the boxing competition, already referred to, which for a time became a feature of the spring term. Meanwhile he had become a full-time instructor during the 1914–1918 war, at the same time undertaking the care of the school grounds and the general supervision of the outdoor staff. He was popular with boys and masters alike: a man who took an artist's pride in his work, it pained him to do a job badly. At the Prize Day gym displays his own performances, even when he was getting on in years, were always impressive to watch. And he was always willing and able to turn his hand to any job that might enhance the appearance and amenities of the school grounds.

It was in November of this same year (1938) that three cases of infantile paralysis developed at B.S.C.: and towards the end of the month the School was saddened by the news of the death of one of these boys, Graham Hodgson by name—a particularly gifted boy who had only just come up to the Main School from the Prep. Meanwhile normal school life came to a halt: the great majority of the boarders went home, and those day boys who continued to attend school were isolated from the remaining boarders. School work was continued by post.

In 1939 the Rev. A. G. Knott, the Congregational minister at Stortford, left the town to go to the well-known Carr's Lane Church in Birmingham. For six years or more he had had close connections with the School, not only at the Sunday services in Water Lane but through the scripture classes he took at the School and through his keen interest in the boys' cricket. He was a personal friend of H. L. Price; and with his going the School's ties with Congregationalism tended to be less close than in the past. In the same year F. W. Grimwade retired from the chairmanship of the Governing Council which he had held since 1928.

He was succeeded as chairman by H. Stanley Tee, who, as an O.S. and a resident in Stortford, was able to keep in closer touch with the School than his predecessors had done; his advice and support were to be of great help to Price during the difficult years of the Second World War.

Meanwhile the School continued to win open scholarships at the universities—in classics (the last, alas, in 1939), modern languages, science and history: at one time there were ten O.S. in residence at Oxford and more than twice that number at Cambridge.

It was to be expected that, under a headmaster who had been an outstanding international player, hockey was likely to be introduced. The School may be said to have had a hockey tradition already in the making; for, as long ago as 1890, an O.S. named Arnold Tebbutt, who was at the N.G.S. in the 1870's, having played ice-hockey in the Fen District where he lived as a boy, introduced that game into Hampshire, and then founded the first ordinary hockey club in that county. Later he captained the first Hampshire County team, and was dubbed the 'Father of Hampshire Hockey'. In 1902 he captained an English ice hockey team against Germany in Berlin: his opponents were interested to learn of the land game, and he sent them the rules translated into German; so that in a sense he may be said to have been responsible for the starting of hockey in Germany as well. To return now to B.S.C., it was in the spring term of 1935 that H. L. Price introduced the game at Stortford, the rugger house matches having been played off, as they always had been in earlier days, in the previous autumn term. At first only the three senior rugger sides were switched to hockey, but in succeeding years gradually the whole school took up the game. Four matches were played in 1936, and by 1939 First, Second and Third XI fixtures had been arranged, to the number of eleven matches in all. In recent years hockey has developed into the major sport in the spring term and is now played throughout the School, including the Preparatory School.

During these pre-war years all forms of sport flourished exceedingly. The rugger of the School perhaps reached its zenith in 1937, when only one First XV match was lost: and at cricket the season or two just before the outbreak of war produced a number of brilliant high-scoring batsmen: one thinks especially of G. J. Adams, L. E. McLean and P. W. Meen: the first mentioned played for the Rest of England Schools *v.* the Lords Schools at Lords and also for Herts County while still at school. In swimming again the year 1937 saw the School successful in winning the Bath Club Cup for the sixth time since the first war, and this success was repeated in 1938. Meanwhile swimmers benefited greatly by the installation of a filtration plant in the outdoor swimming-pool, with gratifying results in the greater cleanliness of the water.

At this time also a big change was introduced in the running of the athletic sports: from 1938 on all events were run on the relay principle, not as individual competitions. Cups were awarded to the successful teams in what was an entirely inter-house contest. At the same time a new system of standard points gave all boys a chance of contributing to the achievement of their Houses in the athletics competition.[1]

Fives was becoming increasingly popular, organized and encouraged by C. L. Howell-Thomas: the first outside match was against Emmanuel College, Cambridge, Howell-Thomas's own college, in 1931. The number of fixtures was gradually increased, but never exceeded more than four or five matches. Fives colours were instituted in 1933. Tennis too was encouraged by the laying down of two hard courts in 1935 to replace the grass courts in the corner by Sparrow's Meadow.

A change was introduced by Price early in his headmastership in the running of the school P.T. Mid-morning break was made longer, so as to enable the whole school to change and do a quarter of an hour's P.T. This was organized on a house basis, prefects and monitors being trained to take charge of the house squads.

Perhaps mention should be made here of various Old Stortfordian activities. In 1934 the O.S. Golfing Society was formed, and the first meeting, attended by twenty-five members, was held at Broxbourne Golf Club early in 1935. In 1937 the formation of an O.S. Freemasons' Lodge was mooted, and in the following year, largely through the efforts of C. S. Colman, the Old Stortfordian Lodge was launched: it was consecrated by Admiral Sir Lionel Halsey, the first Master being Dr Grantly Dick-Read and the first Secretary H. Stanley Tee. In this year too took place the reorganization of the Old Stortfordians' Club: hitherto the O.S.C. itself, the O.S. Rugger Club, the O.S. Swimming Club and, more recently, the O.S. Golfing Society had been independent clubs, with their own officers, rules and subscription rates. The four sections were now amalgamated into a single club, governed by a committee representative of all its various activities, with membership (apart from playing membership of the various sports sections) involving the payment of a single inclusive subscription. The new arrangement, however, led to unforeseen difficulties, and after some years was abandoned.

The hobbies that had been functioning for many years—the Natural History Society, the Dramatic Society, the Architectural Society, the Music, Debating and Gardens Societies—continued to function actively during the thirties; and a new chess hobby was started by H. E. Wall, and flourished especially in the School House. The Claremont camps

[1] In the fifties, however, the old method of individual events was restored.

continued, and concerts were still given at the Mission during the winter. The Gramophone Circle, after some years' intermission, was refounded in 1937 entirely by the boys' own initiative, and also a Glee Club which flourished intermittently. The School House ran a Swing Club, whose members listened to their jazz records, as no doubt do their successors today to their 'pop' music, with deep seriousness. In the gardens, new 'mountains' and pools were still being added from time to time, with the result that they were considered worthy of a special article, with a photograph, in *The Times Educational Supplement*. The art work of the School was well represented at the Public Schools Art Exhibition of 1932, and gained favourable mention in *The Times* report of the show. Other societies—the Science Society, the Wireless Society, the Photographic Society—showed the wide range of out-of-school activities that were catered for: at R.P.H. a model theatre and, later, a model cinema ran for a time. There was an ephemeral jiu jitsu hobby, run by a Viennese P.T. instructor who came for a term or two after Sergeant Salmon's death. The School had an active branch of the League of Nations Union, and also a branch of Toc H, B.S.C. being one of eighteen schools in the country which were awarded the Toc H Lamp in recognition of their participation in some form of social service—in our case the Claremont Mission. The Christian Union also held weekly meetings.

In the late thirties Leo Price, feeling that the boys, apart from the enthusiastic few, tended to drift away from the Saturday evening hobbies, instituted a 'Pioneers' scheme, the object of which was to broaden the boys' interests yet further, and to encourage individual out-of-school activities of a worth-while kind. A list of subjects was drawn up, and this was expanded as time went on until it included archaeology, astronomy, photography, railways, motor engineering, bird-spotting, finding and identifying trees and wild flowers, architecture, literary appreciation, dramatics, carpentry, first-aid and ambulance work, athletics, model-making, sketching and painting, boxing, geology, heraldry, gardening, beekeeping and entomology: a very mixed bag, of which the above is not an exhaustive list. The master in charge of each group gave the boys periodical tests in their knowledge of the subject and their practical achievement in it, those who passed their tests being awarded a proficiency star. Boys were encouraged to move on, term by term, from one activity to another: they could choose any subject, provided the group was not already over-large. (One boy put down boxing as his first choice, and first-aid as his second! Charles Mellows, asked how many boys were on the list for his bee-keeping hobby, replied somewhat testily: 'How many boys? I've got more boys than bees!') The Pioneers scheme, which continued until the outbreak of the Second World War put a stop to it, was independent of the already existing hobbies, though obviously there was overlapping at certain points. There is no doubt that it laid a useful foundation for broadening the boys' interests, even if it did not take them very far along any given line.

Of holiday activities during this pre-war decade, the Duke of York's camps, already referred to, were continued into the early thirties, and boys from Stortford attended them each summer holidays. Holiday parties abroad were organized by various masters, the countries visited including France (many times), Scandinavia, Switzerland, Jugoslavia, Italy and Corsica. In 1934 another kind of holiday party was arranged. In view of the serious distress due to unemployment, Leo Price organized two parties to visit one of the Distressed Areas in South Wales: the boys lived as paying guests in the homes of unemployed men, working during the day at building a road through the local allotments provided for the unemployed: one party went down a coal-mine and saw the conditions under which the miners worked, if lucky enough to be working at all. In 1935, with H. E. Wall, he took a similar party to another Distressed Area, this time in the north, staying at the village of Escomb, in County Durham. Further parties were taken by A. L. Creed in 1936 and H. E. Wall in 1937.

In 1936 and the three following years, three boys and a master attended Easter holiday courses in Paris, arranged for English public school boys by the Institut Britannique.

At the end of the summer term of 1938 a very successful bazaar and flannel dance were organized, to raise funds for a new Day Boy House (the need for which was increased by a fire the following year, which more or less gutted the wooden Day Boy House down by the tuck-shop). For the dance the Old Field was decked with fairy lights and Chinese lanterns and even floodlit: Stortfordians past and present with their partners 'tripped the light fantastic toe' in the academic precincts of the college grounds, while the strains of 'The Lambeth Walk' were wafted on the night air. It was a festive occasion to which those who took part looked back nostalgically in the dark days that were to follow a year later. It had been Price's hope that he would be able to put up a more substantial building as headquarters for the Day Boys: but in the same year came the Munich crisis, and the new Day Boy House had to be relegated to an indefinite future date.

The international crisis of September 1938, at the time of the Munich Conference, found the School, in common with the rest of the country, fitting gas-masks and undergoing gas-mask drill in the anticipation of imminent war, while boys and masters spent feverish hours digging zigzag trenches in various parts of the grounds. These were unfinished when the Conference ended, giving the nations an uneasy breathing-space before the actual outbreak of war a year later. School life resumed more or less its normal routine. Price himself was, most unfortunately, away ill during a large part of the spring term of 1939, F. S. Sutton, second master since Colman's retirement, acting as headmaster during Leo's absence. The following term saw the appearance of concreted underground air-raid shelters in various parts of the school grounds and behind R.P.H., in place of the improvised trenches of the previous year: the shelters were allotted to the several Houses, while to the Preparatory School was assigned the boiler-room under the New Classroom Block of 1932, which was reinforced with heavy iron girders.

Leo Price was now back at his post, and in that last summer term before the war he had the pleasure of welcoming his old headmaster under whom he had worked at Christ's Hospital, W. H. Fyfe, who came to B.S.C. to present the prizes. This was one of our more memorable Prize Days. 'We had been led to expect much of Mr Fyfe,' reported the *Stortfordian*, 'and we were not disappointed. But how can one in cold print reproduce the genial humour and warmth of his winning personality?' Fyfe began his speech with a definition he had recently heard of a public school education: it consisted in 'casting sham pearls before real swine!' And he proceeded to treat his audience to a speech that was both witty and wise.

With the end of that summer term the normal school life of peace time, at Stortford as everywhere else, came to an abrupt stop. On the declaration of war against Germany in September, Grimwade House was immediately thrown open, a fortnight before term was due to begin, for boys, whether from the Main or the Preparatory School, whose homes were in areas thought likely to be subjected to air-raids. (Incidentally this was the present headmaster's first introduction to the School, as a new boy entering the Prep.) Soon Stortford's first air-raid alarm was heard: whereupon, marshalled by Leo Price and Norman Monk-Jones, the whole party trooped down, complete with gas-masks, into the air-raid shelter by the tennis courts, wondering what was going to happen. In fact, as was usually (though not always) the case at Stortford throughout the war, nothing happened, and soon the all-clear sounded. For a short time it seemed likely that the Upper Field might be requisitioned as an airfield: officials from the Air Ministry were closeted with the headmaster: rumours were rife that the School would be evacuated and the boys transferred elsewhere—perhaps to be combined with some other school. Fortunately, however, we were spared that additional

THE CLASSROOM BLOCK completed in 1925 and the Elementary Laboratory (now the Basic Biology Lab.) beyond the main Laboratories.

A. I. Rae winning the Public Schools Half-Mile, 1947.

SENIOR ATHLETIC TEAM, 1925. *Standing:* R. C. Jackson, F. W. Davey, E. D. H. Renton, W. P. Barker, G. V. N. Chadd. *Sitting:* J. D. Kitching, F. B. Arnold, D. G. White (Capt.), C. J. Jackson, W. F. Roberson.

WESTGROVE HOUSE, 1926. *Standing:* B. H. Bennett, W. K. Good, F. Hill, W. R. Murfitt. *Sitting:* E. D. Jones, J. M. Brown, Rev. C. H. Stearn, R. M. Davies, B. J. Davis.

WESTFIELD HOUSE: the Sanatorium from 1926 to 1968, now Sutton House.

SCHOOL HOUSE FIRE DRILL, 1930. J. C. Newbold is looking out of the B Dormitory window, H. H. Wagstaff similarly at the A window (heads of the respective dormitories in charge). T. C. Sanders is holding right hand side of B chute, his brother W. M. G. Sanders is on the left hand side of A chute. This system was discontinued about 1960.

IE PREPARATORY SCHOOL, 1927. *Back row:* J. R. H. Nash-Wortham, R. V. Tipple, S. M. Smith, Heddle, J. K. Tee, R. S. S. Young, D. E. Clodd, D. H. Eggleton, E. A. Bompas, K. W. Bonnar, R. N. :hards, A. K. Horner, C. H. Deverill, D. R. S. Ferguson, B. M. Law, L. K. Dawson, C. A. Paige, J. W. barts. *Second row:* W. L. Taylor, H. M. Knee, P. A. T. Cope, D. A. Fordham, C. N. Brown, G. Oyler, D. F. ck, A. J. Matthews, J. D. C. Joslin, A. Bedwell, G. G. Ivory, H. B. S. Warren, G. E. A. Ralston, R. L. G. wson, J. R. Cherry, S. C. Collins, A. T. Almond, R. C. Macdonald, J. Hotson, A. D. Coates. *Sitting:* M. K. llard, A. T. Appleby, J. P. Shillingford, A. J. H. Palmer, R. R. Pearce, D. C. Lloyd, Mr A. H. Blandford, :s Monk-Jones, Mr N. Monk-Jones, Miss Parsons, Miss Bennett, Mr G. L. Coulson, W. L. Herington, J. E. tchard, H. B. Rowles. *Front row:* R. J. Dawson, A. C. Abbott, J. Hardyman, D. L. Robarts, J. K. Sinclair, B. Pope, M. B. Pope, G. R. Ellis, F. A. M. Docker, A. S. Tee, W. J. Littlewood, H. G. Heyworth, J. R. ttle, A. K. Blake.

;RIMWADE HOUSE after the completion of the private wing, 1931.

W. Rogers, Houseman at G. H., 1919–64.

THE SWIMMING BATH with the old diving boards and the 'boxes' (pre-1933).

With the later alterations (photo 1955). *Ground level:* Mr Mellows, Mr Clare, R. C. Davies, C. J. Wagsta R. V. Westlake, I. J. Beaton, Two unknowns and then P. J. Sabine (*under top board*), T. Hutchinson, H. Garrett, R. W. Gibbons. *Balcony:* R. Wallis (*second from left*), N. T. G. Eggleton (*extreme right*).

Mr Mellows giving instruction in the Open-Air Bath in the early days. A. C. D. Parsons is second to the righ from Mr Mellows.

9: 1. (?), 2. N. L. Good, 3. K. L. Daly, 4. (?), ?. J. C. Wallis, 6. H. L. Greig, 7. R. A. Dean, . J. A. Richardson, 9. J. H. G. Stockley, 10. (?), I. C. Grant, 12. D. Marrack, 13. F. C. Laverack, J. M. Laws, 15. (?), 16. D. J. Meen, 17. C. M. ›hens, 18. G. T. Rolfe, 19. P. B. Mills, 20. C. M. ıchan, 21. J. E. Alexander, 22. J. L. Strachan, G. B. S. Chase, 24. A. F. Harris, 25. D. S. Collett, H. M. S. Hadfield, 27. (?), 28. R. A. Beckett, (?), 30. P. D. Carter, 31. P. G. Blackburn, A. D. Norris, 33. (?).

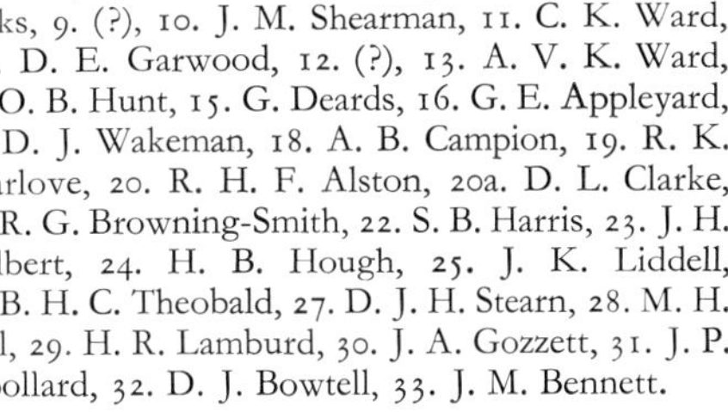

8: 1. M. B. Scanes, 2. T. C. M. Ling, 3. C. N. ›man, 4. M. R. Wilson, 5. B. A. Latham, 6. P. ›hens, 7. N. M. Browning-Smith, 8. N. R. ks, 9. (?), 10. J. M. Shearman, 11. C. K. Ward, . D. E. Garwood, 12. (?), 13. A. V. K. Ward, O. B. Hunt, 15. G. Deards, 16. G. E. Appleyard, D. J. Wakeman, 18. A. B. Campion, 19. R. K. ırlove, 20. R. H. F. Alston, 20a. D. L. Clarke, R. G. Browning-Smith, 22. S. B. Harris, 23. J. H. lbert, 24. H. B. Hough, 25. J. K. Liddell, B. H. C. Theobald, 27. D. J. H. Stearn, 28. M. H. l, 29. H. R. Lamburd, 30. J. A. Gozzett, 31. J. P. ›ollard, 32. D. J. Bowtell, 33. J. M. Bennett.

Chas's camera captures two generations' enjoyment of the Outdoor Bath.

H. L. PRICE,
Headmaster 1932–43.

A. N. EVANS,
Headmaster 1944–57.

P. W. ROWE,
Headmaster from 1957.

HEADMASTER'S HOUSE, 1965.

:HOOL HOUSE, 1932. *Back row:* H. M. Knee, D. L. Robarts, J. Bywaters, G. R. B. Blake. *Next row:* . J. Littlewood, A. Bywaters, J. D. C. Joslin, G. Oyler, H. B. Rowles, G. H. Cooper, J. B. Elton, B. E. G. ake, L. R. A. Styring, A. A. Pearce, F. A. E. James, T. O. E. James, F. S. Laws. *Next row:* F. J. Ohlson, J. R. ray, N. Clark, P. J. Mackay, J. B. Newland, J. Dalrymple, G. C. Rae, R. S. Beedell, J. Hardyman, E. I. asters, J. R. H. Nash-Wortham, J. T. Smith, T. W. Bolingbroke. *Standing on ground:* R. F. A. Sharp, R. B. aze, A. G. Smith, C. D. J. Irmie, G. D. Taylor,A. J. Watkin, R. C. Jenkinson, J. R. Kettle, N. S. Wagstaff, . G. Stevens, P. M. Wright, A. G. Wilks, K. C. Cooper, E. Stratford, A. J. Wills. *Sitting:* B. E. C. Stanley, Hotson, R. J. Wakely, G. W. C. Garrould, J. D. Hennell, D. C. Lloyd, Mr H. E. Wall, Mr H. L. Price, r W. R. Towns, R. R. Pearce, K. W. Bonnar, D. M. McKinnon, H. B. S. Warren, F. H. Davis, S. C. Collins. *front:* K. A. Cuff, D. I. Mumford, R. I. B. Warwick, N. D. Caldwell, W. J. Mohun, L. H. Beedell, D. Heddle, R. Corke, W. R. Driver, M. N. Joscelyne, B. W. Watkin.

THE SCHOOL HOUSE LIBRARY, 1933.

Looking west, 1932.

The Rock Gardens

Charles Mellows, genius loci.

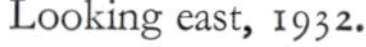

Looking east, 1932.

complication: there were already problems enough for the school authorities to tackle. For the first few weeks of term, boys and staff alike, when not in school, were kept busy with air-raid practices and with the seemingly endless task of making black-out frames and then fitting them so as to black out all windows throughout the classrooms and boarding houses. Gradually the School adjusted itself to the new routines of war time. Land cultivation was started, and working-squads took over, first behind R.P.H. and on the Mountain (behind the Manual Workshop), where increasing quantities of vegetables were grown. Later, through the initiative of the boys themselves, a large field on the Much Hadham Road, south of the present Cable Field, was brought under cultivation: during 1941 sixteen tons of potatoes were harvested from this field alone. Meanwhile under the T.A. Association a Cadet Force was organized, for boys over fifteen, and started functioning in January 1940 under the command of Captain (afterwards Major) A. O. Ward, with W. A. Jones second in command. It was known officially as the 12th Hertfordshire (Bishop's Stortford College) Cadet Corps, and was affiliated to the 1st Battalion of the Hertfordshire Regiment. Membership was voluntary: those boys who did not join were required to enrol in special service squads which undertook various forms of manual work to meet the needs of the community in war time. The expected air-raids did not at first materialize: and a Local Defence Volunteers' observation post on Upper Field, where members of the staff took it in turns to sleep at nights, was discontinued after a few months.

Shortly before the outbreak of war, the Old Stortfordians' Club had organized a special fund to help educate the sons of wartime refugees from abroad at B.S.C. Three such boys were educated here during the first three years of the war, and in 1942 the fund was established on a firmer basis. After the war the fund developed into the O.S.C. Benevolent Fund, and as such is still functioning.

It was not until June 1940, at the end of the so-called 'phoney war' period, that the air-raid warnings began in earnest: detailed instructions were now issued as to the procedure to be followed when the siren went, according to whether the alarm occurred during school hours, or when boys were on the playing-fields, or at night. The writer well remembers having to blow the whistle, when the siren went during a game of rugger, to stop play and send all players into the shelter of the ditch between Upper Field and New Upper Field, there to await the all-clear. Later, games continued unless enemy aircraft actually appeared overhead. Down at the School a brick shelter was erected near the Cinder Track, from which the Headmaster could direct operations during a raid.

Meanwhile lengthening lists of O.S. serving with the forces were appearing in the *Stortfordian*: and frequent staff changes occurred as one by one the younger masters received their call-up papers. The senior masters, in so far as boarding house duties permitted, joined the Home Guard (which had replaced the L.D.V.), or became special constables or air raid wardens. The School organized its own squads, each consisting of a master and three senior boys, to watch for incendiaries during black-out time, the squads being based on the shelter under the New Classroom Block (by now vacated by Grimwade House), where the two not actually on watch had mattresses for sleeping till their turn came. Several boys and indeed masters owed to this nocturnal job their first interest in astronomy, the study of which helped to pass the monotonous hours of night watching.

On half-holidays, working parties were sent out to local farms: and in the summer holidays of 1940 the first of several farming parties were organized to help with the harvest, one being based on the School and another at Little Maplestead, on the other side of Essex, where J. S. Blomfield O.S., who had farmed there all his life, made himself responsible for the arrangements. Successive groups of senior boys, in the charge of various masters, were housed in Maplestead village hall, from which they were sent out daily, in groups of two or three or more as required, to the neighbouring farms. Numerous Stortfordians worked in this way during the succeeding war years: apart from the satisfaction of earning some pocket-money, they got to know something of farming, or at any rate of the harvesting of the different crops, at first hand: and during off-hours, if they were not striking up friendships with the local 'land-girls', they were most hospitably entertained by Joe and Laura Blomfield up at the Hall. Their house stands on the site of a 'preceptory' of the Knights Hospitallers or Knights of St John: thus the fields in which we were working may well have been farmed by the members of this Order in medieval times.

As the days drew in, during the autumn of 1940, afternoon classes were as far as possible held before black-out time. At night the boarders in the various Houses slept downstairs, usually on mattresses on the floor. For a time the Grimwade House boys slept in their shelter under the New Block; but the combined unpleasantnesses of the overcrowded floor space, the ubiquitous dust from the cement floor, the midges and the fumes from the boiler-room finally drove them back to the House, where every available inch of ground-floor space was occupied, mattresses even being laid between the tables in the dining-hall. In the day time the air-raid alerts were becoming more frequent, though chiefly occasioned by enemy planes passing over on their way to or from raids on London. During this autumn term there were no less than a hundred and eighty alerts, averaging about three hours' duration before the all-clear: and it may easily be imagined how the routine of class work was thereby disorganized. After a time the regulations for taking shelter were modified: spotters were sent out when the alarm went, and boys only repaired to the shelters when enemy planes were reported to be actually approaching. This happened comparatively rarely: though on one occasion a German Dornier bomber was chased over the school grounds at tree-top level by British Hurricanes, and on another a German Junkers 88 crashed during the night on the edge of our cabbage and potato field on the Much Hadham Road.

At the end of 1940 it was decided, as a war-time economy measure, temporarily to close down Alliott House as a boarding house, and most of the A.H. boys were transferred to School House. Mr Mellows and Mr Hayward stayed on, and were joined at Alliott's by Mr Ward. The top dormitory became temporarily the Natural History Museum; and the dining-hall was used as an overflow ground-floor dormitory for boys from R.P.H. The rest of the ground floor, consisting mainly of the common-room and studies, was taken over by the Day Boys, who, since the fire of 1939 already mentioned, had migrated to temporary quarters in the old Carpentry Hut down by the fives courts. Their, transference to Alliott House left the Carpentry Hut available for other purposes: it became in fact the headquarters of a platoon of the Home Guard for the duration of the war.

In spite of the alarms and excursions of war time, school routine was carried on, though with severe restrictions as far as outside matches were concerned. But it will be readily understood that throughout this time a very heavy burden of responsibility rested on the shoulders of the Headmaster. Price had been suffering for some time from duodenal trouble, and in the spring of 1941 he was operated on for an ulcer, F. S. Sutton again acting as headmaster during the first part of the summer term: Price was able to be back, however, in time for Prize Day.

Later that year it was considered safe for the boarders to return to their dormitories to sleep. In the following year, owing to the increasing difficulty in getting domestic help of any kind in the Houses, boys were organized in rotas to lay the tables for meals and to clear them and wash up afterwards—a practice which was continued after the war, until the communal dining-hall was opened in 1962. (The waiting at table is still done by the boys.) The boys' Service Squads took over further jobs such as cutting, rolling and watering the school pitches, gleaning at the local farms after the harvest, helping to take up the potato crop or gathering acorns for pig feed. At the same time the school cultivation squads were extending their activities, though at times with a certain lack, if not of enthusiasm, at any rate of skill: this led to a remark by Walter Strachan, after supervising one of the squads at work, when, inverting Churchill's famous dictum, he observed that the boys' attitude seemed to be: 'Give us the job, and we will finish the tools!'—so heavy were the casualties amongst the School's supply of spades, forks, hoes and shovels!

In 1942 Charles Mellows, with his usual energy, organized holiday working parties to help the country's war effort: in the Easter holidays he took a party of boys to work in a munitions factory at Peterborough (this was repeated the following year), and in the summer holidays he took another party to help in the heavy work of breaking up scrap-iron.

At the end of the summer term of 1943 Mr Sutton was for a third time called upon to take over as acting headmaster; for Leo Price, in spite of careful dieting, had again been unfit for some months, a condition which the increasing stresses and strains of running a school in war time did nothing to help. In July he underwent a second operation: this at first appeared to have been successful, but he had a relapse, and shortly before the end of the term the School was deeply shocked to hear that he had died. It would be difficult to exaggerate the loss the School suffered by his death at such a time; while the sense of personal bereavement was shared by Old Boys, present boys, staff and parents alike. The general feeling was summed up in a sentence in the *Stortfordian* editorial: 'We have lost a great headmaster, and many of us have lost an irreplaceable friend.'

In the Leo Price Memorial Number of the *Stortfordian* H. E. Wall, who was not only a lifelong friend of Leo's but had worked closely with him as assistant housemaster in the School House, wrote of him as follows: 'I well remember meeting him for the first time after he had taken over as headmaster, when I came back for the spring term. As I wished him success in his headmastership his reaction was characterized by humility: he was diffident of his abilities and only hoped that he would prove worthy of the trust: that was how he regarded it. He was determined from the first to do his best so that he should be able to carry on the great work of F. S. Young. Those early years were joyous years of promise and achievement. His athletic record and the fact that he was still playing rugger, water-polo and cricket (and hockey, when it started later on) were great assets in getting to know the boys and the Old Boys of the younger generation. This close personal contact, so soon established with masters and boys, he never lost. Even as he got older, and after serious illness, he continued to play hockey and cricket, and turned out for the Masters' XI at both games. But his hold on us was much surer than a mere common interest in games. His interests were varied: he was an able teacher: the charm of his personality was a great factor: but chief was his interest in people as individuals. He was concerned not only in the welfare of "the School", but of the boys in it. Boys soon knew this: his forms realized it—he gave a lot of unofficial private coaching to backward mathematicians in his set—as did the boys he patiently persevered with at the nets, or taught to swim, or took out in his car, or had in to tea or to read of a Sunday evening. The prefects and monitors realized this in their contacts with him; and he worked very closely with them, for he was a great believer in the principle that boys should take their share of responsibility. Boys in the School House had constant evidence of his forethought and kindness, in countless ways big and little—the books he lent, the occasional game of bridge or chess, the help he gave in times of difficulty or trouble, his kindness to them when ill. But with all this it would be a mistake to think he had any sympathy with "spoiling" boys: indeed in an era when "having a good time" was becoming too readily the aim, he was most insistent on the need for discipline and a sense of duty: he recognized the importance of firmness, and had a critical eye for parent, master or educational theorist who wouldn't be prepared to "put his foot down".

'Throughout his years as headmaster, Price formed many ties with the Old Stortfordians. In addition to his own contemporaries and those who were at school under him, he kept in close touch with all generations in a variety of ways: by his hospitality on Whit-Mondays and other O.S. occasions: by his presence at O.S. functions—the London dinners, the Northern dinners, the O.S. dances: and by his work on O.S. committees, where his advice and help were of great value. He visited Hasbro' and became a regular member of the Easter parties, where his enthusiasm was infectious, whether in sailing or in "bridge for all". When during the war it was not possible to run a party at Hasbro', he took a school party to Waxham Hall, and it was a holiday to be remembered.

'His early enthusiasm never dwindled: but circumstances inexorably narrowed the scope for its development. The smaller number of boys entering the public schools, owing to the decline of the birthrate and to the economic depression, led to the closing down of Houses. The process had begun in F. S. Young's time with the closing of the smaller "overflow" houses: under H. L. Price action had to be more drastic: the shutting down of Westfield Lodge in 1933 and of Waytefield five years later meant disappointment for housemasters, boys and Old Boys alike, and, because he realized so fully what they felt, apart from other considerations, it was an even more bitter disappointment to

Price himself. He worked hard, few knew how hard, to fight this tendency: but the difficulties were aggravated by the clouds that darkened the international horizon. New problems developed, which in turn occupied his thoughts when he had already little enough time for any private life of his own. Immediate and pressing financial difficulties confronted the School: rigid and irksome economies became necessary.

'The war of course brought a multiplicity of difficulties and extra work and anxieties. Yet though he was often deeply worried by many apparently insoluble and conflicting problems, he rarely showed it, but on the contrary gave others courage and steadiness by his calm andcheerful demeanour.'

After mentioning the recurring attacks that necessitated the operations to which we have already referred, and from the second of which Leo never recovered, Mr Wall concluded: 'No review of the career of H. L. Price could be complete without a reference to his public work outside the School. He was a keen member of the Bishop's Stortford Congregational Church. For a number of years he was chairman of the Bishop's Stortford branch of the League of Nations Union. He served actively on a committee to help local unemployed. He was a member of the Governing Body of the Herts and Essex High School, and was helpful in many ways to that school. He served on many committees in connection with Hertfordshire education; was an active member of the Headmasters' Conference, and was a great help to the Bishop's Stortford and District A.T.C. as their chairman.

'I feel that there was an element of real hard luck in the fact that, with his natural gifts for doing things superlatively well, he was headmaster at a time when opportunities or means for using these gifts for the progressive development of the School were so restricted. Considering his difficulties, and the handicap of his illness, which he masked so that few guessed his suffering, I say without hesitation that there was something heroic in his character and in the stature of his achievements during those war years that were the last of his life. Although he died before his hopes could be fully achieved, at least he had the satisfaction of seeing the tide of war turned; of seeing the School numbers stabilized; and, after all his patient and unremitting toil, of knowing that the School's finances showed not merely improvement but recovery.[1]

'I know that hundreds of Old Stortfordians, who knew, respected and loved him, will always remember with a thrill of pleasure the pictures that come to their minds of that impressive figure—in the classrooms, in the Memorial Hall, on the playing-fields, or dashing across the lake in the hurly-burly of ice-hockey at Takely. Or they will

[1] This was largely due to the issue in November 1932 of £48,000 Debenture Stock by the Bishop's Stortford College Association.

recall talks with him into the early hours of the morning in his study on their welcome visits as O.S., the badinage of that friendly voice, and the steady gaze in which one could see the humour, the kindness, the wisdom and the strength that so many of us loved.'

We may fitly end this chapter by quoting H. Stanley Tee, who was chairman of the Governing Council during Price's headmastership and, residing as he did in Stortford, was able to discuss with him in detail the innumerable problems that arose. 'Was Leo Price a successful headmaster? Will he be (as one well-known man wrote of him) "rightly judged as one of the great headmasters of his time"? It depends, I think, on what standard is used in measuring success as applied to a headmaster. If you consider that, to be successful, a headmaster must be a great educationist, whose views on educational problems are eagerly sought by his contemporaries, then probably Leo Price will not rank as one of the great headmasters of his time. Had he lived, I believe even by that standard he would have made a great name for himself. He had very decided and progressive views on public school education and in fact on education generally. The development at Stortford of art, manual work, hobbies—teaching a boy, as he expressed it, to teach himself by his hands and his eyes as well as by his mind—bears testimony to his ideas. During the last two years of his life he began to speak in educational circles, and those who really knew, listened: several well-known headmasters wrote regretting his passing just as he was beginning to make a name for himself at educational conferences.

'But if you rank as success an unsurpassed knowledge of boys, a genius for their friendship, unceasing work for their good, and an almost miraculous power of making them strive for the highest in themselves, then there is no living schoolmaster who has achieved more success than did Leo Price.'

9. Scrapbook from the *Stortfordian*

To F. S. Young on his Retirement

The good ship pauses in her steady stride:
Her weathered bulwarks gently ride the swell:
Her crew salute in token of farewell,
As now her Captain passes down the side.
Awhile he muses; gazing on the tide,
Surmising if a later tongue shall tell
Of storms survived and cargoes carried well,
And if his work shall any time abide.

His first command when first he put to sea—
How changed her form! Yet still her oaken core
Lies sound within: no shattered vessel she,
But taut and trim to sail the ocean o'er:
Though guided by another hand she be
He yet may mark her passage from the shore.

G. L. C.

Leavers' Supper

It was my first 'Leavers' Supper' in the School House: there were flowers on the table—what a difference that made! Salmon and cream jellies took the place of the usual piles of bread and other plain foods. But it was not these things that impressed one so much as the atmosphere, the awe of the occasion: on the platform were sitting a distinguished company—the Head, some members of the staff, a handful of ladies and a selection of Old Boys of different years, mostly 'bloods'.

After the supper, while the menus were being passed round for signatures, the Head rose to introduce the speakers. How truly and accurately he portrayed their characters as he alluded to their life in the House and in the School, or to the business or profession that each was choosing. The head prefect followed with his leaving speech: he spoke of things that had recently happened in the House, of things he hoped would shortly happen, of the events that stood out most vividly as he recalled his life at school. Then came the second prefect (something of a hero of mine, as it happened: how often had I watched him, the centre of a crowd round the schoolroom fire). I knew I should not be disappointed: it was a masterly speech, tempered with wit. Obviously he spoke under stress: it was easy to see that he hated the wrench of leaving. Several other prefects and monitors were leaving whose presence would be missed: they were part of the House, and discipline would surely go to the winds after they had gone. So the speeches went on: I noticed that each speaker thanked the Matron 'for what she has done for me', no less than he did the housemasters, and quite rightly.

The less senior boys were also less eloquent: the more raggable form-masters were mentioned, if not by name at any rate in terms that left no doubt in our minds to whom the speaker referred: personalities became rife. It was now long after 10 p.m., but the lights had not been lit, and the last two or three boys—there were even some from the 'C' dormitory—strained to read their notes ('I'm afraid I can't read what I have written') and then sat down amid torrents of applause.

'Auld Lang Syne' followed in the darkness with crossed hands round the dining-room walls, beneath the portraits of unknown Nonconformist worthies of fifty years ago. The darkness was welcome, for I was profoundly moved.

J. F. A.

School House Stairs

N. M. J.
Has an awe-inspiring way
Of getting to the bottom of the stairs,
And a Monk-Jones stride
(Maybe twenty paces wide)
Is apt to take a person unawares.
Bang goes his door!
One stride more
Brings him to the door of the 'A'.
Don't disappear,
For this is what you'll hear
If his whistling doesn't keep the sound away:
Plonk, plonk, plonk
(Done it in three!)
Tonk, tonk, tonk
(At the bottom, you see)
Plonk, plonk:
Tonk, tonk:
(Gone).

A. C. T.

On Leaving School

'Eheu! fugaces labuntur anni' was the lament of Horace some nineteen hundred years ago; and it is at a time such as this that we first begin to note the fleeting years, first begin to look back tenderly upon the days when we were very young. What after all remains to be our heritage from Stortford, what are we to bear away with us into the world of tomorrow? To the glorious few, the pride of high achievement and unfading renown; to the vast majority, the memory of happy days, none the less happy because they were insignificant. To few indeed is it granted to keep the stage for long; but if it has not been our destiny to hear for ourselves 'the thunder of tumultuous applause', still the memories of Stortford remain with us fully as fragrant.

The successful have left 'a memorial more lasting than the Pyramids'; yet perhaps to the rest the quiet confidence in valiant attempt and worthy defeat, in a devotion that was none the less genuine in that it passed unheeded, brings memories of Stortford deeper and more poignant in their mingled joy and pathos. (*From an Editorial*)

A. E. D.

The End of the Holidays

O cara mia! I cannot stay,
For Stortford's calling, 'Come away
And work! You cannot always play,
You slacker!'

What shall I do without you, dear?
No, no, you can't come too, I fear:
For Stortford's laws are too austere
To let you.

The term is long, the long weeks loom
So close ahead; and through the room
My voice sinks down and down; the gloom
Grows blacker.

I'm going now: my blood runs hot
And cold. . . . Good-bye, you're all I've got,
My motor bike! Be sure I'll not
Forget you.

A. O. R.

O. S. Week-end

(1)

'Aren't you coming to bathe, you slacker?' I might have known this would happen. It's about 2 a.m. Sennitt is chanting this little refrain at each bedside that he disarranges. From my end of the Hut I open an eye and watch his progress. John Collett gets him good and proper with a slipper: good for John! He is coming nearer and nearer to my bed. Shall I get up and kill him outright? No, sleep would be impossible after such a burst of energy; and it is sleep that my tissues need most. On the other hand, if I—— Good! Sainsbury has taken the matter in hand: the door slams, and peace reigns again, after a Parthian 'you lot of slackers!' through the window.

(After breakfast) Hallo! a whole lot of boys seem to be clearing off down the drive on bicycles. This is rather a shock. In my young days we never dreamed . . . But after all, bless their little hearts, why shouldn't they? What better way of spending a whole holiday than to mess about in a boat down the green reaches of Sawbridgeworth and Harlow, or lie, towel-girt, basking on the butterfly haunted river-bank to the drowsy murmur of myriads of insects, with the sun laughing in the dimples of the stream and the larks singing overhead? It's better than watching people like me playing cricket! Still, I'm glad the entire school hasn't cleared off. . . .

Let those who will sing of the cricket: of the leisurely white figures moving in the green distance beneath breathless sunshine: of the occasional click of ball on bat: the rattling tins of the scoreboard being changed: the restful applause as someone hits a boundary, or reaches fifty, or gets out: the chatter and laughter from the Pav: of paired Old Boys in conspicuous and famous blazers, wandering along the far hedgerow in contented reunion after many months: of others propelling fiancées or wives from group to group. It is all very pretty, no doubt, and it seems like that forty years on.

But what it really *feels* like is one agonizing expectancy that each ball will be hooked round really hard to square leg (for the umpire doesn't give much cover, after all), broken by moments of mild excitement as you suddenly wake up after the second ball of a new over and try to edge round to your new position without Stanley Tee noticing. Then a wicket falls, and some fat-headed fieldsman amuses himself by throwing the ball straight at you. This goes on for several hours, with intervals for meals. After every half a dozen or so balls we all cross over in silence, smirking at each other: 'There's nothing like a good day's cricketing to take you out of yourself.'

Then comes water-polo. Then comes bed. . . . As I enter the Hut, Sennitt comes across to me, and chants: 'It's been a topping day, hasn't it? Simply grand, wasn't it?' I take him by the hand. 'Sweetheart,' I reply, 'it was.' And it *was*. I enjoyed my visit to the School very much indeed, and I thank them all very much for having me.

G. H. D.

(2)

He had not been down to Stortford for some time and felt considerable uneasiness. Which of the many O.S. hanging about the grounds with pipes dangling from their mouths were fellows he knew, or ought to know, or could not possibly know? Here and there he recognized a familiar face only altered by the addition of a moustache, but not so easy to put a name on it. However, with all those whose faces were those of strangers and who looked as though they had left since he did, some of whom seemed to know him, he launched out into an animated account of the 'A' *v.* 'B' match of 1921, or some such suitable topic.

He passed into the swimming-bath, and here was a whole row of them changing in the boxes and hailing each other round the box partitions. By now he was in training and could handle these situations: he walked smartly down the line, with a half-smile on his face, greeting the occupant of each box.

When he reached the showers a friend drew him aside: 'You know, don't you, that that's the Emmanuel College Cambridge team: we're playing them on Silver Leys!'

J. F. A.

Maths and Science [1]

The House clock was slow, and you couldn't run?
    It's so simple!
Mechanics, page 93, question one—
    It's so simple!
Now which is the problem that nobody sees?
Just simplify this and then cancel the threes.
$\frac{DY}{DX}$ is—stop talking, please!
    It's so simple!

[1] All except very recent Stortfordians will recognize in these two stanzas echoes of F. S. S. and A. D. H.

Where did we get to last time in Light?
    Stop that row, there!
Did you have any trouble in prep last night?
    Stop that row, there!
The drops are excessively spherical spheres . . .
Give in the prep with any arrears.
Your're the worst form I've had for seventeen years!
    Stop that row, there!

J. A. S.

Not 'The Same Old Place' (1933)

How many of us thought on the last day of the holidays, 'Back we go to the same old place—the same old Houses, the same old dormitories and the same old bathrooms.' But when we came back, what a surprise awaited us! We walked into the School House Common Room and stopped dead: the place had shrunk! And where was the wooden library wall with the gap at the top? It had gone! And in its place was a new wall far nearer the door and reaching completely up to the ceiling. We dashed into the library and positively sat down in surprise. Gosh, what a comfortable chair! And—where were all the theological treatises? Gone, every one of them! After a little we missed something else: no longer could we hear the steady buzz of the burning gas—we looked up and, lo and behold, electric light!

Having investigated the library and discovered that the whole House was lighted with electricity, we decided to go for a stroll, and walked into the courtyard. By this time we thought we were fairly acclimatized to the new state of affairs, but even so the sight that met our eyes brought us up short. Before us we saw a building with—two floors: yes, there could be no doubt about it—we were not seeing double, because they were different colours: the ground floor was red brick and the first floor was coated with white plaster. Up the outside were some iron stairs: we climbed them, and entered the new changing-rooms. The place was a positive palace: it was lit by electric light, and radiators were scattered everywhere. Each of us had six pegs, and two special ones over hot pipes for drying wet clothes; and the lockers—why, they were as big as the average study!

Going to bed that night we were still discussing the changes, when we walked into the 'A' bathroom, and there we were given still more cause for discussion. It had been completely done up: gone were the old enamel basins, the taps with the tops loose and the old lead trough. In their place were porcelain hand-basins (would they break?), silver-coloured taps of the latest pattern and no lead anywhere. And the walls were now tiled in spotless white as high as the towel hooks—and what towel-hooks! All new, and of the same pattern and colour as the taps. We felt positively privileged to hang our towels on them.

It was *not* 'the same old place' any longer.

'BURE'

Cargoes

(With apologies to John Masefield)

Hefty fourth-form slacker, barging from the tuck-shop,
Grumbling at the monitor who gave him whacks,
With a cargo of 'herp mags',
Mars Bars, Smith's Crisps,
Baked beans, knucklebones—and sixteen tracks.

Wretched little new bug creeping to his classroom,
Wishing he was back at the good old Prep,
With a cargo of wine-gums,
Stamps, cigarette cards,
Five-stones, inkpots and half-learnt rep.

Stately sixth-form Prefect striding to his study,
Splendid in the tie of the First Fifteen,
With a cargo of House lists,
Greek books, notices,
Toast, silk handkerchiefs and brilliantine.

J. D. A.

Fire! Fire! (1937)

When a fire alarm is given it is often treated as a hoax: but on Wednesday, 20th October 1937 a real fire broke out in the laboratories. Knight, who was calmly devouring his sandwiches in the 'prep' room, was rudely awakened by the clamouring of voices outside: and after he had realized that they were not endeavouring to pull both his legs he proceeded to take action. The fire was raging around the wooden partition in the skylights between the Chemistry Lab. and the Balance Room, and in the exhaust tube from one of the fume-cupboards. 'Jackie' coupled a bunsen jet to the water supply, but was forced to use an extinguisher.

By this time the news had spread: extinguishers arrived from Alliott's and Grimwade House, and the gardeners produced a ladder from thin air. Then the Headmaster, Mr Mellows and others 'went over the top' of the parapet above the laboratories door, and the entire company went into action. The gallant fire-fighters were hampered by the soapy effect that the spent extinguisher liquid had upon the slates, but by hanging on to the skylight with one hand and wielding an extinguisher with the other they managed to produce some effect.

More ladders, more extinguishers arrived, and the fire showed signs of abating. The Headmaster decided to make a job of it, and smashed many panes of glass to increase accessibility to the nucleus of the inferno. A bucket chain was started, and proved very effective. Meanwhile the fire brigade had arrived: the metalwork of the engine gleamed, the firemen looked very efficient, but somehow the connections would not fit the hydrants, one of which blew right off, to the detriment of the firemen concerned. Leaks sprang from the hoses, which the pressure of water hardly inflated. But firemen know their job: within five minutes there was a good pressure of water, they were hacking away charred woodwork, and the fire was extinguished.

ANON.

Stortford Farming Party

On 8th August 1942 some twenty of us assembled at Grimwade House for a fortnight's or three weeks' farming on land at or near Stortford. Wet weather had held up the harvest, and for the first few days very little harvest work was done. However, we were not idle: backs were bent in long hours of weeding and singling: one party did building repairs, others hoed turnips, two of us lifted a field of valuable red clover. And we gathered potatoes. . . .

In the early hours of morning
Rode the throng of happy workers,
Armed with cycles, scarves and mittens,
Gloves and sweaters, garments woollen.
On the road a lorry passed them,
Full of other rowdy fellows,
Went on into Little Hadham
Midst the sound of yips and bellows.
Then they reached the field in Braughing,
Put their bikes among the hedgerows,
Took up pails and, talking, talking,
They began to pick—Potatoes.
   All the morning, gasping, bending,
In the furrows all are seeking,
From the earth the taters grasping:
By midday their backs are breaking.

For an hour midst hay reclining,
Eating, they forget their troubles;
But when they have finished chewing
They must pick up more—Potatoes.
Still the pains of toil enduring
Worked the aching band of heroes:
Where they turned their wide eyes, straining,
All they saw were more—Potatoes.
  Now the day of toil is ended:
Wearily to bikes they stagger,
Shoulders o'er their cycles bended,
Plod towards the School back yonder.
Joyful, seated on the saddle
They forget the dread Potato,
Strength returning, pedal faster
(One bright lad crashed by the wayside).
Finally beneath the showers
Scraping mud from dirty elbows,
They forget the bending hours
During which they picked—Potatoes. ('OBSCURUS')

We worked usually from about nine o'clock till half past six, often much later at the peak of the harvest. Yet I think it will not be the long hours of work that most of us will remember. Many other incidents will stand out long after our work is forgotten. There was the unending 'jam session' on Chiv's gramophone, which slowly drove those who were running the party to distraction, especially on Sundays. There was the famous night when one of our number was the loser in an argument with a car. And the hot baths—such a comfort to the tired worker.

After ten days the party moved into School House, where life went on in much the same way. The food was as good and the baths were as hot; only now the faces were changing—some had gone, others came. And finally there was bridge: night after night, in School House or in Alliott's, a party would pit its brains against the master-minds of members of the staff.

Such was the Farming Party of 1942: a holiday with pay, in which there was never a dull nor a sad moment. C. L. B.

Hasbro'

It all began when early in this century two Stortfordian masters, A. G. Tidmarsh and N. P. Wood (both of them O.S.) got into the habit of running house parties in Norfolk farmhouses during the school

C.S.C. (with J. B. Knight) at the helm of The Moth, 1928.

Holiday Parties

Right: F.S.Y. on Great Gable, 1930, with J. H. Johnson, J. D. Hennell, H. J. S. Wilson, Mr C. L. Howell-Thomas.

Above: A.O.W. with G. H. O'Brien, C. W. C. Miller, M. A. Edwards in Jugo-Slavia, 1936.

Below: Helping the Unemployed in the Rhondda Valley: Three unemployed miners with (*left to right*) J. E. H. Jones, J. M. Paterson, D. W. Smith, E. Ll. H. Jones, J. Ferguson, N. G. Longdon-Thurgood, 1937.

Some Masters off Duty

Above:
A.D.H., A.O.W., W.J.S., N.M-J., 1929.

Right:
G. H. Rhoades, near his H.Q., the old Art Hut.

Left:
H.L.P. at Hasbro'.

Below:
Easter Party at Hasbro': (*left to right*) A. E. (Drew, B. J. Greenhill, A.O.W., W. F. Mauger, J. R. Braybrooks, R. J. Johnston (*on ground*), R. E. Clark, D. G. White, F.S.S., F. H. Sutton.

ɩurch Farm.

M., J. C. Wilkerson, J. Glyn Jones, F. H. Sutton, H.E.W., J. R. Braybrooks, L. J. Widdicombe, C. G. ɔothroyd, R. G. Brady.

Iasbro' Summer Party

Egyptian Fantasy'.

Claremont Week

1938: Orderlies off duty on the old Elm stump with H.L.P. *Back row:* A. P. S. Sanders, A. M. Smith, J. N. Dupont, R. V. Bennett, R. C. Farrow. *Sitting on stump:* R. A. Green, G. H. O'Brien, M. B. Horsfall. *On ground:* J. Ferguson, C. M. Stephens, J. P. Tolson.

1934: Breakfast under the Oak. The 'Orderlies' are: J. B. Elton, T. W. Bolingbroke, (D. G. White, O.S., looking in from the Past and Present Party), B. B. Dyke, A. A. Pearce, R. S. Beedell, L. A. Coote, G. R. B. Blake (*low down*), H. M. Knee, H. D. Logan.

Below: 1920: J. F. Attenborough, D. E. de Rusett, R. H. C. Archer, M. C. Nokes (O.S.), A.G.T., J. T. Clark, R. H. Pumfrey serving dinner near the Old Gym.

Left: NATURAL HISTORY EXPEDITION TO WICKEN FEN, 1929: (*left to right*) C.M., visitor to B.S.C., H. B. Rowles, H. B. S. Warren, C. H. Deverill, E. J. N. Cakebread, M. G. Stevens.

Below: SKATING AT TAKELEY. 1929: J. C. Newbold, C. M., F. H. S. Stephenson, E. F. Hatch, J. H. Johnson, 1935: C.S.C., N.M-J., F.S.S., H.L.P.

'WILL YOU TAKE THE CHAIR,' produced in the Memorial Hall, 1925. *Back row:* R. M. Arnold, J. R. Cuff, G. W. Creighton, M. W. J. Laws, O. M. Mathews. *Sitting:* O. W. Reynolds, A. C. Taylor (author), C. K. Vartan. *In front:* W. G. Williams.

'ALL CLEAR!' after the first Air Raid Warning at B.S.C., 7 a.m. 6th Sept. 1939. H. D. V. Chappell, A. C. Hay, R. A. Beckett, M. F. Butler, R. H. Edgley, B. M. Gray, G. C. J. Midgley (shading eyes), D. A. Knock and P. W. Rowe (both obscured by Midgley's arm), J. D. Bury, J. B. Chaumeton, D. J. Morris (shading eyes), A. B. Laws, Mr H. L. Price, G. A. Knott, J. W. Rowe, Mr Sandford (Head Gardener). Note boxes containing gas-masks; also the entrance to the Air Raid Shelter on right. The unfinished south end of the Prep. School side of the Library Block is beyond the Air Raid Shelter. The row of elms has now gone.

THE OLD PAVILION, 1928: The first three are R. Collett, W. G. Williams, L. S. Squires.

OPENING OF THE DOGGART PAVILION, WHIT MONDAY, 1933. D. F. Cock leads the School team on to the field. C. S. Colman in panama hat is standing by the clock.

A. G. Doggart and H. L. Price go out to open the O.S. innings. On their left: A. Wherry and D. A. R. Wherry (father and son). To the right of H. L. Price is H. S. Evason (master, 1927–37).

1st XI CRICKET, 1933. *Standing:* H Watson (Groundsman and Coach), A. S Tee, F. J. Ohlson, N. S. Wagstaff, E. M Zelley, R. L. G. Dawson, R. F. A. Sharp *Sitting:* M. B. Rowlands, J. D. C. Joslin D. F. Cock, A. Bywaters, S. C. Collins.

PRACTISING FOR PRIZE DAY MAS P.T., 1931.

THE LAST WESTFIELD LODGE GROUP, 1933.
Back row: S. D. Church, D. V. Knight, J. M Henry, V. C. Meeson, J. F. Sexton. *Next row* F. W. Burton, P. G. Bisset, P. L. Bookless W. P. Dockray, M. Bisset, H. D. Logan D. W. Robinson. *Sitting:* F. G. Miller, L. A Coote, Mr J. D. Craig, Mrs Craig, G. D Hutchings.

holidays. To these parties they invited people they liked and respected: certain Old Stortfordians and a few fairly senior present boys. Prowess in the classroom, in the swimming-bath or on the playing-field carried no weight with them. You had to be, in some unspecifiable way, acceptable; and it was a tremendous accolade for a present boy to be invited. If you proved a palpable misfit in the party you might be invited to pack up and quickly disappear. This happened only once or twice: more likely you would stay the course without comment, but you would never be asked again. Having been a guest at three summer parties, you were recognized as 'one of the family', and were welcome to come whenever you liked without further invitation. By then too you would have a say in the choice of future guests. There were no written rules, no protocol: it was all very informal, and it worked.

What happened at these parties? Simple unsophisticated 'fun and games': farmyard cricket, podex, 'lurkey', beach-bathing, and sailing expeditions on the Broads. In the evenings round games, charades, mock trials, super-chanteys with outrageously funny impromptu acts, and lots of Gilbert and Sullivan. In those oil-lamp and bicycle days we had no money, no cars, no holidays abroad: and we undoubtedly matured much later than is fashionable today.

It went without saying that these Norfolk parties were annual occasions for reviving old friendships and creating new ones. You met and ragged about with Old Boys of earlier vintages, with more recent Old Boys who were heroic figures at school when you were a new boy. You established warm fraternal fellowship with masters whom in the classroom you might have previously feared and detested. No enmities or rivalries could survive in that atmosphere of tolerance, good humour and laughter. As the years rolled on you encountered those who were new boys when you were a prefect and (in their eyes at least) a 'terrific blood'. Later still you got to know those who hadn't even been born in your time. Hasbro' friendships are undoubtedly deeper, more vital and more enduring even than those made at school; and Hasbro'-ites like to feel that they may be helping to perpetuate some of the more worthy Stortford traditions.

The time came when Tidmarsh and Wood relinquished the reins. To take their place a 'Norfolk Stortfordians' Club' was formed, with chairman, secretary, committee and code of rules. Finance proved a growing problem, and the Club was forced to let its premises during the earlier summer months, chiefly to members and their families, in order to pay the rent, rates and upkeep of Church Farm and to maintain our permanent housekeeper. Graver difficulties arose in the wise selection of present boys for invitation. Latterly too it has seemed as if simple, home-made fun has gone out of fashion: past is the Golden (but Penniless) Age.

And yet in spite of everything Hasbro' still goes on. The Club membership numbers one hundred and forty, of whom rather more than half are life members. The year 1962 marked the fiftieth anniversary of our tenancy of Church Farm, and to the Jubilee Reunion came sixty-six Hasbro'-ites from far and wide, of all ages between nineteen and seventy-six, and representing sixty-three consecutive years of Stortford schooldays. For the past twenty-two years (apart from the war years) the 'Antiques', a sub-group of mostly pretty elderly gentlemen now, have assembled to spend the first week-end of January at the Farm. Not one of them will miss it if he can possibly help it: for it is for most the only chance of keeping in touch.

G. H. D.

LE PANTO-MIME

(Night Ops. with the Combined Cadet Force)

Faint sharp orders pronounced with Essex tongue,
Where only in a C.C.F. the tocsin bell has rung,
The pupils of a public school have heard the urgent call,
And twice a week they take their hats and tunics off the wall;
And once or twice a term they meet for company parade,
And march across the grassy sward erect and unafraid;
And once a year they muster all to wander in the dark:
They trample Stortford Cricketfield and stamp on Stortford Park.
The cries of terror from the east[1] are unperceived and faint,
But Bishop's Stortford C.C.F. are putting on their paint.
  Bad eggs flying through the cold moonlight:
The men of Bishop's Stortford are learning how to fight:
In their tens and in their twenties they swarm across the land,
They plunge through thorny bramble-beds, by subtle sergeants scanned.
Their eyes are fired by Freedom's flare, their faces painted black,
They light the world with Verey lights and move to the attack.
  Smoke streams thinly as the strong men talk:
  Fumes may affect their breath,
  Thunder flashes make them deaf,
But Bishop's Stortford C.C.F.
Are putting on their cork. . . .
The Union of the Soviets has crumbled and declined;
The Cadets of Bishop's Stortford still are Forceful and Combined.

'RATSNACH'

[1] The reference is to the Cold War of the early 'fifties.

Leo Price at Oxford

At the time of Leo's death, R. C. Robertson-Glasgow, who was up at Corpus with Leo, wrote of him as follows:

What a man he was, and what a player! He looked and was magnificent. There was one Easter term, 1921 or 1922, when on four Saturdays of one month he played in turn rugger and hockey for Oxford and rugger and hockey for England. At rugger he was a wing-forward of the sort that gives argument to the critics. But in Corpus Christi College there was nothing to argue about. He was the finest thing we knew or hoped to see; and for us there was no athlete in Oxford or Cambridge to touch him, for he had it all.

He was fast, tall, quick in device, sure of hand; with the speed of a centre three-quarter and the strength of a forward. At Twickenham against Wales in 1923 he scored a wonderful try: England kicked off against the wind, Price followed at speed, wrenched the ball from a Welsh forward's hands, dropped at goal, was short, followed up again, gathered and scored by the post.

At hockey, as a centre- or wing-half, he was grand, combining skill and strength to a rare and formidable degree; and if play became excitable or tough, it was not Leo Price that went under. He represented Oxford also at water-polo and, sometimes, at cricket, though he never went to Lord's against Cambridge. At stump-cricket, with a hockey stick and a battered fives ball in the Fourth Quad, he was in a class alone.

Beyond all this he had a clear and balanced brain; and his character was pure gold. He was loved as much as he was admired, for he was as modest as he was great. He had a genius for friendship; and the influence of his fine and sympathetic character will live on in the hearts of those who knew him in the carefree years.

10. A. N. Evans: 1944–1957

ALTHOUGH Mr A. N. Evans was appointed headmaster in 1943, the interregnum under F. S. Sutton continued throughout the autumn term of that year and the spring term of 1944. The war-time routine continued, relieved by the innovation of a dance at Hockerill Training College to which for the first time members of the Sixth Form were invited. School outings were still of course impossible; but Mr Strachan organized a series of interesting exhibitions covering such subjects as calligraphy, book-jacket designs and typography, which stimulated the artistic activities of the School. At the end of his term of office as acting headmaster, Mr Sutton was presented by the boys with a gramophone record cabinet, in appreciation of the splendid work he had done for the School during two difficult terms.

A. N. Evans, who took up his post as headmaster in the summer term of 1944, was educated at St John's School, Leatherhead, and at Keble College, Oxford, of which he was an exhibitioner in Classics. After a period of teaching at Christ's Hospital, where incidentally he was on the staff with H. L. Price, he went to the preparatory department of St Paul's School, Colet Court, of which he was headmaster at the time of his appointment to B.S.C. Like his two predecessors, he was not only a scholar but a good all-round athlete, who for many years had captained the St John's Old Boys' cricket team against his old school at Leatherhead. Unlike previous Stortford headmasters, he came of an Anglican family and was himself a member of the Church of England; with the natural result that, from this time on, stronger links were formed with the parish church of St Michael's and its successive vicars. But Mr Evans was no sectarian, and there was no break in the School's connection with the Nonconformist churches, especially the Congregationalists, which had existed ever since the days of the old N.G.S. Indeed from the first Mr Evans identified himself with the traditions of the School and with the Old Stortfordians' Club.

It was no easy time for a new headmaster to take over. After four and a half years of war, administrative and, especially, staffing problems were at their most difficult: and the advent of the 'doodle-bug' flying bombs, chiefly at night, did not make things easier. As long as the war lasted, new building was of course at a standstill, though the disbandment of the Home Guard in 1944 set free the old 'Carp Hut' for use as a Hobby Hut for the Prep.

Meanwhile temporary masters came and went; but 1944 saw the retirement of a member of the staff who was anything but temporary, who was indeed one of the outstanding personalities at Stortford throughout the first half of this century. A. G. Tidmarsh had joined the staff as early as 1905. We cannot do better than quote here the article that H. E. Wall, a former pupil and later a colleague of Tid's, wrote about him in the *Stortfordian* at the time of his retirement.

'Mr A. G. Tidmarsh retired at the end of the summer term, and from the School has gone a familiar figure and a talented personality. He was at Stortford as a boy from 1894 to 1900, and after some five years in the publishing business with the firm of John Lane, came back on the teaching staff in 1905. His work was principally music, but he was also a full member of the staff, taking art classes as well as ordinary classroom teaching. He devoted his varied abilities to developing musical interests in the School, as well as teaching it to the specialists. He founded the Musical Society: his enthusiasm built up the orchestra, and his fondness for Gilbert and Sullivan made Stortfordians familiar with these rollicking operas. Frequent and enthusiastic chanteys became a feature of the School, and his superb singing voice was a delight. He was, besides, a gifted actor, and helped in the production of many dramatic performances, especially *Mundus et Homo*. Within a few years his had become a name to conjure with. A born raconteur with a colourful turn of phrase, his study would rock with the joyful laughter of a crowd of Old Boys. He played rugger for the O.S. 1st XV, having been one of the original members of the O.S.R.U.F.C. Indeed, he continued playing on Senior Side up till 1919: he also took a keen interest in the swimming of the School.

'Early in the 1914–1918 war, Tid with several other O.S. joined the Universities and Public Schools Brigade of the Royal Fusiliers, but had to leave the army owing to illness. He returned to Stortford to run the music again, to continue as senior housemaster in School House (where he had gone in 1913), to help with the Cadet Corps, and to run the *Stortfordian* while Nevil Wood was in the army. Before this he had started the *O.S. Quarterly*, which later as the *Old Stortfordian* became a popular feature of our Old Boy community. For many years he also ran the Claremont Camps and organized the Claremont Concerts at the Mission in a poor area of London: their success owed much to his inspiration.

'In 1919 he married Gladys Palmer, sister of two Old Stortfordian brothers, one of whom, Wilfrid Palmer, was later to become chairman of the Governing Council; and they settled in Wynch Cottage. Both old and present boys enjoyed their hospitality in this house with its charming garden, and "Mrs Tid" was soon to become almost as much a part of the School as Tid. Owing to a patch of bad health he gave up the post of Director of Music, though he still continued to teach and to take a lively interest in all things musical: it was largely his efforts that enabled the School to buy the organ for the Memorial Hall.

'In 1923 he became the first Housemaster of Robert Pearce House, and he and Mrs Tid, who acted as matron, took a great pride in running it. They threw themselves with great zest into organizing and building up the traditions of the new House, and were always keen on developing individual interests—witness the R.P.H. Hobby Hut and the Model Theatre. Indeed, in the hobbies scheme in the School as a whole, Tid had been a moving spirit: and he was aptly chosen as the first president of the Gramophone Circle.

'At Hasbro' in that carefree and genial atmosphere, surrounded by friends and kindred spirits, Tid's genius for light-hearted amusements—charades, games, music, laughter—reached its height. His could be a truly amazing performance as "the life and soul of the party". For many Old Stortfordians that is perhaps the picture of Tid that will come chiefly to mind: and surely forty, years on, they will bear the echoes of that magnificent voice pealing out "Follow up!"'

On giving up the Housemastership of R.P.H., Tid with Mrs Tid had returned to Wynch Cottage. 'After his retirement from the staff in 1945', wrote his school contemporary and lifelong friend, Professor John Morley, 'Tid kept in touch with what went on in the School, and played an active part in the artistic and musical life of the town, as well as keeping busy in his beloved garden. He was always in demand for songs at O.S. chanteys or Club dinners, for his baritone voice was one of unrivalled beauty and power. Meanwhile to the end he kept up the flow of letters that always delighted his friends—for he was the very prince of letter-writers.' He died from heart-failure in 1954.

The end of the war, or at least of the fighting in Europe, on 8th May 1945—'V.E. Day'—was marked by a thanksgiving service at the School, after which the boys all went home. That evening for the first time after five and a half years the black-out was lifted and the school lights shone forth once again: the Library was floodlit, and we at Stortford shared the universal feeling of thankfulness that the war was over, and that some at least of the austerities of war time could be relaxed. 'At last', wrote the *Stortfordian*, 'victory in the west has come.

No longer will muffled figures, moaning over their hard lot, stagger down the dormitory to the mournful wail of the sirens: no more will very small boys struggle with very large black-out screens. And, overshadowing these trivialities, battle and all its horrors is at an end. We are both proud and happy: proud of those who have fought and those who have died for us, especially those from this school; happy that at last the menace to our homes and to mankind is over.' In all, well over seven hundred Old Stortfordians had served in the armed forces, of whom some ninety had given their lives. Decorations won included three D.S.O.'s, four O.B.E.'s, three M.B.E.'s, five D.S.C.'s, eight M.C.'s, ten D.F.C.'s, one A.F.C., one D.S.M., one D.F.M., one B.E.M.; also three foreign awards—the American Legion of Honour, the American Bronze Star for Valour and the French Croix de Guerre, with Oakleaf; and a Certificate of Merit. In addition, twenty-two were mentioned in Dispatches.

On Prize Day in the summer term of 1945, Mr H. S. Tee, the then chairman of the Governing Council, made an important announcement affecting the School's future. The Council, he said, had decided that Bishop's Stortford College should no longer be, as it had been since 1920, a Direct Grant School, but should become an 'Independent' school as provided for in the recent circular sent out by the Minister of Education.

Perhaps it may be of interest to explain here the meaning of this change. Between the years 1919 and 1926 the Board of Education (as it then was) made administrative changes affecting schools in receipt of financial assistance from the Board. A number of schools, including B.S.C., exercised an option in favour of receiving aid in the form of a direct capitation grant from the Board of Education, instead of through local education authorities. These schools became known as 'Direct Grant Schools', and by 1944 their number had risen to 232.

In that year the final report of the Fleming Committee, appointed to consider the relations between the public schools and the general educational system of the country, stated that the Direct Grant list as it then stood could not be justified, and recommended new conditions for schools receiving this grant. The Minister of Education accepted these recommendations, and during 1945–6 a new Direct Grant list was compiled. The Governors of B.S.C., together with those of a number of other public schools, now decided, in the interests of greater autonomy, to give up the grant; and the College has since that time been officially an 'Independent' school, though the Governors have continued to act in close co-operation with the local education authorities.

Mr Tee also made the further announcement that, as part of the School's War Memorial, an Endowment Fund had been established, to be used primarily for the education of sons or brothers of Old Stortfordians who had lost their lives in the war, and thereafter to help towards the education of relatives of O.S. generally.

In June 1946 a memorial service was held in honour of the Old Stortfordians who had fallen. The Headmaster conducted the service, and his tribute to those who had died, among whom he included his predecessor H. L. Price, put into words most effectively the feelings that were in so many hearts. All those present were deeply moved by this very simple but most impressive service. Three years later commemorative panels were placed each side of the entrance doors of the Memorial Hall, containing the names of the Old Stortfordians who had lost their lives in two world wars. The panels were designed by Percy Delf Smith, one of the foremost experts in lettering at that time in England, and were carved by Angelo del Cauchferta: and they superseded the old panels set up after the war of 1914–1918. The unveiling ceremony, like the earlier memorial service, was again all the more moving because of its simplicity. Charles Mellows, who had himself served in the 1914–1918 war, and had known personally all those whose names were commemorated on the panels, wrote an account of the ceremony in the *Stortfordian*, full of personal reminiscences of those who had died: the names he mentions must inevitably be to a later generation names only, but to older Stortfordians they recall poignant memories of school friendships which made the whole ceremony a personal rather than a merely official act of tribute. He wrote as follows.

'After a brief and eloquent speech by Wilfrid Palmer, the two roll-calls were read faultlessly and very sympathetically by J. M. Rae, the Head of the School, standing at the top of the Memorial Hall steps. First came the list of our old friends and school companions of the First World War, calling up a vivid memory, if sometimes a little blurred by the years, of those whom we had loved so well and found it so hard to lose. There they were: Eric and Urban; Dick, who was never bored, never had an enemy in the world; dear old E. A. K.; Sydney Price and "Jumbo" and "Dan"—names one could still associate with gallant and high-hearted happiness. And one in especial, who had endeared himself to us all,[1] and whose joyous and charming personality had made him the life and soul of our early Hasbro' parties: he died

[1] S. J. Linzell.

as he had lived, unselfish and unwearied in discharging his endless self-imposed tasks. ("Toujours", the citation ran, in a language more eloquent than our own—"toujours il se portait au secours des blessés et de la population civile".) And now, the first roll-call over, there came the second, longer and more familiar than the other; and as I listened I seemed to trace in this list of our dead the progress of that grim war. Earliest of all came Bob Hammond, who died gallantly fighting over Heligoland: then Stanley Laws, one of the devoted few who tried to hold up the advance of a victorious German army on the fatal canal bridge; and "Johnny", and Alan James and the others who died in the struggle against hopeless odds, that led to the days of Dunkirk. Some fell in the Norway campaign: one in the Greek war. There were fighter pilots who fell defeating the Messerschmitts over Britain, and those who flew Blenheims to bomb the barges and save England from invasion, and ground troops killed in bombed London. One went down with H.M.S. *Hood*, another in the battle round Crete, others while bombing German battleships in French harbours. We had many in the Eighth Army: one perished in the fatal Battle of the Cauldron, one at Alamein, one at Mareth: a war poet who had already achieved a national reputation died in the fighting in the Apennines.[1] At sea, some fell in the battles of the Atlantic, and another in the dreaded "Bomb Alley" on the way to Malta, bringing help to the garrison that contained so many of Stortford's sons in that island of the George Cross. Some of those in the roll-call were killed in the battles with Japan, some in the training camps of India. A great number died in the liberation of France and Norway and Holland and in the final invasion of Germany.

'Pericles, in the most famous speech in history, told his Athenian compatriots that "heroes have the whole earth for their tomb". Well, here were the names of those who perished not only in and over their own country, Scotland and Ireland, France and Belgium and Holland; but in the Arctic Circle and on the mountains of Norway; far out in the Atlantic or off the West African coast; in Greece and Albania, Roumania and Italy, Egypt and Libya; in Malayan jungles, on Indian plains and on the far China seas. In these countries and no doubt elsewhere in the world could be found "some corner . . . that is for ever England" and that our School might well in some measure call her own.

'We were grateful for the words of encouragement and inspiration spoken as the tablets were unveiled. It was right that John Morley should do this for us. Thirty-five years ago in the Gallipoli campaign he first displayed the skill which made him one of the foremost surgeons

[1] J. D. Allison.

in our country. His own son, of rare promise and universally loved, died from a tragic accident in the second war. Who had a better right than Dick's father to bid us remember our Christian verities, and not to sorrow as they that have no hope?[1]

'The unveiling done, there came from within the building the opening bars of the finest of all the war-memorial hymns "O valiant hearts", sung softly and very beautifully by the choir as the large congregation slowly filled the Hall. Then followed "Heroes"; after which we heard Milton's famous lines from *Samson Agonistes*, "Nothing is here for tears, nothing to wail"—words which were quoted by Sir Arthur Quiller-Couch when he opened the Memorial Hall nearly thirty years previously.'

The ceremony was brought to an end with an address by the Headmaster. Of those we were commemorating Mr Evans said: 'Here they spent some of the most important years of their life: here they lived and laughed, made their friendships, learned to live together. In this Hall they learned to worship: they sat where you sit: their names are on the chairs, and now their names are enshrined in the entrance porch of the Memorial Hall. They are indeed the Sons of this House, and today we dedicate their names with pride and thanksgiving to commemorate the sacrifice they made.'

With the return once more to peace-time conditions, Mr Evans's headmastership naturally saw a series of staff changes. In July 1945 G. H. Rhoades retired, having been art master for fifteen years: as a teacher, as an original artist, above all as a personality of great charm and a certain ripe wisdom, he left his mark on both boys and colleagues. (Some of us still recall with delight memories of Geoffrey Rhoades retailing, in that slow, almost indolent voice, punctuated with quiet chuckles, some ribald yarn which he often had difficulty in finishing because both he and his hearers were reduced to helpless laughter long before he reached the climax of his story!) His place as art master was taken by Mr A. J. Hunt.

In the same year masters began to return from the Services: T. C. Sims came back to the Prep; and in the following year S. W. Woodward and D. T. Newton returned, the latter transferring shortly afterwards to the Main School (he had come to Grimwade House a year before the war). At the same time L. G. Soady joined the modern languages staff, and P. S. Burns took over the history department from W. A. Jones. It was Burns who founded the Ten Club, which in some ways

[1] Professor Morley endowed the Richard Morley Scholarship, for the sons of Free Church ministers and missionaries, in memory of Dick.

revived the traditions of C. S. C.'s Carlyle Club, though the subjects discussed were historical or social rather than literary. The Club was taken over by A. E. Charlwood when Burns left, and later by A. Lee, who now runs it.

We should mention here also D. B. Fielder, who took temporary charge of the music until the return later in the year of R. G. E. Oakley: he only stayed in fact two terms, but his wide culture and charm of personality left a definite mark on the music of the School as well as on all those with whom he had personal contacts.[1]

In these post-war years also the staff lost several members who had loomed large in the life of the School. We have referred above to W. A. (Bill) Jones, who after ten years at Stortford left in 1946 to become headmaster of Staveley Grammar School. Bill Jones was a vigorous personality, both as a teacher and as a gifted all-round athlete. 'In September 1936', wrote F. S. S., 'four rather obstreperous "new boys"[2] appeared in the Masters' Common Room, at once lowering the average age of its inhabitants considerably and adding greatly to the gaiety of that institution: one of their number was Bill Jones, who was taking over the work of the History specialists.' In the following decade his brilliant teaching produced a remarkable record of university scholarships in History. He played a prominent part too on the school playing-fields: he both played and coached rugger with tireless energy, helped with the athletic sports and ran the hockey and the cricket with great success, but latterly, owing to the exigences of war time, with very little assistance. It was a deep sorrow to his many friends at Stortford, and a tragedy for Staveley, that he died two years after leaving Stortford, after a complete breakdown in health due to continued overwork.

In 1946 also the Preparatory School lost the services of Miss G. E. Parsons, who retired after no less than thirty-six years' teaching, having joined Mr Hurst when the Prep was functioning in Newbury House on the Hadham Road. Generations of young Stortfordians owed to 'Nips' (as she was always known to the boys) their first grasp of the Four Rules in arithmetic and their first interest in English history. Right up till the time of her death in 1963, Miss Parsons continued to take an interest in 'her' Old Boys, and to attend regularly all school functions.

In the same year another familiar Stortford figure passed away with the death of Albert Fordham. He first joined the School House domestic staff in 1910: after the 1914–1918 war he was made responsible for the cleaning of the classrooms. Twenty years later, after Sergeant Salmon's

[1] Mr Fielder returned as Director of Music in 1968, in succession to Mr Warburton.
[2] G. A. Goodban, W. A. Jones, L. P. Madge and S. W. Woodward.

death, he moved into the Lodge, and took over much of Sergeant Salmon's work. He was latterly dogged by ill health, and boys and masters alike had at times to put up with a certain brusqueness of manner on his part. But he was a most reliable and loyal servant of the School, and many generations of O.S., recalling that well-known figure in cap and green baize apron, will remember 'Ham' with affection.

Fordham's place at the Lodge was taken by Mr F. W. Jordan, who also took over the supervision of all the outdoor staff and became Clerk of Works to the School. But indeed it is impossible to list the jobs that fall to Frank Jordan: any task not specifically assigned to anyone else will be carried out, most competently, by him. He is the link too between the teaching staff and the outdoor staff of laboratory assistants, gardeners and engineers—the men whose work makes possible the functioning of the school community. Some of these men we have already mentioned. Many will recall other names—Ted Gillett, for instance, laboratory assistant in the twenties, and Jack Knight—both of them not only most competent technicians, but school personalities as well. Ted Gillett eventually left to take up a senior position in the laboratories at Stowe School. Jack Knight left only in 1966, having presided over the Labs, apart from a few years' absence, for something like thirty years. In addition to his official work, Jack helped with numerous school activities, e.g. the radio and film hobbies, the Science Society, the Motor Transport Section of the C.C.F. He was a skilled craftsman too in wood, metal or glass, and a resourceful mechanic, electrician and chemist. Others will remember too the gardeners—C. Sandford, for instance, and M. Phillips, both of whom served the School for many years, the latter for over forty. Then there was W. Parkin 'the Engineer', who came at the beginning of the first war and looked after the Bath for fifteen years or more; and Henry Wacey, who came in 1939 and is still going strong (for some years now he has had his son Roy working with him); and A. J. Elderton, tall ex-police sergeant, who was Tuckman for some years in the twenties and thirties. And finally we do not forget W. Wedlock, who started before the first war as boot-boy in the School House, but later looked after the classrooms; and 'Bridge' Hummersone, assistant groundsman since 1949.

In 1947 three more masters left. Dr W. V. Lloyd, after fifteen years as senior Chemistry master, was appointed headmaster of a new Day Continuation School at Welwyn Garden City. 'Doc' Lloyd was president of the Photographic Society, of the Science Society, of the Dramatic Society; assistant Day Boy Housemaster; secretary of the Old Stortfordians' Lodge; a senior air-raid warden during the war; an officer in the school C.C.F.—a man of manifold activities, who subsequently built up a most successful school, known now as the Mid-Herts College of Further Education, at Welwyn Garden City. He died, suddenly, in 1966.

Another master who left at the same time as Dr Lloyd was S. W. Woodward, who became headmaster of Wem Grammar School in Shropshire: indeed B.S.C. seems at this period to have supplied headmasters for schools all over the country. The modern languages side of the school, the C.C.F., the hockey teams, the Architectural Society all felt the loss of Wyndham Woodward's help and ever cheerful presence. He subsequently moved from Shropshire to Lincolnshire, where he has for some years been headmaster of Spalding Grammar School, as well as a leading figure in the civic life of that town.

The third to leave was J. D. Craig, after thirty years on the staff teaching chiefly English and History. In the later years of the 1914–1918 war he had taken charge of a small waiting-house for new boarders at 68 Hadham Road. Shortly afterwards he took over Westfield Lodge from F. B. Shawe and, with Mrs Craig acting as matron, ran it for fifteen years until, owing to reduced numbers in the School, it had to be closed down. Many old W.L. boys (the initials will be unfamiliar to later generations of Stortfordians) will remember 'Jimmy' Craig's speeches at House suppers, for he had a pretty turn of Caledonian wit. His place as senior English master was taken by an O.S., C. D. Ross Murray.

In the same year T. A. Grocock joined the staff: he went first as assistant housemaster to Alliott's, later joining Mr Ward at R.P.H. In 1950, on Mr Sutton's retirement, he became senior mathematics master: he took an active part in out-of-school activities as well, refereeing or umpiring games, speaking at debates and, more particularly, organizing and encouraging square-dancing. It was in 1947 too that T. A. Davies joined the Modern Languages staff.

While masters were thus leaving or coming, various changes were occurring amongst those who stayed. In 1946 Norman Monk-Jones retired after nineteen years from the Housemastership of Grimwade House, which was taken over by T. C. Sims: he remained head of the Preparatory School. In the same year H. E. Wall married and left School House, where he was succeeded by P. S. Burns. And in the following year W. J. Strachan retired from the Housemastership of R.P.H. after ten years, in order to be able to devote more time to his other multifarious activities. He was succeeded in R.P.H. by A. O. Ward, with L. G. Soady as assistant housemaster.

During these years it was the task of Mr Evans to switch the School back to peace-time routine. The general economic situation precluded any new building; but it was a welcome sign of the return to normal conditions when in January 1946 Alliott House, after nearly six years' occupation by the Day Boys, was reopened as a boarding house under Mr Mellows, its former housemaster: the Day Boys meanwhile transferred to Waytefield, recently de-requisitioned by the military authorities. In the summer holidays of the same year Mr Ward once again took a holiday party abroad, the first for seven years. And in the following autumn the O.S. Rugger Club started up again—another sign of the return to peace-time activities.

In 1947 the School once again won the cup at the Bath Club Public Schools Invitation Race—a welcome revival of the School's pre-war swimming prowess; and indeed it proved to be only the first of three successive wins. In that year Mr Ward, after seven years of most efficient work in establishing and training the Cadet Corps, handed over the command to S. W. Woodward, from whom shortly afterwards it was taken over by L. G. Soady. At this time P. S. Burns left School House to get married; P. W. Meen O.S. now joined the staff and took Burns's place as Housemaster in School House.

Meanwhile important changes were taking place on the Governing Council. In 1947 Mr H. Stanley Tee, who as chairman since 1939 had had the critical task of leading the Council in its handling of the manifold problems of war time, felt that he must give up the chairmanship owing to ill health. His conscientiousness and unremitting work as a Governor were shown by his remarkable record of only one meeting missed, whether of full Council or of innumerable sub-committees, during his thirty years' service. His affection for the School was proved by an even more remarkable record: not only did he regularly watch matches on Upper Field whenever time permitted, but over a period of no less than fifty-eight years he never missed an O.S. Whit-Monday match—an astonishing instance of loyalty in an Old Boy. He continued to put his great experience and wise counsel at the disposal of the Governors till his death in 1960: at that time A. G. Doggart, who had been Stanley Tee's colleague on the Council for many years, wrote of him as follows: 'Perhaps it could be said that during the six years between 1939 and 1945 two of the most important decisions in Stortford's history had to be taken; and it was largely on Stanley Tee, as Chairman of the Governors, that the responsibility of taking them rested. The first, in 1939–40, concerned the possible evacuation of the School, which was on the outskirts of the London defensive zone: after the most exhaustive deliberations by the Governing Council, the Headmaster and the staff, it was fortunately decided to carry on at Stortford. The second decision arose in connection with the 1944

Education Act, when it had to be determined whether to continue as a Direct Grant school or to become fully independent. It was largely due to Stanley Tee's courage and conviction that we are now an Independent School, with the unbounded advantages that spring from independence; with the added assurance that, so long as we provide the type of education rightly expected from a Public School, our amenities and facilities are bound to continue in demand by parents as well as by the Local Education Authority itself. It was Stanley Tee's vision that we should emerge from World War II as a Public School of which Hertfordshire and Essex could feel justifiably proud, and on which they could depend for developing local talent to the greatest advantage and in the best possible way.'

Stanley Tee was succeeded as chairman of the Council by W. E. Palmer, with Professor John Morley as his vice-chairman—both of them prominent Old Boys of the School.

In the following year the Governing Council and the School suffered another great loss in the death of A. H. Mellows as the result of a motor accident. Arthur Mellows was not only a prominent figure in Old Stortfordian circles, and an outstanding citizen of his native Peterborough (of which he had been mayor, as well as chairman of the City Education Committee): he was also for some thirteen years an active member of our Governing Council. Stanley Tee wrote of him: 'It did not take us long to realize that Arthur Mellows was a man of outstanding ability and one who had a deep love of the School. At meetings of the Council as a rule he said little, but what he did say always commanded the respect and attention of every member. He usually listened quietly to a debate, and then at the end in a few well chosen words he would sum up: and we all realized that his legal training had given him the unusual power of making the whole matter under consideration appear quite simple, so that we sometimes wondered why we had debated it at all.'

It was in 1948 that N. Monk-Jones retired from the chairmanship of the Games Committee, which he had held for twenty years, to be succeeded by P. W. Meen; and that H. E. Wall, likewise after twenty years on the job, handed over the running of the *Stortfordian* to C. D. R. Murray. The latter was already making his mark in the life of the School, especially through the Dramatic Society: it was in this year that he put on a quite outstanding production of *Hamlet*, which those who saw it will not easily forget. Meanwhile Grimwade House and the Prep staff were 'enriched', as the *Stortfordian* aptly phrased it, by the arrival of J. H. P. Dawson. He eventually took over not only the mathematics department of the Preparatory School but also at one time or another the running of the Prep rugger, hockey (he was himself a county hockey player) and cricket. In the realm of sport, 1947 saw successes in the public schools sports, where a Stortford team won the Mile Medley Relay, and A. I. Rae won the Half-Mile. The year 1948 too was a good year: not only did B.S.C. win the Bath Club Cup again, as already mentioned, but in hockey both the Firsts and the Seconds were unbeaten, winning seven out of eight matches and drawing the eighth.

An innovation[1] in the activities of the Old Stortfordians' Club at this time was due to the initiative of Sir Henry Collett, then president of the Club. He organized a dinner in London for the older generation of Old Stortfordians—the 'O.O.S.' as they have come to be called—which was limited to those who were at Stortford before or during the 1914–1918 war—'Thirty Years On' in fact. The experiment proved a great success and further such reunions have been held since. In 1954 Sir Brett Cloutman arranged another similar function: this time it was a luncheon, held in Stortford at the Chequers Hotel; and in 1958 yet another reunion—now known as 'Forty Years On'—was held, again in Stortford. Of this gathering Sir Brett wrote: 'It has certainly been a privilege for those of us who saw the beginnings of F. S. Young's plans for the development of the School, to witness their flowering half a century later. And "flowering" was the right word on that Saturday afternoon, when the great rose beds on the terraced New Field were in their glory and scented the air around. They formed the lovely centre of as beautiful a setting as you will find anywhere in Hertfordshire.' The last O.O.S. reunion, organized by H. E. Wall, was held in 1966, this time in the new school dining-hall, where nearly one hundred people sat down to lunch. Of this reunion R. B. Cawood wrote afterwards: 'Of all the people I met, there was only one I had seen in the last forty years; and yet when I was talking to them it only seemed as though one or two years had elapsed. I had been very happy at school: I regained some of that happiness, and the day will always remain in my memory.'

To return now to the forties: in 1949 the swimming team did the hat-trick at the Bath Club by winning the cup for the third time in succession—a feat not previously achieved by any school. Our natural jubilation led to a correspondent reviving, in a letter to the *Stortfordian*, the age-old controversy between the swimmers and the cricketers (how well some of us still remember the acrimonious discussions on this subject at Hasbro' in the years immediately after the first war!). He ended by declaring that our specialization in swimming was often

[1] Actually an 'O.O.S.' Day was held at Stortford as early as 1912, for those who were at the School (i.e. the N.G.S.) before 1890.

rs F. S. Young speaking at the opening: 1936. Mr and Mrs Young's children are on the left: Freda, Frances ıd Russell. In the doorway is Albert Fordham (School Porter). In the centre of the picture are Mrs Price ıother of the Headmaster), Mr Grimwade (Chairman of the Governing Council), Mr R. C. Foster (Architect) ıd Mr H. L. Price.

The Francis Samuel Young Memorial Library

ıe interior, taken 1950. On the left is the reading stand given to the School in memory of M. E. Power, who ed on active service in the Second World War. The cup is the small replica of the Bath Club Cup, and was presented to the School by H. M. Wagstaff, member of the winning teams, 1926 and 1927, on behalf of Old Stortrdians, as a tribute to Charles Mellows' outstanding contribution to Stortford swimming.

THE YEO CUP: the Senior Cross, March 1937, approaching the Bury Green road. P. F. Thompson leading followed by G. H. O'Brien. P. M. Edes, the eventual winner, is directly behind O'Brien. Running thi is D. R. Jeffryes. The spectator looks like J. M. Henry.

ALLIOTT HOUSE, 1938. *Back row:* D. A. Knock, G. T. Rolfe, P. D. Carter, A. F. Harris, J. C. Dunhan M. D. Jacobson, D. R. F. Macdonald, C. J. Garlick, D. A. E. Smith. *Next row:* P. F. Wherry, M. Shepher G. H. James, R. V. Bennett, J. H. H. Smith, D. L. Pascall, B. B. Rackstraw, H. L. Henry. *Sitting:* W. Nixon, G. H O'Brien, A. P. S. Sanders, Mr W. A. Jones, Mr C. Mellows. Miss Molony, F. F. Bonsall, R. C. Farrow, R. A Green. *In front:* A. E. Ewens, G. W. Burns, P. H. Vincent, M. F. Butler, A. R. Galbraith.

ɪst XV, 1937 (Unbeaten until last match v previous captain's XV) *Back row:* G. Rackstraw, D. E. Wills, C. G. Smith, J. P. Tolson, S. D. James, C. M. Stephens, M. D. Green, L. G. Wilson. *Sitting:* J. N. Dupont, P. W. Meen, G. J. Adams, M. B. Horsfall, C. C. Bryan. *In front:* R. R. Hammond, G. W. Mohun.

WAYTEFIELD REUNION AND FAREWELL GROUP, July 1938. *Back row:* R. R. Perry, G. B. Padwick, A. W. de Rusett, J. D. de Rusett, J. Marriage, P. D. Davey, F. W. Bateman, R. W. Horner, W. N. White, G. R. Ellis, K. T. Lockhart, K. W. Wells, K. N. Blake, A. B. Savage, A. K. Horner, M. G. Hall, V. Marriage, D. H. Godkin. *Next row:* M. D. Green, W. M. Hartley, D. J. Young, D. W. Edgley, B. A. Ferguson, R. Turney, D. C. Pritchard, H. Poulter, T. D. Stewart, E. N. Davey, W. R. Lee, A. W. Claypole, Mr W. R. Bion, F. H. Sutton, J. Glyn-Jones, W. A. Pritchard, J. S. Padwick, W. E. Bruce, R. H. A. Cave, J. H. Peters, A. H. Mogford, A. J. Warren, D. F. Cock, M. B. Horsfall, J. N. Dupont. *Sitting:* R. G. Fuller, H. S. Widgery, G. W. Pritchard, J. A. White, A. O. Russell, C. A. Yeo, W. M. White, T. C. McIlroy, Mrs Sutton, Mr Sutton, Eileen Sutton, A. N. Todd, A. E. Drew, D. G. White, E. W. Ferguson, J. B. Martin, G. A. Rowe, A. A. Lockhart, R. J. Johnston, N. D. Lockhart, S. D. James. *In front:* A. M. Smith, O. P. Folkard, B. R. Black, E. F. Kirby, R. H. Edgley, G. Rackstraw, R. M. Hicks, J. B. Barber, R. A. Beckett, R. A. Dean, A. C. B. Horsfall, G. O. Sharpe, D. W. Dupont, M. L. Woods, R. H. Adams, G. F. Allen, A. C. Hay.

CADET CORPS, 1915. *Names of those sitting:* S. F. Prior, W. R. Bion, M. C. Nokes, C. E. Schnadhorst, R. Morton, Lt E. A. Knight, Capt. F. M. Kingdon, C.S.M. Salmon, A. G. Doggart, P. O. Davies, L. F. Clar F. W. Day, C. G. McLachlan.

C.C.F., 1942. *Names of those sitting:* C. A. Martin, N. M. Hart, J. W. Wigg, D. E. Gunner, G. D. Luton, G. B. S Chase, J. D. Bury, 2nd Lt G. W. Cartwright, Capt C. Mellows, Capt A. O. Ward, 2nd Lt W. V. Lloyd, Under-Officer D. S. Collett, J. W. Rowe, J. F. F. Clark, M. H. Mayer, O. F. Hutter, R. H. Beale, J. S. G. Smith.

NING ROOM, 1933.

Robert Pearce House

·USE GROUP, 1944. *Back row:* A. J. Soper, J. St Lawrence, C. J. Norris, N. W. Palmer, R. I. Mussellwhite, . Payton, R. F. Burlinson, W. B. Wailing, B. R. Hall, D. A. Fothergill, P. N. Broad. *Second row:* R. C. Wilson, . Howe, L. R. Kirby, J. E. Smith, A. H. Webb, J. A. Baldwin, J. S. Wesson, J. C. Hall, G. S. Irving, A. E. F. rn, A. F. Waterston, G. R. Spaulding. *Sitting:* R. S. T. Luget, H. Gaydon, J. N. Minnis, Mrs Strachan, Mr J. Strachan, Mrs Medway, J. E. Reeve, C. A. Fothergill, B. C. Hale. *In front:* C. N. Stephens, C. A. Meadows, R. Clapham, W. A. Jeffrey, H. C. Hay, J. A. Winter, R. H. Stearn.

SCHOOL HOUSE, 1945. *Back row:* T. N. F. Butcher, M. R. Gale, J. A. Howard, T. W. Harbage, T. S. Blaydes, J. M. Rae, P. M. T. Leith, B. H. Wales, J. M. Shearman, J. M. Wilkinson. *Next row:* G. W. L. Pry R. H. Swinstead, J. P. S. Maber, W. W. McDougall, J. A. Sinclair, R. J. Deards, G. W. Rowley, J. H. Gre acre, R. G. Browning-Smith, G. A. Clarke, C. Parker. *Next row:* W. F. Harris, D. J. Power, M. H. Powell, J. Rendle, E. A. Bright, E. J. T. Davies, F. R. Ridley, R. T. Trigg, J. C. Graves, G. M. Carter, D. G. Rose, G. A. Searle, G. Lusty, A. G. Smith, R. H. Berendt. *Standing on ground:* K. D. Reckhouse, J. A. Vivers, T. C. Ey J. C. Fenton, E. J. Ronalds, A. I. Rae, H. P. Joscelyne, K. G. Luckin, A. C. Blaxill, A. R. Itter, R. R. Lac R. M. Ross, I. C. McDougall, G. D. M. Nunn, M. S. Claridge. *Sitting:* M. J. Mynott, E. A. N. S. Jeffries, C. Kennett, J. B. Chaumeton, P. A. A. Cullen, Mrs Jones (Matron), Mr H. E. Wall, Mr A. N. Evans, Mrs Eva Miss Ashwell (Assistant Matron), P. W. Rowe, A. J. Richardson, J. A. Mynott, A. P. Power, A. R. Blair. *In fro* L. N. Franklin, W. P. Cowell, G. L. Lennox, J. K. Liddell, A. L. M. Stockley, T. C. Borgman, S. P. Rice, J. Woollard, B. W. Eves, M. A. Yeo, J. M. Collett, C. A. Poulter, A. R. Edmonds, D. J. Wakeman.

MANUAL WORKSHOP. Mr P. Carlaw (Instructor, 1921–63), R. J. G. Lusty and B. J. Heddle.

OBERT PEARCE HOUSE, 1951. *Back row:* D. Paterson, M. Broad, C. R. Isbell, K. A. G. Day, N. C. Iacmillen, J. F. Rowley, A. Appleyard, M. F. T. Brownhill, P. Stacey, S. J. A. Robinson, M. B. Rutter, D. V. runt, M. G. H. Winton, M. Pickthall. *Next row:* W. C. F. Butler, C. J. H. Wagstaff, M. J. Schwier, D. T. Earey, . E. Borrett, P. R. Thompson, S. F. Leaver, R. A. Arnold, G. M. Eadie, C. S. Wiseman, C. D. Jones, A. A. endle, E. P. Connelly. *Sitting:* M. F. Rowley, B. D. Muddell, J. M. Palmer, Miss Frost, Mr A. O. Ward, Mr '. A. Grocock, D. K. Smith, G. H. Toye. *In front:* D. J. Cove, D. Campbell, B. M. Boyd, T. M. Sloan, G. Stacey, . F. Sharp, M. J. J. Maskell.

LLIOTT HOUSE, 1951. *Back row:* B. C. Abbott, C. S. Hills, J. R. S. Reid, W. L. Wild, A. V. K. Ward, . T. Ling, A. L. Wright, R. L. G. Lasseter, R. J. Blackall, N. E. B. Swan, R. W. Boardman. *Next row:* D. L. ›nes, J. J. A. Cave, B. Hall, D. B. Wright, A. T. Gear, J. W. Saxby, D. J. Bowtell, G. M. Liddell, D. R. How, . I. M. Jones. *Sitting:* P. J. Simor, M. K. Ward, A. M. Grant, Miss Jackson, Mr H. E. Wall, Mrs Wall, Mr T. A. avies, D. T. Kilian, B. V. Floyd, D. L. Clarke. *In front:* I. M. Brown, C. C. D. Cain, R. C. Davies, R. J. Carter, . H. Swain, J. Warrington, D. T. L. Spires, R. Wallis, A. van Bruggen, B. Scott.

DAY BOY HOUSE, 1951. *Back row:* D. Watts, M. Hatton-Ward, D. A. Eagling, B. B. Sell, T. C. Hazzar W. H. A. Larrett, J. Simpson, O. Marrack, R. A. Millar, A. A. Trigg. *Next row:* D. J. Brown, B. L. Molliso P. A. Thompson, J. B. C. Atkinson, R. F. Preston, M. A. Palmer, G. J. B. Jones, R. Kerr, R. F. Gunn, I. J. F Palmer, P. G. Kirkby. *Next row:* E. B. Natley, V. D. Clarke, J. H. Kemp, M. J. R. Hart, R. Squires, J. E. Vile R. A. Marshall, J. G. Strachan, B. W. Crisp, T. F. Taylor, A. G. Lewis, J. M. P. Lloyd. *Standing on ground:* B. W Partridge, R. J. Franklin, C. J. Mitchell, J. P. Gawthorn, P. J. Burleigh, J. M. Gibbins, J. F. Morton, M. S Gunn, R. J. Perry, P. E. Wellings, J. S. L. Bewers, C. E. A. Burgess, C. G. B. Beales, D. J. Meredith, I. D Newman, D. Oldacre. *Sitting:* J. N. Turner, M. J. Turvey, P. T. G. Chastney, J. N. Davis, D. T. Briggs, M A. D. Hayward, I. McE. King, G. H. B. Sell, B. D. F. Mansfield, J. Hayden, A. C. Taber. *In front:* C. J. Elliot M. J. Travers, M. G. G. Chapman, R. J. Brinton, P. J. Barker, H. G. James, G. A. Barringer, J. W. Appleyard J. B. Johnson, F. G. Perrin, M. T. Hutchinson, B. K. Walker.

C. COVILL, 1936–62.
Groundsman and Cricket Coach.

UPPER FIELD, 1953: 1st XV v Mr C. Mellows' XV. *Below:* On the field of pla from right: D. B. Wright, H. W. Lambert, Mr F. D. Bryan-Brown (Referee) M. F. T. Brownhill (third from left) and D. A. Watson at full-back for the schoo are recognizable. On extreme right of picture, Mr N. Monk-Jones.

regarded by other schools as something of an eccentricity, and urged that the balance between promising young swimmers and the then much fewer promising young cricketers needed to be redressed in favour of cricket. The question was one of priorities: now that so many more schools have come to realize the importance of swimming, our emphasis on it at B.S.C. no longer seems anything other than a normal school activity, and the question of cricket versus swimming, once so hotly debated, is now largely an academic one.

Tennis was encouraged after the war by Dr Gammie's presentation of a House tennis cup. Lighter forms of sport also flourished ephemerally about this time, especially on Saturday evenings in the summer terms: e.g. rounders, of which a highly popular series of 'Test' matches were played off between the Houses, and the favourite campers' game of puddox.

The hobbies were encouraged by Arthur Evans as they had been by his predecessor, and by now had reached their pre-war standard both in variety and in achievement. On Speech Day, 1949 (the name 'Prize Day' was dropped soon after the second war in favour of 'Speech Day'), the activities of two interesting new groups—the Pottery Hobby and the Puppetry Hobby—were on view: indeed the number of hobbies, though varying from time to time, tended still to increase.

The later years of Mr Evans's headmastership saw the steady building up of the numbers in the School, though few additions to the buildings were as yet possible. In 1951 a spacious art-room and a large classroom were added, as southward extensions, to the Main and Preparatory School wings respectively of the Library Block. But it was not until the very end of Mr Evans's time that a major new building was added to the general layout of the School. This was the new gymnasium, built in memory of the Old Stortfordians who fell in the Second World War and of H. L. Price, whose death was felt to be in a sense as much a war casualty as were those whose names were on the panels on the Memorial Hall. Known as the Leo Price Gymnasium, it was only completed in the spring of 1957, during Mr Evans's last term: indeed the official opening did not take place till after he had left. It was Mr Evans too who was responsible for the negotiations with the trustees of the Industrial Fund for the Advancement of Scientific Education in Schools, which resulted in a generous grant towards the rebuilding of the school laboratories. Here again, however, the results of his planning were seen only after his departure.

This decade also saw further big changes in the staff, the most notable being the retirement at last, in 1949, of F. S. Sutton, after no less than forty-five years' service on the staff. Educated at Bristol

Grammar School, Mr Sutton won an open scholarship in mathematics at University College, Oxford; we have referred already to his outstanding record, both academic and athletic, at the university. After a brief period of teaching at Newcastle-under-Lyme, he came to Stortford in 1904. 'For forty years he did full-time work on the staff,' wrote C. S. Colman, 'including three periods of acting headmastership, and he continued to do a considerable amount of teaching until the end of 1949. That period of service to the School is unmatched in all its history, and has rarely been approached. He was one of Mr Young's earliest appointments at a critical moment in the School's development, and there could not have been a happier one. It would not be easy to overrate the value of the service that he gave, quite apart from its length. From his first coming he gave himself unsparingly to his work, in school time and out, in form room and in games. No budding mathematical genius could have asked for a finer coach. At cricket for some thirty years he came with absolute regularity to the nets, and bowled and coached for hour after hour, with an energy provided by his keenness for the game and for the credit of the team. Not the smallest part of his value to the School was his influence on the staff: friendly with all men, never wishing to take offence and never likely to give it, he was a great uniting influence in the Common Room.'

At Waytefield his position had been in many ways unique: for he was its first and only housemaster, and he and Mrs Sutton ran it almost single-handed from its opening until it was closed down, as already noted, in 1938. In that connection we have already referred to his outstanding qualities as a housemaster: here we may add a tribute from Sir Dick White, written at the time of his final retirement. 'F. S. S. created Waytefield during the First World War. He began with two borrowed prefects and seventeen new boys in part of a large Victorian house in Hadham Road. On opening day the interior, fresh from its conversion by carpenters, smelt strongly of creosote and knew nothing of boys or of school traditions. Yet to the seventeen new boys it possessed from its earliest beginnings a happy atmosphere, which it is still easy and delightful to recall. Creators and maintainers of this atmosphere were the Sutton family: F. S. S. and Mrs Sutton, who managed the House with skill and kindness to all, and Eileen and Frank, then under six, whom one encountered playing in the very pleasant gardens.

'In a remarkably short space of time the Housemaster shaped his bewildered new boys into a school community, capable of holding its own with other Houses of the School. What they achieved thereby is now a part of school history. Looking back, I would say the House had a pronounced individuality of its own; certainly its qualities expressed the personality of the Housemaster. It worked hard and it played hard: it won inter-house shields and nurtured young scholars. If it gave scope to individuality, there was F. S. S.'s wisdom and tolerance to account for it. As a housemaster F. S. S. steered his House rather than commanded it. Seeing him pottering in his garden in the long summer evenings, you might have thought him detached from the life of the House. But if you got that idea, you were in for a big surprise at the end of the term when he handed out, together with the travelling money, his penetrating assessments of each boy's school performances. It was the accuracy of these assessments which impressed, and their special value that they came from someone who obviously had the boy's best interests at heart.' Mr Sutton lived to enjoy sixteen years of retirement, during most of which time he lived at Bishop's Stortford.

Charles Mellows succeeded Mr Sutton as Second Master; and in the following year (1950) he gave up the housemastership of Alliott House, a position which he had held (apart from the war years when, as we have seen, the House was closed) since 1931. He was succeeded at Alliott's by H. E. Wall, who had similarly taken over from C. M. at School House. In 1953 Charles partially retired from teaching, though his time was still entirely devoted to the School.

New arrivals on the staff during these years included A. K. Hardyman O.S., who joined the Prep staff in 1949; A. Darlington, who took over the Biology department in 1950; W. E. Clare, who became senior Chemistry master in 1952 and at the same time took over from Mr Mellows the responsibility for the school swimming (he was himself a county and England swimmer); and, also in 1952, Captain A. W. Mack, whose boundless energy and enthusiasm soon communicated itself to the school's P.T., gymnastic and athletic activities. In that year the school's music suffered a loss in the death of Frank Greenfield, who for just on twenty years, ever since the death of his friend Percy Green, had taught the violin at B.S.C. and led the orchestra at school concerts. Several times he brought down the full Harlesden Philharmonic Orchestra, of which he was the conductor, to play at the School. His place as violin teacher and leader of the orchestra was taken by Jack McDougal.

In 1953 F. D. Bryan-Brown, a classics man, came to B.S.C. from University College School, where he had also been the master in charge of rugger. He now took over the Upper Fifth from C. M. In that year the School lost a good friend by the death of Rev. E. T. Killick, the vicar of St Michael's Church. A Cambridge cricket blue who had also played for England, he had often helped with coaching at the nets on Upper Field. He developed a close association with Mr Evans and with the School, an association since maintained by his successors, Rev. Charles Hooper and the present vicar, Rev. David Farmbrough.

Two masters left in 1953, T. A. Grocock from the Main School and Clifford Sims from Grimwade House. The latter took up an appointment for five years as headmaster of Prempeh College at Kumasi, on the Gold Coast. Apart from the war years Clifford had been assistant housemaster and then housemaster at Grimwade House over a period of eighteen years. In addition to his keenness in the classroom he was an energetic games player and coach. On his return from the Gold Coast (Ghana) five years later, after one or two temporary posts he was appointed headmaster of the Grammar School at Swanage, Dorset, where he is a prominent figure in the civic life of the town.

His position as housemaster at Grimwade House was filled by Mr G. K. Bond, who came to us from the Royal Masonic School at Watford, a historian who had also been in charge of the hockey at the R.M.S. It was Mr Bond who introduced at Grimwade House the 'Ladders' and the 'Chronicle'. In such games as chess, draughts, table-tennis and billiards, the names of the players are pinned on to 'ladders' on the Common Room notice-board, and as a boy succeeds in defeating the boy above him, his name is moved up; so that the respective order of merit at any time can be seen at a glance. The 'Chronicle' is a day-to-day record of events in the Prep, which is written up by a senior boy and is read out each week (to encourage if not to inspire home letters!) on Sunday morning. Mr Bond also took over from Mr Sims the running of the Christian Union, of which he has been president since he came to Stortford.

Shortly afterwards another familiar figure in the Prep said goodbye to Stortford, when Miss E. M. Watkins retired after having been matron at Grimwade House for no less than twenty years. Many Old Boys could testify to the way 'Ma Wat' smoothed out the difficulties of their first term away from home as boarders. She had come to identify her own interests entirely with those of the School, and still, in her retirement at Hove, she takes a keen interest in all things Stortfordian.

In 1954 Mr A. E. Charlwood joined the Main School staff as senior mathematics master, and as assistant housemaster in R.P.H. In that year too Mr Bryan-Brown took over the rugger from P. S. Burns, who left in the following year, after nine years on the staff, to take up a senior post at Caterham School. Burns was succeeded as senior history master by Mr K. A. Hearne. In the same year Mr M. S. Maxwell joined the Prep staff as geography master.

In 1956, after thirty-six years' service in the Bursary as Clerk to the School, Mr B. J. Adams retired. 'Bertie' Adams was not only a highly competent accountant, who also taught shorthand, typing and book-keeping to many a Stortfordian, but a man of wide interests—a musician who regularly played the violin in the school orchestra, and a keen botanist who specialized in the study of grasses. Above all, he was every man's friend in need: many of the teaching staff will remember with gratitude how readily he always put at their disposal his detailed knowledge of the business side of schoolmastering; and the College servants, in whatever capacity they served, brought all their troubles to him. It was indeed fitting that on his retirement the Old Boys marked their appreciation of all that he had done for the School by making him an honorary member of the Old Stortfordians' Club.

Meanwhile the School lost another good friend by the death in 1954 of Rev. H. C. Carter, whose association with B.S.C. dated from the early days of the headmastership of F. S. Young. His own son had been at Stortford; during a long ministry at Emmanuel Congregational Church, Cambridge, he himself had been in touch with many generations of O.S. undergraduates from before the first war until the end of the second; and during the last years of his life, having retired to Bishop's Stortford, he had renewed his active interest in the School.

Two more men whose names have figured prominently in these pages also died at this time. C. S. Colman, after nineteen years of retirement, died, as we have said, in 1955: he had been to the last a familiar figure in the school grounds and at matches on Upper Field, the playing-field which he had himself been mainly instrumental in securing for the School: it was a happy thought to rename it, after his death, Colman Field.

In the same year A. D. Hayward, who for so many years had been C. S. C.'s faithful henchman at Alliott's, underwent an operation which caused his first absence from school for more than a day or so (apart of course from his war service) during his forty years and more on the teaching staff. He was back in harness in 1956, but fell ill again and died at the end of the spring term. A scholar (in mathematics and science) of Queens' College, Cambridge, he came to Stortford in 1914 to teach physics: he followed E. A. Knight as assistant housemaster under C. S. C. at Alliott's: and returned there after seeing active service with the R.G.A. in the 1914–1918 war. 'While in Alliott's', Charles Mellows wrote of him, 'he fell very much under the spell of his Housemaster: he imitated much of his philosophy. Hayward made many lifelong friends in Alliott's and did very much for the life of the House before he left it to take on the Day Boy House. Here he did fine work and devoted to the House and the Science Labs the best years of his life. He was also for many years an enthusiastic Scoutmaster and it was a great disappointment to him that the School later gave up scouting.

'He was a familiar figure in many scenes of Stortford life. Equipped with a battery of stop-watches fresh from time-testing in the Labs, he stood on Upper Field or by the side of the Baths time-keeping in school sports. Every March a stentorian "NO JUMP!" dashed the hopes of ambitious long-jumpers. On starry nights if you went to the rose-beds, a dark outline was visible displaying the wonders of the heavens with a telescope to a party of young astronomers: next morning the same figure was in view, making his way towards the Young Memorial Library—our meteorologist was taking the daily readings. If you drove along the lanes in the district, or indeed much farther afield, a solitary cyclist might often be met (or passed, if you drove fast enough), on his way to study churches or to botanize in familiar haunts. He was not a cricketer, but he loved watching cricket on Upper Field. He had little use for films (he was inclined to damn them all as 'tomfoolery'), but sometimes you might see him at the Phoenix or the Regent—and then you knew the Housemaster was on business!'

Of Hayward as Housemaster J. K. Tee, a former head of the Day Boy House, wrote: 'A. D. H., or "Bilsh", as we used to call him, was Housemaster of the D.B.H. for nearly thirty years. When he took it over, the largest House in the School, its members were rarely accepted as equals by the boarders. The House had the reputation of producing a few "swots", of being no good at games, playing no part in School affairs, and having produced few if any school leaders. A. D. H. set out to alter all that, and alter it he did. Those of us who knew him well will never forget his joy and pride when the time came that members of his House took their rightful places in the School, so that it was the accepted thing for a day boy to be Captain of a school team or Head of the School.' As treasurer of the Old Stortfordians' Club for the last two years of his life he had renewed contact with many whose membership had lapsed, and the Club's finances greatly benefited thereby. His memory was fitly honoured at B.S.C. by the renaming of the Day Boy House, to which he had devoted so many years of his life, as Hayward House.

Academically, as we have already noted, there were during Arthur Evans's headmastership a number of scholarships and exhibitions won at Oxford and Cambridge in history and modern languages, with a few in the natural sciences. In classics, on the other hand, the last open award gained was an exhibition in 1940: this no doubt reflected a trend that was general, at any rate in the smaller public schools such as Stortford. At the same time, owing to the increasing competition for admission to the two older universities, even as commoners, there was a tendency, which has continued up to the present time, for more and more boys to go to the newer 'redbrick' universities.

In the realm of sport mention should be made here of B. M. Gray O.S., who in the early fifties, after a brilliant record in club and county rugger, played in successive England trials but just failed to gain an international cap. The introduction of hockey in the Preparatory School in 1947 marked the final development of this game as a major sport at B.S.C. In 1954 a school hockey team went on tour in the Easter holidays to Belgium and Holland, and had a successful time, especially as they were playing mostly against more experienced (men's) teams. In swimming the standard continued to improve: so, however, did the general standard throughout the country, and with more schools taking up swimming seriously the Bath Cup since the forties has eluded us. But we won the Public Schools' Medley Relay in 1953 and again in the following year, when our team was the fastest the School had ever had, with the free-style, orthodox breast-stroke and hundred yards back-stroke records all broken. A very successful water-polo team ended up their season with an East Anglian tour organized by Bill Clare in the summer holidays, in which all the matches were won. In tennis there were keen House contests for the Gammie Cup. The fives courts, after long desecration as store-rooms in war time and then as bicycle sheds for the Prep, were at length put into order again. The Prep bicycles were relegated to the shelter of the miniature rifle range: and under the coaching of Mr Burns the game of fives was revived; so also was squash racquets, played as before the war on the town courts behind Waytefield. It was in the forties and fifties too—to mention a very minor form of sport—that table-tennis began to be played intensively in the Houses, especially by the day boys. (In 1950 one of their number, J. A. Hunt, reached the final of the Junior Metropolitan Table Tennis Championship, and won the Hertfordshire Junior Championships—singles, doubles and mixed doubles. He was also televised playing a demonstration game in the Children's Hour programme.)

An unusual expedition was made to the east coast in the spring term of 1953 when, in response to the appeal for voluntary labour to help repair the breaches in the sea wall made by the disastrous storms and high tides in February of that year, a party of three masters and more than fifty boys shouldered shovels and set off for 'Operation Fillbag': they spent the day near Stansgate Abbey, on the Blackwater estuary, helping to fill sandbags with a peculiarly malodorous, black, slimy clay.

Of the school societies mention may be made here of the Typographical and Calligraphic Society, the Natural History Society and the Archaeological Society. The first-named, founded by Mr Strachan in 1948, has designed a B.S.C. Christmas card every year since that date: rhyme-sheets have been conspicuous at the exhibitions on Speech Day, and for the last ten years or so an annual rhyme-sheet competition has been held. The School came to be well known among calligraphic connoisseurs, and was indeed one of the first schools to encourage the Italic hand: in 1953 Mr Strachan's enthusiasm and the School's achievement were recognized publicly, when the Italic Hand Society held its first exhibition at the School.

In the Natural History Society Mr Darlington's energy inspired a lot of original work on the part of his biologists, and in 1954 no less than four prizes were won by members of the School N.H.S. in the competition sponsored by the Association of Schools' Natural History Societies. In the same year the Society's annual report, previously cyclostyled, first appeared in printed form under the title *Coturnix*: the high scientific standard and the wide range of biological studies which it covered were fully maintained in subsequent numbers. At this time too field-work was started on the ecology of Dernford Fen, in Cambridgeshire: this was to culminate a few years later in the publication of a comprehensive biological survey of that area.

The Archaeological Society, in the course of many afternoons spent digging down in the Meads, discovered Roman pottery (chiefly of the first to the third centuries A.D.) in considerable quantity: this was reported to the Ordnance Survey, and it was largely owing to the Society's discoveries that in the third edition (1956) of the Ordnance Map of Roman Britain Bishop's Stortford for the first time is marked as a Roman settlement.

In 1954 the first American exchange student [1] came to B.S.C. through the good offices of the English-Speaking Union: his impressions are worth quoting. 'After two terms here at Stortford', he wrote, 'the number of activities you carry on seems, for a school of this size, really impressive: the hobbies on Thursday afternoons, the debates, from loud and boisterous to tame and devious, the films, the concerts, the sports—hockey, athletics, seven-a-side rugger all going on at the same time even when there's six inches of snow on the ground—these and all the other activities really keep you busy. Nevertheless, I feel that there is something lacking, something that we had at my old school

[1] H. C. Cook.

in the States, namely dances with girls. In our Southern States we still have some segregation of white from black, but it never occurred to me that some people believe in separating boy from girl.' Perhaps it was our American boys, whom Arthur Evans had been instrumental in bringing over, that persuaded him to encourage at Stortford the group interested in square-dancing and reels: this soon led to an invitation to a dance at the Herts and Essex High School and a return invitation to the girls to a dance at the College. Shortly afterwards lessons in ballroom dancing for senior boys were initiated, for whom the wives of some of the younger members of the staff acted as long-suffering partners: and further dances with the High School were arranged. These and similar social functions have long since become a normal part of school life, and have been followed by other contacts between the two schools, in combined debates and at occasional lectures, and regularly in the Dramatic Society's productions.

Another American student [1] had some interesting remarks to make about our attitude to sport. 'I was surprised at the casual approach to sport, and the high standard achieved. With no real intensive training in athletics, for instance, most of the boys coming fresh from the hockey season, we were able to perform feats of prowess which would be unheard of in the United States without several weeks of training first. Therein lies the main difference between America's and England's approach to almost all sports. In America, winning is the one and only object of any sort of encounter with the opposition, sometimes at the cost of the personal enjoyment which always seems to be present when an Englishman "has a bash".'

In this connection one recalls an article by an O.S., J. M. Rae (the present headmaster of Taunton School) in *School and College* a few years back, written at a time when he was coaching both rugger and swimming at Harrow. Rugger, he maintained, was a game to be enjoyed, and a school coach should play down the idea that the school's prestige is at stake in every inter-school match—he had sharp criticisms to make of the publicity given in the press to what he called 'prestige rivalry'. But of course a school team must play to win, which means taking risks. 'If the school's attitude is right, the various school teams will have the confidence to play attacking football, because they know that the world will not come to an end if they lose.'

A third, more recent, exchange student [2] was chiefly interested in the disciplinary methods and the monitorial system at Stortford. 'In my school in the States, smokers and drinkers were rusticated on a

[1] R. G. Messer.

[2] E. S. Greene.

first offence, expelled on a second. Here "whackings" are the most popular solution, and rustication or expulsion is only used as a last resort. For offences in the States there is a system of "hours", which are worked off as tracks are here: there are no fines, detentions or beatings at all. School leadership is handled in a rather more democratic way than at B.S.C. There is a school "Student Council", and members are elected from a list of nominees provided by the equivalent of the Upper Sixth boys at Bishop's Stortford. The Council has wide powers, and has changed rules, disciplined boys and even overweighed the Headmaster's wishes. This system has one great advantage over the College practice of the housemasters choosing monitors: that is, that boys look up to someone they have chosen, and will obey him because they chose him. In practice, personal malice is almost always outweighed by a boy's leadership qualities.'

We have quoted at some length from the impressions of our exchange students: partly because it is salutary at times 'to see oursel's as others see us', and partly because their reactions are of interest in view of the increasing influence that American methods are having, for better or for worse, on English education—witness such recent innovations at Stortford as the Language Laboratory and the School Council; of which more later.

Holiday parties during these years visited Derbyshire, the Lake District and Snowdonia, and, on the Continent, France, Switzerland and Italy. More specialized parties, combining a first-rate holiday with detailed ecological survey work, were organized by Mr Darlington for his biologists: they visited such unusual and out-of-the-way places as Great Saltee Island, off the south-east corner of Ireland, Bardsey Island at the northern point of Cardigan Bay, the Isle of May in the Firth of Forth and the Aran Islands off the west coast of Ireland. A rather different type of holiday activity took place in 1956, for the first but not by any means the last time, when senior members of the School attended the Christmas holiday lectures organized by the Council for Education in World Citizenship: these were attended by some two thousand boys and girls, mostly from grammar schools, and were concerned with various social and political problems throughout the world.

Meanwhile Mr Evans's tenure of office was drawing to a close. He had always maintained that ten years was the optimum time for a headmaster to remain at one school, and in fact he had, on this ground, offered his resignation to the Governors back in 1954. The Governors at that time urged him to stay; and though his health had been giving cause for anxiety he decided to remain, as he was apparently making a good recovery. He had for some time, however, made up his mind that he wished to take Holy Orders; and in 1956 the chairman of the Governors announced that Mr Evans was seeking ordination and that the spring term of 1957 would be his last at Stortford. Mr Palmer spoke of Arthur Evans's outstanding sincerity, modesty and charm, and of Mrs Evans's kindness and hospitality which had endeared her to all Stortfordians. 'Mr Evans' thirteen years as Headmaster in the difficult post-war years', he wrote, 'have been distinguished by a remarkable understanding of the traditions of the School, and we have much to thank him for.'

Perhaps that understanding showed itself especially at Old Boys' week-ends when, term after term, Arthur and Mrs Evans laid themselves out to entertain personally the hordes of Old Stortfordians who descended upon the School, most of whom were, of course, strangers to them at first, though they soon ceased to be so. At the chanteys which were then usual on these occasions Arthur delighted to compère the show or conduct the singing: and afterwards he and Mrs Evans, and indeed the Evans family generally, held open house for any Old Stortfordians—and they were many—who cared to drop in.

This hospitality was extended to all those with whom his work brought him into contact. Typical of him was the institution of At Homes at the beginning of each term, before the staff meeting, when the masters and their wives, the house matrons and the members of the office staff were all made welcome in the headmaster's house.

The same friendliness inspired his unfailing interest in both school and O.S. rugger and cricket. Every Christmastide for a number of years he might be seen on Upper Field, braving the elements to referee the traditional Boxing Day rugger match between J. C. Collett's team and an O.S. team: he never failed to turn out, even when the pitch was covered with snow and the bitter winds blowing, surely, straight from the steppes of Russia had driven the spectators into the pavilion. At cricket he played regularly in Past and Present week, and on alternate years took the team to his old school at Leatherhead to play against an Old Johnians' eleven.

In the town he was well known not only at St Michael's Church but on the Bench, where he devoted a lot of his time to the work of the Juvenile Court. He was a Governor of the Herts and Essex High School, and a regular supporter of the local United Nations Association and of the Bishop's Stortford and District Musical Association.

For some years now Mr Evans has been living at Hove, where he is the incumbent of St Andrew's Church. O.S. who have called on him from time to time have found him happy in his work, and all Stortfordians will wish him many more years of service.

We may end this chapter by referring to a practice that Arthur Evans introduced at B.S.C. which is characteristic of him, and which has added greatly ever since to the impressiveness of the last Assembly of each term. On such occasions he read out a solemn charge to those boys who were about to leave. 'Each of you, whatever his position in the School, has added something to the life of the School, and for that addition the School is grateful. Now that the time has come for you to leave, it is my duty to charge you never to forget the benefits that you have received in this place—benefits which bring with them a responsibility. You take with you the name of the School: it is your duty to see that you keep this name high, and never let it down by any future conduct on your part which might bring disgrace upon it. On the contrary, you should always seek to raise it higher.

'With this charge I bid you go forth into the world in peace. Be of good courage, hold fast that which is good, render to no man evil for evil; support the weak, comfort the faint-hearted, help the afflicted, honour all men; love and serve the Lord, rejoicing in the power of His Holy Spirit. And the blessing of God Almighty, the Father, the Son and the Holy Spirit, be amongst you and remain with you always.'

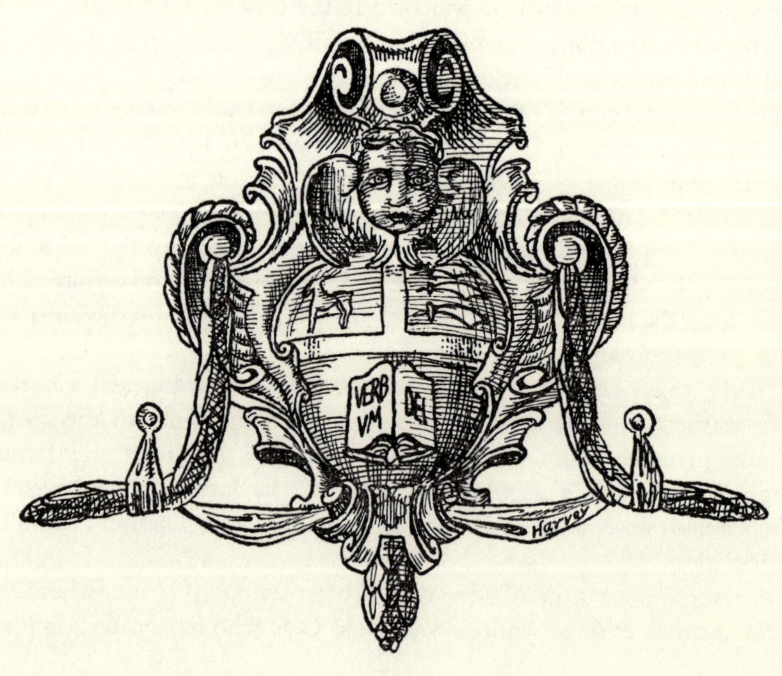

11. Some School Societies

WE have already seen what a big part the various hobbies have always played in the life of the School, from the early days of the N.G.S. up to the present time. Recently, under the title 'Taking Stock', the *Stortfordian* printed a series of articles on four of the more important school societies, written by some of those who for longer or shorter periods had been responsible for running them. In this chapter, at the risk of some repetition, we are reprinting these in whole or in part, adapting them and expanding them where necessary to bring them up to date.

It is fitting that we should begin with the Natural History Society, for Richard Alliott was himself an eager all-round naturalist, and F. S. Young a systematic botanist; while a succession of masters have been enthusiasts in one section or other of the Society's activities. Of the N.H.S. Charles Mellows wrote as follows:

The Natural History Society

Bishop's Stortford is a good district for naturalists, and the College N.H.S., founded before the first war, has played an important part in the life of the School. For convenience it was subdivided into four sections, dealing respectively with birds, other vertebrates, insects and other invertebrates, and plants. These sections worked independently, but joined for major excursions, and especially for the exhibitions on Prize Day which have become traditional. F. S. Young, the Headmaster, presided at weekly meetings in his study, taking a special interest in the rock gardens and in a small school museum of local specimens, dead or alive. He was a member of the Alpine Club, and his prefects and some junior masters went with him on climbing holidays, at Wasdale, in the Highlands or in the Alps. When his usual large post arrived, we were left to our own devices and encouraged to be naturalists: and we brought home to England fauna as well as flora. Lizards were exciting creatures to catch and easy to transport, and for years they were naturalized, along with the Alpine plants, in the rock gardens. Once in the New Forest we helped an expert adder-hunter catch a dozen adders; and soon a member of the N.H.S. was feeding and even breeding adders, kept in a padlocked cage in the museum.

We made a good many experiments with the rock gardens as a vivarium: there were nearly twenty ponds, and each had different residents. Many botanizing holidays spent abroad with an import licence to England explain the large numbers of Alpine plants—from the Pyrenees or from many localities in the French, Swiss and Italian Alps. A knowledgeable visitor would notice in the ponds a number of characteristic flowers of the Norfolk Broads, especially when buckbean, bladderwort and pygmy water-lilies were in flower.

I wish I could do justice to the work of the bird section, but must leave that to others. Here I may mention that ringing began in the first year or two of the Society's existence: in the grounds, aviaries could be seen which housed young hawks, owls and jackdaws: there was a brisk trade in the two latter, the local churches being visited not only by architects but by bird-fanciers. Little owls were much commoner then locally than they are today. Nightingales sang in the school grounds; kingfishers and herons visited our ponds; I recollect red-backed shrikes, long-tailed tits and goldcrests nesting in the grounds. In the twenties we had an outstanding ornithologist in R. W. Hale, who while at school twice (in 1926 and 1927) won the Public Schools Essay Prize, given by the Royal Society for the Protection of Birds: this success was to be repeated thirteen years later by S. E. Linsell. Both have maintained their keenness on birds: Hale is a prominent member of the London, Linsell of the Essex, Natural History Society.

The railway banks of the old Dunmow and Braintree line (now defunct) were worked for lizards, slow-worms and grass-snakes. A surprising number of mammals also lived in and immediately around the school grounds. Foxes, weasels and stoats were common (not so long ago a mother stoat was seen parading her family round the School House courtyard). An injured badger was once brought to me, at another time a young otter. Hedgehogs and most of the rodents have always been common. The red squirrels were very tame: we got no nuts from the School House walnut tree, for the squirrels got them all!

The moth collectors had not far to go, for thousands could be caught in a walk up the rough field-track which is now Maze Green Road. One curious change has struck many observers. As a boy I had reason to regard this part of Hertfordshire as the worst I knew for butterflies: there were a few of interest, especially white-letter hairstreaks, holly blues and large tortoiseshells (all in the school grounds), but in Long Meadow, for instance, none but the commonest insects. In twenty years all this changed: one after another the rarities of the New Forest and other southern woods came to live with us—it was quite uncanny how they found us out. One year a grass field on the cross-country run was bright with devil's-bit scabious, the food-plant of the locally rare 'greasy' (marsh) fritillary, the very last species I expected to see at Stortford: next year the fritillaries swarmed. Then came the war: the field was ploughed up, and I have never seen one since. The beautiful white admiral appeared in Hatfield Forest one year and soon grew to be quite common: I have seen very few there lately. These curious local conditions led the ardent collectors to go farther afield. We went to the chalk country round Fleam Dyke and Therfield Heath; or the fascinating Breck Sand area around Mildenhall and Brandon, usually making Wicken Fen our last port of call; we would go up the Great North Road to Monk's Wood and Castor Hanglands, or the Purlieus and King's Cliffe—Northants woodland at its best: several of these places justified our choice and have been made nature reserves.

I have said nothing about fish, and would have liked to discuss our success with the rainbow trout and failure with the brown trout made over to us by the Biology Labs. We had no running water, only a spray fountain. With most coarse fish we were fairly successful, as were our forefathers many centuries ago with their stew-ponds.

The College has produced some first-rate botanists who astonished us with some of their finds. It seemed remarkable that the London clay could produce so many orchids—we had some strange experiences with the seeding of some of the wild orchids, especially the eccentricities of the bee orchid and the fragrant *conopsea.*

I remember one especially interesting holiday in Provence, when I went with Mr Ward's party as naturalist. We visited, near Orange, the home of the famous Henri Fabre: his favourite creatures were all there —cicadas, scorpions, dung-beetles; burying beetles and pine 'processionaries'; praying-mantises and all sorts of hunting-wasps. But what we did not expect at all was an encounter with the French C.I.D. The Foreign Minister M. Barthou and the King of Jugoslavia had recently been assassinated, and itinerant foreigners were apparently suspect. 'Pourquoi cela?' shouted their chief man, snatching a butterfly-net and making it plain that we were under arrest. Hesitantly I replied, 'Pour attraper les papillons.' With immense scorn he almost spat the words at me: 'Pour attraper les papillons? Pourquoi?'

We got away after an uneasy ten minutes: but I have never really found an answer to that rhetorical question.

C. M.

Since 1950, when Mr Darlington arrived at B.S.C. (we are now quoting C. R. Beaufoy), the Society has made contacts for itself all over the country by joining in several national schemes. There were the four national surveys, for example, in which it took part—the nocturnal migration of redwing; regional variations in the nesting habits of rooks; the distribution of mistletoe in Britain (the Forestry Commission used some of the Society's information in their handbook on diseases of forest trees, because they found it more up to date than anything they had); and the survey on certain orchid variations in Britain, which the Society organized through the Association of School Natural History Societies. One should add the work on the migration of insects, carried out for the Royal Entomological Society. As for the nest-record card scheme, Stortford has for many years held the record for the number of cards kept by any school N.H.S. That people trust the accuracy of our observations is shown by the number of research workers who have written to the School asking for material.

Naturally Stortford is well known to the A.S.N.H.S., of which we were one of the founder members. We have regularly taken part in the Association's annual exhibitions and essay competitions, and have won many awards and prizes—more in fact than any other school.

The Society's survey of Dernford Fen was regarded by Mr Darlington as 'the best thing we've ever done' (though that was before the similar survey of the Naze on the Essex coast had been undertaken). As a result of it, he will tell you with pleasure, the area was saved from development. 'And ah, yes: the boy who fell in the peat bog *was* rescued!' Talking of surveys will remind some boys, and many Old Boys, of summer expeditions: to Great Saltee (twice), the Aran Isles off Galway, the Isle of May, and Bardsey Island off the coast of the Lleyn Peninsula in Wales.

Individual pieces of research that stay in the mind are too numerous for a full list to be given. But after some quick thinking Mr Darlington will mention R. T. Ling's work on burying-beetles; D. R. How's study on gall-causing wasps; and R. W. Boardman's work on the liverworts, mosses and ferns of this district, carried on by P. B. Freshwater and M. Downing. The latter showed originality in marking fishes in the Stortford area: then, switching to botany, he became remarkably expert on orchid variations. That a schoolboy can break fresh ground is shown by J. A. C. Kew's discovery, while working on the distribution of ferns, that there are species to be found below ground (in drains, for example) that do not appear elsewhere.

Coturnix, the N.H.S.'s annual report (the name remembers the rare event of a quail nesting in the district), is a specialist publication for specialists. That it has earned respect as a serious journal is shown by the fact that a letter was received from Poland asking that copies should be sent regularly to the library in Warsaw.

But more important than any exhibition or any individual piece of research has been the routine all-the-year-round work, such as the checking of changes in the status of animals and plants, both land and aquatic, over the years. Painstaking 'office-work' of this kind may not be exciting, but it gives a schoolboy the feeling that he is taking part in a long-term piece of research which may produce exciting results long after he has left school.

C. R. B.

More recently the Natural History Society has done further work on the non-vascular plants (liverworts, mosses, ferns, lichens and fungi) and on various forms of aquatic life, especially in Hatfield Forest, on behalf of the National Trust, where the Society has worked in co-operation with the Bishop's Stortford and District N.H.S. Preliminary studies have also been made, under Mr Darlington's guidance, of the various types of galls found in the Stortford area, in addition to those caused by the gall-wasps.[1]

But the major achievement during the sixties was undoubtedly the publication in 1963 of a very full and detailed Survey of the Naze, at Walton on the Essex coast. This strip of saltmarsh and coast had already been pronounced a 'Site of Special Scientific Interest': now, largely as a result of the school N.H.S.'s survey, it has been bought by the Essex County Council, to preserve it from 'development', and has been declared a Regional Open Space.

The Architectural Society

The following article on the Architectural Society is from the pen of Walter Strachan, who himself founded the Society more than forty years ago.

Our first expedition took place on 8th June 1927: it was to Horham Hall and Thaxted. The report by the first secretary, John Bourne (now a portrait-painter) ends: 'We returned to our char-a-banc, and after a comfortable ride reached B. S. about 6.30 p.m.' (How Edwardian it sounds!) Society members gave talks at irregular intervals. The minutes of one, 'delivered' [*sic*] on Stained Glass by E. G. Collieu (now senior don at Brasenose College, Oxford) begin: 'Mr Johnston was in the chair and he called upon the secretary to read the minutes, which he was very naturally unable to do, having none. . . .' During

[1] See *Plant Galls* by A. Darlington (Blandford Press 1968).

the next vital year while I was away at Giggleswick, Mr Hayward piloted expeditions to Southwark, Ely and Long Melford. On my return I started a Saturday evening hobby 'for novices and all others who cared to come'. Expeditions continued, extensive in time and place: one remembers with particular thrill those to Penshurst (1930), King's Lynn (1931) and Peterborough (1932). On the first of these we had the guidance of Leslie Martin O.S., and enjoyed the hospitality provided by his wife. (Leslie for many years encouraged the Society by giving prizes for the best illustrated architectural essays.) It would be an ungrateful survey that failed to mention some of the teas so generously provided for us—from the strawberry tea on our visits to Little Hadham Hall as the guests of the Minets (the last private owners) and to Gifford's Hall, where Mrs Brocklehurst entertained thirty of us, to more recent occasions, notably at Standon Hall and at Cammas Hall, where we were the guests of another O.S., J. M. Lukies. But tea is not always forthcoming, as I discovered at Rupert Brooke's Grantchester, where I had to announce to the hungry multitude that the host of the Lion had failed to book the date and . . . could not oblige!

The programme in the earliest days, conditioned as it was by a non-daylight time for the hobby, was inevitably taken up largely with semi-academic work—the drawing of ecclesiastic and domestic subjects centred round a theme. Some of these were ultimately made into film strips, and 'Classical Tradition in Architecture' or 'Local Tradition in Building' are still shown to successive generations. Experiments were made with modelling in plaster of Paris—fonts, mouldings, etc., and one real masterpiece by Tony Harrington, of a Crusader on his tomb. Out of doors we recorded almost exclusively by photography, and on the grand scale: in 1930 I find a note to the effect that three hundred and thirty photographs were shown in our Prize Day exhibition.

Right up to the war the Society also ran at least one annual expedition to see pictures: parties saw every international art exhibition from the Dutch to the Chinese, for which we were prepared beforehand by Percy Horton or Geoffrey Rhoades. Among other distinguished lecturers we had Stephen Gooden, the famous engraver of the Windsor Castle Library bookplate and designer of the George Medal. His first lecture, on engraving, was described in the minutes as 'sprinkled with humour'. Of his second I recall his dictum that architecture should be 'a good shape, suited to its purpose and its setting'. What an antidote to our only disastrous lecture, by a professional architect with a military title who wanted to cover the countryside with neo-Tudor houses: the discussion afterwards was heated! Real heat was generated inadvertently on another occasion, during another lecture by E. G. Collieu, who was blissfully unaware that a page in a valuable book borrowed from his College library at Oxford was gradually browning in the overheated epidiascope which he was operating. A year or so later D. L. Robarts, now, alas, dead, and R. G. Coleman left their mark in the shape of first-class drawings which are still treasured and shown.

John Ferguson, an outstanding secretary (1937–9) proves my theory that by sheer persistence anyone can learn to draw: for he regularly won the Leslie Martin essay competition. He was an admirable organizer of our exchange visits to Felsted School History Society, with which we also ran joint expeditions. ('What boots it', writes the secretary in his report of the one to west Suffolk in 1938, 'to relate of the president's terrifying skids, or his race with Mr Sutton. . . .') Senior members of the respective societies lectured at each other's school: how we envied Felsted their 'Bury' for their hobby activities.

The war years were difficult, but we continued the Saturday evening hobby, and kept our Prize Day exhibitions going from drawings made, of necessity, within cycling distance (I remember the sight of an immaculate Bill Marlow hurtling down the hill to Barwick Ford, followed by the secretary, Bobby Swinstead, who plunged straight in!). These full-scale sketching tours, covering fifty to sixty miles of architectural terrain, have become a feature of our summer programme, a particularly pleasurable and useful one.

After the war Town Planning was in the air, and the Society made it a theme for the year under the guidance of John Bury: I shall always be grateful for his enthusiasm and his practical help, which continued after he had left. Another former member, Nelson Foley, F.R.I.B.A., now chief architect of Trust Houses, also kept us up to date on modern developments, which were to become a preoccupation of an outstanding secretary, Paul Thompson and of his gifted apprentice Christopher Hewett: the latter contributed to the *Architectural Review*, while still at school, an article on the industrial landscape of Bishop's Stortford, and thereby first drew the attention of Nikolaus Pevsner to our work. Christopher staged a revealing local Subtopia exhibition during his time as secretary. We watched developments at Harlow New Town and began to model some of the new buildings there. Each secretary illuminates some aspect of a many-faceted subject: the two last-mentioned with their rapid pen-and-wash sketches also introduced a new style and standard of recording, to supplement the more exacting technique of more formal drawings. Of our modellers one of the best was Peter Burleigh, whose 'magnum opus' was St Michael's Church: a later secretary, George Wood, followed this lead with a superb model of Much Hadham Church—work which he combined with the study of

Le Corbusier! Roger Peers, now chief curator of Dorchester Museum, threw light on the historical as well as the aesthetic interest of church brasses, and later at Oxford edited a fine series of reproductions of brass-rubbings.

By this time an increase in the intake of junior members was made possible by the help first of Mr Woodward and then, for many years, of Mr Newton. The latter will recall some of the perils of cycling in droves: the advance guard is not necessarily the most discreet body, and I expect Mr Newton like myself has still a vision of that angry vicar who, gesticulating at boys hanging over the parapet of Great Easton Church tower, shouted at me: 'I've had half the parish ringing me up about lead thieves!' Later, thanks to Mr Burrell and then to Mr Beaufoy with his great modelling skill, an even larger number of boys can now enjoy a hobby that, out of doors invariably and indoors more often than not, extends its interest beyond trade union hours.

Impossible here to record gratitude to all the friends who have helped us with prizes, car transport, lectures; but I must mention the school architect, Mr R. O. Foster, in the latter connection, as well as Alec Clifton-Taylor O.S., whose generous gift of books to the architectural library is proving most useful: as likewise is R. D. Knight's gift of specimens of building stone, supplemented later by another O.S., B. J. Greenhill. The Society has accumulated over the years its own records of local buildings and features of interest, from malt-houses to cast-iron pumps, from pigeon cotes and windmills to bus shelters, from historic farmhouses to modern churches.

We are particularly proud that so many former members have come back from time to time to talk to us on some interest of their own in the architectural field; for we take this to be an act of faith on their part, that they believe in our main purpose, which is to teach the pleasure of seeing intelligently and with discrimination.

W. J. S.

More recent expeditions have included visits to Coventry to see the new cathedral, and to both Oxford and Cambridge to study the extensions and new buildings that have been erected in the last few years.

The Dramatic Society

Charles Ross Murray, who was for so many years a most enterprising president of the Dramatic Society, wrote of it as follows:

To look a long way back, there was little attempt at serious drama before the 1914–1918 war; for until then the only hall available for acting was the present School House Senior Common Room; though Mr A. G. Tidmarsh and others were always at hand to encourage any enterprising group of players. But when the Assembly Hut was erected in 1919, with a small stage or platform at one end, a new era of highly successful performances began. Those days will be particularly associated in the minds of then-Stortfordians with Mr E. W. Edmunds' remarkable *Mundus et Homo* morality play, which was to have quite a vogue in the twenties. (When later it was moved to the Memorial Hall, however, I am told it lost something of the freshness and spontaneity of its appeal, and of that close contact, physical and mental, between audience and players—the sense of mutual contribution—which is at the heart of artistic achievement.) In the Memorial Hall one remembers Aristophanes' *The Frogs*, played in Greek under Mr Pond and Mr Monk-Jones; and John Glyn-Jones's most moving speech as the Inquisitor in the trial scene from Shaw's *Saint Joan*, produced by Mr Pond; and a number of French plays put on by Mr Bluett, also in the twenties. The *Stortfordian* reports a long series of productions during the thirties, often with the help of Mr H. R. Spencer: when he left at the beginning of the war to join the Air Force, the Society carried on very successfully unassisted by any adult.

Joining the staff from a place where everything was master-sponsored, I considered this a praiseworthy achievement, and lay very low. But a few weeks after my arrival someone sidled up to me and announced that he was the secretary of the Dramatic Society, that they were going to do *Hamlet* next term, and would I produce it? 'You appear to get on very well without masters,' I said, 'so why bring them in? And *Hamlet*', I added sourly, 'is a star out of your sphere. You'll never do *Hamlet*.' '*Hamlet*,' he replied: 'and we can't do it alone.'

One cannot go on stone-walling this brand of mulish persistence indefinitely; and break was drawing to a close. Not weakening, but with the intention of ending the stultifying conversation by administering the *coup de grâce*, 'And who', I asked, 'do you suppose would take the name part? Me?' 'Well,' murmured the secretary tentatively, 'I was wondering if I could have a bash. . . .' So that was it: megalomania: a stage-struck egocentric! 'I don't think you could take the part; and anyway you can't do this play; and if you did, it would be a dreadful flop.' But he could, and they did; and it wasn't. . . . I still remember with respect Nigel Palmer's Horatio, Derek Beales' Polonius, Geoffrey Strachan's thirteen-year-old Ophelia; and a Christopher Stephens who as Hamlet moved with grace, and developed a certain youthful and touching beauty of person; who felt and projected to the audience the complex emotions in that distracted orb—but felt too the poetry. (Not seldom, even on the professional stage, Shakespeare is well served in the one direction but at the expense of the other.) It was Shakespeare's miracle of course: and even the busy stage-hands knew they were in the presence of something great and exciting.

I dwell at some length on this production of long ago, because it introduced me to something that was symptomatic of the Society then as now—a flood of selfless enthusiasm that has carried us along on the crest of a wave: and that is admirable even if waves do have a habit of sometimes toppling.

I found it was a good plan I had inherited, to have a genuine Society of volunteers who had to submit to an audition and could only then be elected as members; and even so were not cast for a part unless they agreed to give up almost all their spare time, including if necessary their Long Sundays, during production. The result has been a group of dedicated, loyal people (and this of course includes the back-room boys). They have not always been successful: I remember a *None but the Brave* which masqueraded as a farce but was seldom funny. One is tempted to make the diagnosis that the Society rises to a great work of art or a noble theme (I suppose that *St Joan*, with the *Hamlet* already mentioned, was one of our outstanding successes), were it not that that rather spurious play *The Amazing Dr Clitterhouse* was one of our high spots, and *The School for Scandal* a rather tedious performance.

The move from the Hut to the Memorial Hall had transformed the techniques of production as well as altering the atmosphere. There came such problems as the adapting of a vastly high proscenium arch, a shallow, sharply tapering stage and the lack of any elbow room in the wings or rear. Wonders were done with makeshift equipment and primitive lighting. In the early fifties Grahame Liddell, one of the Society's most skilful and resourceful electricians, built a first-rate switchboard and dimmers; and an apron stage gave more room and mobility. But without a cyclorama the difficulty was always with outdoor scenes, and choice of play was somewhat conditioned by this consideration. Then came our second move, to the Leo Price Gymnasium: which with its special equipment gave the Society tremendous opportunities. The strange thing is, however, that the standard of performance has shown no noticeable advance, though the performances may be technically slicker. It is good to have a cyclorama at last, and room beside and under the stage. On the other hand, the lighting supplied by the contractors was an unimaginative, stereotyped issue to schools: much of it we do not use because it lacks flexibility and selectiveness, and consequently we hire extensively—which is absurd.

One of the most valuable traditions which I inherited when I took over as president was that whereby boys and not masters take complete charge of all departments of what is really a complex, diverse and major industry. Boys build and paint the sets; boys are entirely responsible for lighting and sound effects; and stage-hands are a close and jealous confederation, given to strange headgear, a secret way of life and a language of their own. A boy stage manager controls all these, and is solely responsible during the run of a performance. This I do consider an achievement: the producer's responsibility finishes (save perhaps for some savagery at an inquest) as the curtain rises upon the dress rehearsal. I am proud of the fact that I can watch shows from the back of the audience; that if there is a crisis (and there always is), it is coolly coped with by the stage manager, and only one perspiring and half-dead person in the house knows that a fatal moment has been deftly handled by steady nerves and quick thinking.

I am supposed to be 'taking stock'. Briefly, then, in the present and the immediate past we have been too conservative and cautious: the choice of play has been limited and obvious, the handling conventional and unadventurous, the staging traditional, attempting a realistic approach which is inimical to speed and the influence of suggestion. We have had Shakespeare, Sheridan, Shaw; Rattigan, Daviot, Gogol; only one play by a genuinely modern author, Ustinov.

Of the future it is scarcely for me to speak. But I hope we shall move towards the briskness and intimacy of the theatre 'in the round'—not very well suited to the Leo Price Gymnasium, though a start can be made there. But a new building has lately arisen, intended as a place for eating, though anyone with half an eye can see at a glance that it is simply created for the drama; destined, surely, not for the mere satisfaction of animal appetites but to be dedicated to the cult of Thespis! Finally, is it not time that a school which built its own swimming-bath should now construct, perhaps west of the fives court on land that has never yet been utilized, its own outdoor theatre?

C. D. R. M.

Charles Ross Murray's last production, the *Merchant of Venice*, was thought by many to be second only to his *Hamlet*. As to his suggestions, though no open-air theatre has been constructed nor has the Dramatic Society appropriated the school dining-hall for its own purposes, Roger Beaufoy, who succeeded Ross Murray as president, experimented with the theatre in the round when he produced *The Man who was Thursday*; and in tackling *An Angel comes to Babylon* by the Swiss playwright Friedrich Durrenmatt he was certainly not guilty of conservatism in his choice of authors. John Cole, who took over from Beaufoy, inspired a School House group with his own enthusiasm when they gave us *She Stoops to Conquer*. Other group activities have included *The Long and the Short and the Tall* by Willis Hall, most convincingly realized both by actors and by John Cole as producer (rehearsed in a mere ten days by boys who had been taking their 'A' Levels); and the production by the Cercle Français of Molière's *Le Médecin Malgré Lui* and *Le Bourgeois Gentilhomme*, and of two short plays by Ionesco, *La Leçon* and *La Cantatrice Chauve*. A Shakespearean play usually considered difficult for schools, *The Winter's Tale*, was recently put on most successfully, again by John Cole: and we look forward with interest to his forthcoming production of *King Lear*.

In most of these and other plays various local girls' schools have collaborated, and the Society has had the help of gifted actresses from the Herts and Essex High School, St Mary's Convent School or Chantry Mount.

The Archaeological Society

Finally, H. E. Wall wrote about the Archaeological Society (or, as it has recently come to be called, the Archaeological and Local History Society), which he ran for some twenty years:

The roots of the Archaeological Society are to be found in the archaeology section of the Pioneer Scheme of the thirties. At that time we scanned local churches for evidence of Roman brick (the fine Saxon chancel-arch at Great Hallingbury, for instance), and traced the line of Stane Street west of Stortford, digging somewhat desperately and unsuccessfully (as perhaps A. F. Minnis will remember) for evidence of Roman road-metal under a remote cart-track.

The enthusiasm of D. J. Emery, P. G. Collett and P. Stephens was largely responsible for the actual formation of the Society after the war. Mrs Cippico, the owner of Walbury Dells, very kindly allowed us to survey the Iron Age camp and do some digging there. Our lack of experience and the time taken in cycling to and fro seriously handicapped our efforts: but the incentive given by this impressive local earthwork gave us a good start.

Then came my chance observation of a pile of oyster shells dug from an electric cable trench in Rye Street, near the line of the Roman Stane Street. The Surveyor's Department of the Bishop's Stortford U.D.C., the Eastern Electricity Board and the archaeological staff of the Ordnance Survey (summoned by phone to pronounce upon the significance of the oyster shells!) all helped us in a quick dig in Goodliffe's Nurseries. However, the finds—some bits of drainpipe, and willow-pattern china—somewhat damped our ardour! But Mr Watts, the deputy surveyor, examining some rabbit-holes in a bank on the other side of the Meads by the railway, had his appetite whetted by seeing more oyster shells dug out by the rabbits, and searching further found also some pieces of ancient pottery. We gained the permission of Mr Charles Edwards O.S. to dig near by, and soon found a few coins and enough fragments of pottery to establish the fact of a Roman settlement of some kind. The advice and help of Mr John Holmes, of St Edmund's College, Ware, were invaluable to us, and through him we had a visit from the Curator of Verulamium Museum. Later, British Railways rented us a piece of land, alongside the line, which was built up from material from the cutting. As the latter probably went through part of the Roman site, we had hopes of finds here before reaching the Roman levels below. It meant some tough digging, and after the harvest we also made some brief digs in the fields east of the railway; but, although we found bucketfuls of broken pottery of various types, including some interesting pieces of Samian ware, we were never lucky enough to find many pieces that fitted together.

Then came the development of a big building site on these fields to the east of the railway, and though not able to dig we were allowed to search for anything the bulldozers revealed. A Romano-British brooch was picked up, which the British Museum asked to be allowed to photograph for their records; and an exciting search at dusk by keen-eyed enthusiasts produced sixteen fragments which, when stuck together, formed half a Samian bowl, with the potter's name RUFI[ANUS] stamped on the base. We had the privilege of a visit from Mr C. W. Phillips, the head of the Archaeological Department of the Ordnance Survey Office, to give us advice on the site. [It has already been noted that, as a result of his visit, Bishop's Stortford was marked on the new Ordnance Survey Map (1956) of Roman Britain.]

In March 1956 some workmen digging a trench put Mr Watts on to the discovery of a Roman stone coffin and skeleton. This, thanks to Mr Seymour, father of an O.S., who owned the building site, we were able to get moved by means of a mobile crane lent by the Stortford stationmaster: it now has its second resting place in Classroom 10.

One should not forget some stimulating expeditions farther afield: to Colchester and to the Roman remains at Verulamium; to Grimes Graves (neolithic flint-mines); and to Braughing, where we saw Mr Brodie Henderson's fine collection of Romano-British pottery found on his land. The Roman settlement at Braughing was extensive and still awaits systematic excavation.

H. E. W.

(Our account of the Society's activities is continued by K. A. Hearne, who for a short period took over the presidency from Mr Wall.) When the Society helped to unearth the Roman coffin, we were still able to excavate on both sides of the railway line, between Rye Street and Parsonage Lane; but since then the area of excavation has of necessity been curtailed by the building of the Stansted Road housing estate. The outlook did not appear too bright when we were restricted to a small stretch of land on the Rye Street (west) side of the railway embankment. Our fears too seemed justified by the results: we found odd fragments here and there, and occasionally came across pieces of more significance: but very often a Friday afternoon's dig was a frustrating experience. Indeed, as our Secretary Roger Madsen observed in thoughtful mood, one got the impression that, in Stortford at any rate, the Romans did little else but break up pottery and throw it away, for, apart from three coins, we have found only pottery. But our faith has been rewarded, for more recently we have unearthed a practically complete Romano-British basin-like jar, as well as a much rarer spherical jar with a narrow opening, such as contained liquids; together with more pottery that we have been able to reconstruct.

The reader will appreciate from all this that our activities are essentially of the hit-or-miss variety, in which more recently we have been on target. We have no maps to help us, and only the line of the Roman Stane Street to guide us. But from our excavations we would hazard a guess that it is under the Meads and in the Cannon's Mill Lane area that the core of Roman Stortford may lie buried.

K. A. H.

Since Mr Hearne's departure, Mr Wall and his archaeologists have had the welcome and enthusiastic help of Mr A. Lee, who became joint president of the Society with Mr Wall. More recent finds have included a Roman copper pin of unusual type, a large fragment of a Roman quern and a late (fourth century A.D.) Roman coin. An attempt was made to preserve a second Roman sarcophagus which was uncovered on another building site, some distance to the east of the burial mentioned above, but unfortunately it had been too badly broken up by the bulldozers. The main objectives of these digs in the Meads are still to trace the line of Stane Street to the point at which it crossed the river, and to determine the exact location of the Roman settlement.

12. P. W. Rowe: from 1957

Mr P. W. Rowe, who became headmaster in the summer term of 1957 at the age of twenty-nine ('the youngest headmaster in England'), was an O.S. and son of an O.S. At school he had had an outstanding career both in scholarship and sport. He had been Head of the School, and captain or vice-captain of rugger, cricket, hockey and athletics; and he had crowned his career by winning an open scholarship in history at St John's College, Cambridge. Before going up he served for two years in the R.A.S.C. At Cambridge he obtained a First Class in the history tripos. He represented his college in various forms of sport, and was a university trials man in rugger. On going down he taught for a time at Brentwood School and then at Repton, where he was senior history master at the time of his appointment to B.S.C. It was while he was at Brentwood that he got married, and the happy family life he enjoys with Bridget Rowe and their three children provides a most valuable background to a man carrying so much responsibility.

The appointment of such a man was popular with masters, boys and Old Boys alike. His outlook on religion is that of a tolerant but far from apathetic mind: an Anglican, he has shown himself aware of certain valuable strands in the traditions of what was a definitely Nonconformist foundation. He is a good public speaker, and his speeches at Old Boys' dinners, on the school Speech Days and similar public occasions have always evoked interest.

Peter Rowe's first four or five years saw striking additions to the school buildings, many of them long overdue but of necessity postponed owing to the war; indeed the spate of new building throughout Mr Rowe's headmastership has been greater perhaps than during any other decade of the School's history, though as we have seen there was a comparable period of rapid growth after the First World War. Reference has already been made to the Leo Price Gymnasium, which, completed during the last term of Mr Evans's regime, was officially opened in the first term of his successor. The opening ceremony was performed on the Whit-Monday of 1957 by Leo Price's sister, Mrs Ling. The Gymnasium, contemporary in style yet harmonizing with the older buildings of the School, was designed by Mr R. O. Foster, the school architect, to serve a dual purpose—as a theatre and concert-hall as well as a gymnasium: the building thus assumed many of the functions previously fulfilled by the Memorial Hall. The stage curtains were presented by Mrs Tidmarsh in memory of her husband—a fitting as well as a most welcome gift, in view of the leading part A. G. T. had played in his time, both in the dramatic and the musical activities of the School.

In that year also an advanced biology laboratory was built over the boiler-room (to be extended northwards ten years later). In 1958 the splendid new physics and chemistry laboratories were built, thanks to the substantial contribution made, as we have mentioned, by the Industrial Fund for the Advancement of Scientific Education in Schools: they were officially opened by Father Trevor Huddleston, who had recently returned to this country after his great work in South Africa.

About this time two new houses for masters were built, in Maze Green Road; and in 1960 important extensions and alterations were carried out in Hayward House. These were officially opened by Mr J. K. Tee, a member of the Governing Council and himself a former head of the Day Boy House: they comprised a library, monitors' common-room, and a sixth form library.

In the same year the Governors decided, with the support of the Old Stortfordians' Club, to launch a development plan which was to constitute the first phase of the celebrations to mark the School's approaching centenary. A Centenary Appeal Committee was formed, under the chairmanship of Mr T. K. Collett O.S.: the target was set at £100,000, and by 1961 the appeal was well under way. To mark the launching of the appeal fund, *Stortford Miscellany* was published (compiled and edited by W. J. Strachan): it consisted of articles by several O.S. eminent in the world of literature and the arts, together with excerpts from recent numbers of the *Stortfordian*.

The personal approach, through local committees up and down the country, to Old Stortfordians, parents and other friends of the School, not only did much to ensure the success of the fund, but renewed many valued contacts with old friends of B.S.C. Meanwhile the Governors did not await the outcome of the appeal, but, with a fine faith in its ultimate success fully justified by the event, proceeded at once to put in hand the first part of the development scheme. The Preparatory School wing of the Library Block was evacuated and handed over to the builders, to be extended and raised to two-storey height; and by the autumn term of 1961 the new classrooms and assembly hall were in use by the Prep—none too soon, for numbers were increasing rapidly. By the beginning of the spring term of the following year the corresponding extensions of the Main School wing had been completed: these included on the upper floor a music-room and a geography room.

But the chief item in the development scheme, that which impinged most noticeably on the daily life of the School and was to be visually the most notable of these additions to its buildings, was the new communal dining-hall. Not only did this provide accommodation for the whole School, boarders and day-boys, to take their meals together (the catering being done by an outside firm), but also, the House dining-rooms and kitchens being thus superseded, it meant that space was released in the Houses for much-needed amenities. These varied from House to House: they comprised more dormitories, more common rooms, more studies (including even some 'bed-sitters'); new recreation rooms, new reading-rooms, new changing-rooms, new central heating; so that, especially perhaps in School House, the interior accommodation of the House was largely remodelled. The new dining-hall itself has by now become so familiar a feature of the school scene that there is no need to describe it in detail here. Suffice it to say that, whether viewed from outside or within, its general plan and design and its internal furnishings, including the kitchen arrangements, have met with universal approval. An incidental amenity has been its convenience for periodical exhibitions of paintings, by local and other modern artists, on the inside walls left and right of the entrance.

In the autumn term of 1962, when the dining-hall came into use, the usual O.S. gathering became a Thanksgiving Week-end.[1] On the Saturday evening each House played host to its former members, who inspected, sometimes with mixed feelings, the transformation of their old haunts. There is no doubt that many felt, and still feel, that the meals taken together in the House dining-hall were an integral part of boarding-school life, and that the homelike atmosphere of the individual House must suffer when all its members, as it were, dine out. But their successors today, never having known the so-called 'good old days', do not regret them. The effect of the new arrangement on the *esprit de corps* of the House communities does not appear to have been of any consequence, though housemasters sometimes regret that they no longer automatically meet the whole House together as often as in the old days. From the financial and the administrative point of view,

[1] The Centenary Fund at this time stood at something over £107,000.

here as increasingly at other public schools, there is no doubt that the communal dining-hall has justified itself.

The same evening some three hundred people attended the Thanksgiving Ball, which was held in the Leo Price Gymnasium. On the Sunday morning a special service was held in the Memorial Hall, taken by the Headmaster: in the course of his address, he spoke of this 'dramatic act of rededication of the School, with all its new premises and facilities, in the same spirit as that of our fathers who founded the School and with much self-sacrifice kept it alive'. After the service a large crowd of boys, masters and Old Stortfordians gathered round the steps of the new dining-hall for the opening ceremony. The Headmaster first expressed his thanks to the school architect, Mr R. O. Foster, for his 'inspiring and practical design', and to Mr T. K. Collett for the tremendous amount of work he had put in as chairman of the Development Fund Appeal Committee. Mr Collett then declared the dining-hall open: after which the company filed inside the building for the inaugural lunch.

Library Block classrooms; increased House amenities; communal dining-hall—already the development plan, thanks to the generosity of so many friends of the School, was materializing in terms of bricks and mortar. In the following year two more houses for masters were built in Maze Green Road, the first of four envisaged under the development scheme: and in 1964 a new wing was added on to Grimwade House on the west side of 'clink'. (To make room for this the old changing-room hut was removed bodily by a motor-crane: it was a fine sight, greeted by cheers from the spectators, when the hut became airborne, to be dumped temporarily on another part of the playground.) The new wing was ready for occupation after the summer holidays: it comprises splendid changing-rooms and showers on the ground floor, a dormitory above with partitioned-off beds, more baths, and rooms for another assistant housemaster. At the same time the G. H. Common Room was renovated, with new floor, new desks, new furnishings; and an oil-fired heating system was installed. The House was now able to accommodate seventy boarders.

In 1965 a new house for the Headmaster was built in the east corner of the Sanatorium grounds. This was in accordance with the Governors' decision that in modern conditions it was undesirable that the Headmaster should continue to act as housemaster as well. Mr Potts had already taken over full responsibility for School House. He was married in 1965, and now he and his wife took over the upper floors of the Headmaster's old house, which had been converted into married quarters for the housemaster: at the same time the ground floor was remodelled so as to provide rooms for bachelor masters. Another pair of houses was built for married masters, as planned some years previously, in Maze Green Road; and in 1966 'Helmdon', the house which had been occupied by Mr Mellows and by Mr and Mrs Sutton, was taken over by the School, and provided further accommodation for unmarried staff.

Meanwhile changes were taking place in the school grounds. In 1959 the last marks of war time had disappeared with the removal of the air-raid shelters beside the tennis courts, their site being put down to grass. Now, in 1964, Charles Mellows's once famous rock gardens, which, alas, had fallen on evil days, were bulldozed out of existence, and hard tennis courts and a hockey practice pitch (usually referred to as 'The Hard Surface') were laid down in their place. In the same year the old Preparatory School playing-field of pre-war days, which for a quarter of a century had reverted to agricultural uses, was levelled and resown with grass, to be brought into use again as a playing-field in 1966.

Mr Rowe's early years also saw big changes in the staff: first and foremost, the retirement in 1957, at long last, of that much-loved, almost legendary Stortford figure, Charles Mellows. His place as Second Master was taken by W. J. Strachan.

Of Chas the *Stortfordian* wrote: 'This term we said goodbye to "Chas", retiring from teaching after forty-five years' service to the School. We make no apology for referring to C. Mellows, Esq., M.A., by that single affectionate syllable. Chas he always has been: Chas he always will be: Chas he is here.' And indeed over a period of sixty years and more, wherever Stortfordians have been gathered together, not many minutes have elapsed before Chas's name has cropped up, followed by the latest Chas story, sometimes apocryphal, but generally, though incredibly, true. H. E. Wall wrote of him at greater length: 'I have been asked to sketch a word-picture of Charles Mellows in a few pages: but were I given even a hundred the task would be impossible. How can one give a lifelike impression of this eccentric genius with as many interests and facets to his personality as a kaleidoscope? Like Proteus, it is bewilderingly difficult to get a proper hold of him, for he seems to have so many forms (I doubt if even Proteus could change his clothes as quickly!); and even while you are having a conversation with him, he will walk away from you backwards as though trying to escape while talking, or start pulling up weeds in a spasmodic sort of way, or neatly capture a moth from the wall in a pill-box: he is quite incalculable, and you never know what he will do next. I doubt if anyone can have had a greater number of amusing stories told of him. To adapt a phrase, one might say that Chas is incident-prone: and what extraordinary incidents they are! No doubt many become exaggerated in the telling by others; but even if you get back to the source and hear them from his own mouth, they rival the *Arabian Nights* in fantasy, and the tales of Saki in their surprising twists. He is a living amalgamation of paradoxes. Although Chas has a reputation for absent-mindedness, he has an amazingly good memory. Although by nature a shy man, he can preach a sermon or make an after-dinner speech with most telling effect—perhaps it is because he is himself such a good speaker that he has always taken such an interest in the Debating Society, and run it for such a long period so well. Because he has been a schoolmaster for so long at the same school, one would assume that he would be very set in his ideas. But no schoolmaster that I know, of any age, is so essentially progressive or more prepared to try out new methods. His mind is fertile in invention to a marked degree. In all sorts of difficulties and problems at B.S.C. the solution has frequently come in a suggestion from C. M., at once brilliantly unorthodox and absolutely sound.

'Charles Mellows's success as a schoolmaster has been largely due to the wide range of his interests, which has brought him in touch with so many boys of different types. He had his contacts with the scholar in his classical teaching in the Sixth Form. As form-master of the top stream of the Upper Fifth for over thirty years he could, while inspiring the cleverer boys, push the slower ones over a number of important hurdles in the School Certificate, especially Latin. This he achieved partly by his system of individual coaching in the evenings, when he went through their proses and heard their "rep" (rep was a feature of his English teaching). He developed his form's literary interests by his Junior Carlyle Club and, when he was housemaster at Alliott's, by giving members of the House free access to his well-stocked library. Amongst the juniors he would be teaching Latin with astonishing devices of his own creation, to keep the form awake and interested (the "Sword" playing its own particular part); or he would get them to learn biology in the guise of running their own form natural history society. If a boy had brawn rather than brains, C. M. was quick to recognize his merit as a worker in the rock gardens, or on service squads during the last war, or on working parties since. Chas carried out the prodigious expansion of the rock gardens with great success—he himself would range the peaks of the Tyrol, the Dauphiné, the Pyrenees during the holidays, and bring back rare and delightful plants in profusion. He was also the moving spirit in the Natural History Society between the wars: how well one remembers those delightful expeditions to Wicken Fen, King's Cliffe and Little Baddow! He is interested and knowledgeable in most branches of natural history;

O.O.S. GROUP, 1954. 1. I. G. B. Garrould, 2. J. D. Kitching, 3. A. H. Jackson, 4. N. Monk-Jones, 5. R. E. Banyard, 6. J. A. White, 7. B. Tilley, 8. L. C. Sennitt, 9. N. S. Rook, 10. W. R. Brackett, 11. J. R. Adams, 12. W. M. Hartley, 13. J. D. Craig, 14. A. O. Russell, 15. J. C. Collett, 16. H. T. Seal, 17. J. C. Wilkerson, 18. J. D. Butcher, 19. C. W. Grose, 20. R. J. Newcombe, 21. S. N. Salmon, 22. F. M. Woollard, 23. J. S. Blomfield, 24. W. E. May, 25. R. W. Glendinning, 26. S. H. Ormerod, 27. H. E. Wall, 28. H. S. Collett, 29. H. L. King, 30. B. M. Cloutman, 31. J. B. Salmon, 32. K. T. Boardman, 33. C. D. R. Murray, 34. W. E. Palmer, 35. D. A. Palmer, 36. J. A. Smith, 37. R. H. Wall, 38. L. S. Palmer, 39. F. M. Cheshire, 40. B. Blaxill, 41. W. E. H. Garner, 42. J. A. Jones, 43. J. C. Brown, 44. A. F. Wilkerson, 45. A. N. Evans (Headmaster), 46. H. Read, 47. C. Mellows, 48. W. E. Wilkerson, 49. H. B. Edwards, 50. J. M. Fellows, 51. A. D. Hayward, 52. F. E. Rogers, 53. H. N. Brown, 54. L. G. Hayward, 55. G. D. Martins, 56. H. S. Bryan, 57. G. D. Read, 58. R. C. Williams, 59. G. T. Nunn, 60. F. W. Lloyd, 61. G. M. Dyer, 62. G. Featherby, 63. F. W. Martin, 64. A. S. Poulter, 65. W. H. Jones, 66. A. P. Holtom, 67. I. J. Girling, 68. A. G. Tidmarsh, 69. C. H. Joscelyne, 70. W. J. Pascall, 71. J. Morley, 72. F. S. Sutton, 73. F. H. Maud, 74. C. S. Colman, 75. F. F. Ashwell, 76. A. M. Hay, 77. A. R. Kelsey, 78. A. Handford, 79. J. H. Abraham.

'OLD STORTS', 1889. H. E. Newsum, W. N. Rook, L. C. Cropper, C. D. Whittaker, S. Hampton, H. Colman, F. Theobald, (?), J. R. K. Duff, H. G. Cribb. *Sitting:* F. S. Culley, H. Hampton, A. Tebbutt, C. Newsum, H. D. Tuck.

(H. Hampton carved the bust of Richard Alliott in the School House Library and J. R. K. Duff painted portrait of F. S. Young in the Memorial Hall. A. Tebbutt, 'Father of Hampshire Hockey', see p. 108.)

PAST AND PRESENT CRICKET TEAM, 1895, at Shelford. *Back row:* A. H. Windsor, W. B. Mar
G. L. Moore, J. A. Alliott, C. D. Whittaker, G. B. Newport, H. C. Colman. *Sitting:* F. M. Kingdon, F. Wilso
(?), H. Wilson, W. C. Jackson. *In front:* F. Baker, F. S. Young, C. S. Colman.

XI HOCKEY, 1953. *Standing:* P. C. Rumney, M. M. Rafi, D. Paterson, D. A. Watson, J. J. A. Cave. *Sitting:* F. Preston, M. F. T. Brownhill, C. I. M. Jones (Capt.), T. C. M. Ling, B. Scott. *Absent:* M. Pickthall.

CHOOL HOUSE AT LUNCH. At High Table (*from left*): Mr J. F. Phillips, Mr A. N. Evans, Mrs Evans, orman Evans, Captain Mack. A. A. Coote is at the head of the nearest table. On his left (looking down) E. N. ook. On Coote's right C. M. Bateman is looking down, and two from him is J. C. Nevell. At the head of the ble behind Coote is R. G. Turnbull. J. C. S. Addyman is below Mr Phillips, and facing Addyman is P. J. bine. M. Phipps is on the right of the left-hand pillar.

1953. Mr W. E. Clare teaching in the old Chemistry Lab. *From left:* J. F. Sharp, M. T. Hutchinson, C. E. A. Burgess, D. T. L. Spires, E. N. Rook, P. I. Khorram, J. M. J. Garner.

In the Laboratories

1953. Mr A. Darlington teaching in the Biology Lab. (before the alterations). Two faces are completely hidden, the rest are recognizable. *From left:* F. J. W. D. Dicum, R. G. Turnbull, R. C. Davies (standing), C. J. H. Wagstaff, T. S. Herring.

Mr H. D. J. McKeown teaching in the new Advanced Physics Lab. 1960. *From left:* R. F. Jameson, R. P. Jackson, S. M. Gregory, D. R. H. Hogsflesh, Mr McKeown, P. J. Cooling, R. E. Jones, A. A. Jiwa.

C.C.F. SHOOTING EIGHT, 1955. J. F. Sharp, P. H. Venn, J. R. Dent, J. M. J. Garner. *Sitting:* J. B. C. Atkinson, H. W. Lambert, T. S. Herring, W. H. A. Larrett.

SENIOR ATHLETIC TEAM, 1956. J. C. Watt, W. H. A. Larrett, R. B. Cannon, J. S. Thorogood, B. A. Beckerleg, W. K. Hall, M. T. Hutchinson. *Sitting:* G. E. Bucknell, M. J. Covill, M. S. Phipps (Capt.), R. H. D. Wall, M. J. Weedy. *In front:* T. L. Hickling, P. L. Maslen.

SCHOOL HOUSE, 1957. *Back row:* P. H. Tidey, P. W. Andrew, D. E. H. Wagstaff, R. R. Wayman, D. J. Green, G. G. Lintott, A. D. Bell, A. F. Jennings, H. W. Slorach, A. G. Quartermain, A. Wickison, R. G. Muir, N. H. Felstead. *Next row:* T. D. Bowden, R. F. Jameson, H. T. E. Masterson, J. W. McInlay, C. R. Wright, R. D. H. Wiseman, P. A. H. Warnes, N. C. Bond, J. G. Stirling, G. L. Eaves, P. A. Newbeggin, J. N. Castle, H. P. Rowles, P. J. Lawrence. *Next row:* R. G. Wakely, R. L. Ashton, P. G. Glegg, G. L. Atkinson, R. H. Coucher, M. Hamidullah, R. N. Lee, O. B. Jones, N. A. Truman, J. A. G. Bilton, P. B. Freshwater, D. W. Neilson, C. A. Bull, M. G. Gregory, P. J. Campion. *Standing on ground:* J. R. Sainsbury, D. G. Creasy, A. D. Foster, W. R. Wayman, F. S. McNamara, S. A. Hart, R. C. Anthony, D. E. Pressland, D. I. Strachan, C. J. H. Pratt, M. J. Downing, D. R. G. Lintott, F. Hamburger, W. G. Bourne, K. M. Boyd. *Sitting:* M. L. Merritt, G. A. Read, J. H. M. Duke, D. I. Wark, G. E. Bucknell, Miss Laing, Mr P. W. Rowe, Mr F. D. Bryan-Brown, P. J. Llewellyn, J. D. Stirling, W. J. Davies, D. H. Mann, D. A. Sharp, J. M. Pascall. *In front:* D. H. Barnard, G. J. Pullen, G. E. C. Cotgrove, C. D. Boothroyd, P. J. Davies, R. E. Jones, A. E. Thomas, M. P. R. Welch, W. J. Porter, B. W. Green, T. N. Warren, H. T. Kaye, C. P. Wheldon-Wright, A. R. King, G. F. Green. (Absent: T. L. Hickling, N. Tweedie.)

1st XV, 1958. *Standing:* S. Kazaure, E. H. Carter, M. J. Bennett, O. B. Jones, D. I. Pressland, P. I. Szilagyi, T. D. Bowden, G. T. Beckerleg, M. Morton, R. L. Ashton. *Sitting:* P. A. Dempsey, D. A. Lancaster, F. S. McNamara (Capt.), D. I. Strachan, P. J. Whyte.

xterior

The Leo Price Gymnasium, 1957

terior

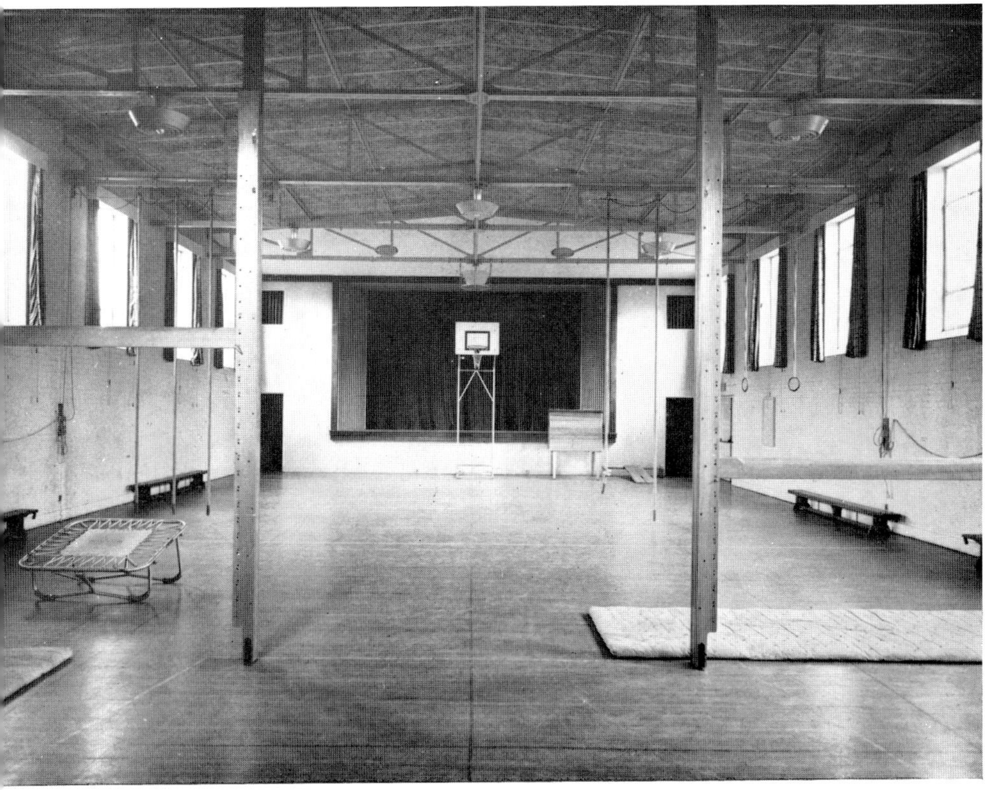

1st SWIMMING TEAM, 1960. O. B. Jones, D. G. Creasy, S. H. Wood, J. R. Beardsley, D. E. H. Wagstaff *Sitting:* P. H. Byers, D. R. D. Steel, L. A. T. Aston (Capt.), P. I. Szilagyi, P. H. Tidey. Winners of Public Schools Medley Relay Race and 2nd in Bath Club Cup. Water Polo VII won all nine matches. All swimming fixtures won except v Otter S.C.

1st XI CRICKET, 1964. Mr C. I. M. Jones (Master in Charge), J. E. B. White, J. B. M. Tidd, M. S. Barrand, R. J. W. Deans, P. E. Evans, G. V. Gilmour, P. J. Sharp (scorer), Mr E. G. Witherden (Groundsman and Coach). *Sitting:* S. J. Lander, B. N. F. Mills, R. H. Edmondson (Capt.), G. J. Deal, A. J. Faure.

and it was through his enterprise that a natural history museum was built up. In entomology he is an expert: who but he would take a party of entomologists to the Isle of Wight and back in one day? He is also an indefatigable bee-keeper, who receives stings with Olympian detachment. When hobbies were put on a more regularly organized basis, he started pottery in Alliott House, and made the generous gift to the School of the pottery kiln; under his inspiration a number of Alliott House potters achieved great success. He also got bookbinding and basket-making going, setting rooms aside for this in his private house, "Helmdon". During the war he put tremendous energy into the cultivation of vegetables, taking charge of service squads and himself doing far more work than anyone; and he also developed "the farm" so as to produce more food during those difficult times.

'On the games side he was for a number of years rugger coach of the School, from which stemmed the traditional match *v.* C. Mellows's XV at the beginning of each season: his own outstanding merit as a hooker made him a valued member of the O.S. 1st XV for many years.

'But naturally one thinks of Chas primarily as associated with swimming. He took over the coaching of swimming after the 1914–1918 war and ran it until 1952, with such conspicuous and well-known success that no underlining is needed here. This high standard was largely maintained through another product of his creative imagination, the Eighty Club, to be a member of which a boy has to swim a total of eighty practices, of a minimum of eleven lengths each, during the winter and spring terms. It was he who launched the splendid project of the open-air bath (in modern parlance the outdoor pool). And besides all this he established life-saving classes as a tradition: his own grim experience in the Mediterranean during the war, when after the torpedoing of the transport he was on he saw men drown for the simple reason that they could not swim (his own skill and stamina enabled him to save the lives of many), made him put life-saving high on the list of priorities.

'One remembers too Chas's holiday trips abroad: his hospitality to boys in his study or at "Helmdon", and in entertaining the Eighty Club or the "Farmers" to supper: his parties on Barton Broad in his houseboats—the *Pax* and then the *Hoopoe*. From Barton one's memory naturally travels to Hasbro', and one thinks of what he has done over the years for the Hasbro' Club, for the O.S. Rugger Club, the O.S. Swimming Club and the Old Stortfordians' Club itself. Of all of these he has been president, and he is also a mason and has been active in the O.S. Lodge.

'As a member of the staff, if on occasions he could be somewhat exasperating to his colleagues by his erratic behaviour, C. M. won their respect and affection by his undoubted talents, his single-mindedness, and his devotion to the School. He served the School most ably as Second Master, and was a popular president of the Masters' Common Room.

'Charles Mellows's association with B.S.C. covers a unique span, including all its headmasters: he was a boy under Mr Alliott, Head of the School under Mr Young; and he served on the staff under Mr Young, Mr Price, Mr Evans and Mr Rowe, having himself taught Mr Price and Mr Rowe as boys. To the life and traditions of Stortford he has made a contribution so valuable that he takes his place without question amongst those half-dozen or more imperishable names which in any history of the School would deserve to be written in letters of gold.'

For some years Chas continued to spend many hours working in the School gardens, and he rarely missed any school function. But after a spell in hospital it was felt undesirable that he should continue to live alone; and in 1965 he moved to a nursing-home in Northampton. Here he was always delighted when friends from Stortford dropped in to see him; and he never tired of talking of the old days at B.S.C., fifty years ago and more. He died in 1967.

At the same time as Charles Mellows retired, D. T. Newton left Stortford, after nineteen years on the staff, to take up an appointment as headmaster of Endsleigh Preparatory School in Colchester. He had joined the Prep staff at B.S.C. in 1938 and was for a short time assistant housemaster at Grimwade House. After six years' absence on army service he returned to Stortford to join the Main School staff, where in addition to his mathematical teaching he gave invaluable help in the coaching of games (especially cricket and hockey—he was a delight to watch on the hockey field), and also in the C.C.F. Other staff changes were due to the retirement of A. O. Ward from the housemastership of Robert Pearce House, which he had held for ten years: his place at R.P.H. was taken by L. G. Soady, whom T. A. Davies now followed as housemaster of Hayward House.

The year 1958 saw the arrival of C. R. Beaufoy, who forthwith took over the treasurership of the *Stortfordian* from Charles Ross Murray; and the departure of A. K. Hardyman after nine years on the Prep staff, to take up a teaching appointment under the Kenya Government. Keith Hardyman's work as an O.S.C. committee man and as O.S. representative on the *Stortfordian* earned him the thanks of all O.S. At the same time N. Monk-Jones retired, after thirty-nine years at B.S.C.; the headmastership of the Preparatory School being taken over by G. K. Bond, who had already been housemaster of Grimwade House for five years.

N. M. J. spent the whole of his teaching life at Stortford. A classical scholar of Merton College, Oxford before the 1914–1918 war, he came to B.S.C. in 1919, joining Charles Mellows in School House as assistant housemaster, and for the next eight years he was form-master of the Lower Sixth. For more than twenty years he was chairman of the Games Committee; he also ran the rugger for a couple of seasons, but gave this up when he took over the Preparatory School in 1927. After nineteen years in Grimwade House he gave up the boarding house in 1946, but remained headmaster of the Prep till his retirement.

Of his years in the Main School Alec Clifton-Taylor wrote of him in the *Stortfordian*: 'What did N. M. J. stand for, to us of the School House in the early twenties? To me, a rebel against many of the institutions of the Establishment, he and his friend R. E. Pond were two invaluable allies. Not that they were in the least disloyal; but if one voiced criticisms, one felt that they understood and were not shocked. My ideas were callow and no doubt often foolish; but they listened patiently, commented freely, and seemed the very embodiment of tolerance, reason and good sense. They were also generous lenders of books.' And two of his former pupils who were afterwards for many years his colleagues on the staff, H. E. Wall and C. D. Murray, added in a joint tribute: 'Alec Clifton-Taylor spoke of M. J.'s help to him as a "rebel": we were in no sense rebels, yet he appealed to those of us who were more conventional just as much. He was unconventional, but in such a natural way that whatever he did went down well, because of the absolute sincerity that animated his conduct. Here were dignity and self-confidence, without the slightest trace of false pride or conceit. His personality so many-sided, his intellect so invigorating also inspired in us great affection. His is undoubtedly one of the great Stortford names.'

W. J. Strachan wrote of his rugger, and of his later years at the Preparatory School. 'At rugger M. J. won the distinction of an Eastern Counties honours cap: it is good to have this opportunity of reminding ourselves of what a fine forward he was, and of his coaching of the First XV and later of the Prep. And there could have been no fairer or more wide-awake referee for the many school matches he reffed.

'His marriage to Betty Ashford in 1926 and the subsequent birth of their three daughters provided him with the happy family background which has meant so much to them all. After a year in private residence came the offer of the headship of the Preparatory School. For the Prep it was a great gain, for few prep schools can have had the services of such an able scholar and fair-minded headmaster. His IIa (then the top form of the Prep) in particular was to benefit from his classical scholarship in Latin, and in French his service with the Friends' Ambulance Unit in France during the First World War had certainly familiarized him, a classics man, with the spoken language, to the advantage of his pupils. So the Main School's debt to him is great, and the number of scholarships won by Prep boys as well as the general standard attained in the Common Entrance Examination are ample testimony to the work he did himself and inspired in his colleagues. Nor did it stop there: M. J. had wide interests, and initiated his boys into the mysteries of biology, especially in ornithology and botany, and grounded them in heraldry, or whatever happened to be his enthusiasm of the moment.'

Since his retirement he has often been recalled to do part-time teaching in both Prep and Main School, and for the last decade he has been responsible for the Old Boys' section of the *Stortfordian.*

N. M. J.'s retirement was followed a year later by the departure of R. G. E. Oakley, who except during the war years had been Director of Music since 1935. 'He was a brilliant pianist,' Charles Mellows wrote of him, 'not only as an accompanist of the famous soloists which the B.S.C. Music Society, largely his creation, attracted to the School, but as a soloist himself, giving immense pleasure by his piano-playing at innumerable concerts as well as by the organ recitals which he gave from time to time after Sunday evening services. And his personal friendships with a number of leading musicians greatly enriched our musical experience over many years.' Reg Oakley now transferred his activities to a partly administrative post with the Hertfordshire County Council, which involved giving lecture recitals and generally supervising the musical activities of L. E. A. schools throughout the county. He was succeeded as Director of Music at B.S.C. by Mr C. S. Bishop.

In the same year the School lost the services of Albert Carter, an old retainer who had served the school faithfully for more than forty years. Many O.S. will remember him as butler in the School House in the years after the 1914–1918 war, and will recall his never-failing courtesy of manner as well as his genial wit. At various times he served in the school tuck-shop and looked after the school stores: latterly he had been houseman for the Day Boys in Waytefield. As the *Stortfordian* remarked when reporting his retirement, the famous quip made by a S.H. prefect in his leaving speech, that he had always supposed the School House grace 'Benedicto benedicatur' to mean 'Thanks be to Carter', aptly summed up the School's sentiments towards him. After his retirement Carter continued to live in Stortford, but suffered increasingly from ill health and died a few years later.

In 1960 A. O. Ward retired after thirty-three years on the staff as geography master. He came to Stortford in 1927, and a year or two later he took over successively a number of jobs, in all of which his meticulous care for detail stood him and the School in good stead. In 1929 he succeeded Mr Colman as master in charge of athletics—an onerous duty which he continued to discharge for twenty-five years. In the same year he took over the management of the school tuck-shop. In 1936 he became the first librarian of the Young Memorial Library, and this job he carried on for many years. With the advent of the Second World War A. O. W. was asked to organize a company of the Army Cadet Force, of which he became the first Commanding Officer. Not only did he run this very efficiently, but he also commanded a company of the local Home Guard. In 1947 he handed over the Cadet Force to L. G. Soady, having been asked to take over the housemastership of Robert Pearce House when W. J. Strachan gave it up in that year: he remained as housemaster for the next ten years. 'What were the qualities', asked F. S. S., writing in the *Stortfordian*, 'which ensured success in so many and diverse capacities? A rare talent for organization and an almost passionate love of order and tidiness were certainly two important ones, most conspicuously shown, perhaps, in the arrangement of school parties abroad. These holidays, planned down to the smallest detail, were a joy to all those whose good fortune it was to share in any of them; and large numbers of O.S. will look back to them as some of the greatest pleasures of their schooldays, with thanks in their hearts to A. O. W.' Old Stortfordian Freemasons have further reason to be grateful to him for his work as Honorary Secretary for many years of the O.S. Lodge. He was also (in 1959–60) Provincial Junior Grand Warden for the Province of Hertfordshire. He continued to live in Maze Green Road till his sudden death in 1967.

Mr Ward's name will always be especially associated in the memories of many Old Boys with the Cadet Force: and perhaps this is a suitable place to outline the subsequent history of the unit. Major Ward was succeeded as C.O. for a short time by Major S. W. Woodward and then by Major L. G. Soady, who undertook the somewhat thankless task of maintaining keenness at a time when the stimulus of the war years had been removed after the cessation of hostilities, and enthusiasm in consequence tended to flag. In 1948 the Cadet Force ceased to operate under the administration of the County Territorial Association, and became from then on a unit of the Combined Cadet Force. The main problem during these years was no longer, as it had been earlier, shortage of equipment, but rather a superfluity of official letters, of documents to be studied and forms to be filled in. More storage space for equipment became necessary, and was provided in the basement of the Library Block. By 1953 Cadets were attending Junior Leaders', Signals and Certificate T courses: the miniature range was completed, and the summer camp at Pirbright was hailed as the best organized of recent years. In 1955 'postal' shooting matches were arranged with St Edmund's, St Alban's and with Hertford Grammar School; and the unit competed in the *Country Life* inter-schools competition. It was about this time that a contingent under Major Soady visited Paderborn in occupied Germany: they were attached to the Rifle Brigade, and stayed with units of the B.A.O.R., with whom they took part in various operations. This experiment was so successful that it was repeated a year or two later, the Stortford contingent being attached this time to the 1st Battalion of the Suffolks, which was stationed at Wuppertal, near Düsseldorf.

In 1958 the strength of the unit was 181. But in that year the Governing Council decided that, with an increasingly congested programme of school work and numerous outdoor activities as well, the time devoted to C.C.F. work could more profitably be used in other ways. And so, after eighteen years' activity, the Cadet Force was disbanded.

Mr Ward's place as geography master was now filled by Mr C. I. M. Jones, who had returned to the School as a master in 1959. 'Kim' Jones had been captain of cricket at school and then at St John's College, Cambridge, where he also played on occasion for the university and regularly for the Crusaders. From 1959 onwards he played for Hertfordshire. But he was even more outstanding as a hockey player: after captaining the Cambridge University team in 1958–9, he played for England from that year until 1964, taking part in the Olympic Games at Rome in 1960 and at Tokyo four years later. On his joining the staff at B.S.C. he immediately took over the running of the hockey, with results that will be mentioned in due course: and in 1963 he became master in charge of cricket as well.

Other staff changes included the appointment of Mr A. C. Johnson as Bursar in 1961, and the retirement in the same year of H. E. Wall from the housemastership of Alliott House, which he had held for eleven years. He was succeeded at Alliott's by W. E. Clare. At the same time F. D. Bryan-Brown left School House, after five years, to get married, his place being taken shortly afterwards by A. M. L. Potts.

The two following years brought changes in the Governing Council, due to the sudden death of its chairman, Mr W. E. Palmer, in 1962 and that of the chairman of its Finance Committee, Mr A. G. Doggart, in 1963. Both men were Old Boys of the School to which they had given such long and invaluable service. Of Wilfrid Palmer, the deputy chairman Professor John Morley wrote as follows: 'For many years a Governor of the School, "Wep", as he was known to his friends, was unanimously elected chairman of the Council when H. Stanley Tee had to retire owing to ill health, a few years after the last war; and he continued to act in this capacity with the greatest zeal and enthusiasm to the day of his death. He was an ideal chairman, for he had not only sound judgment based on his wide business experience (he was managing director of a big firm of glove manufacturers, and Master of the Worshipful Company of Glovers), but also an unaffected geniality and a genius for friendship. He was always ready to help anyone, but he delighted particularly to help Stortford. His driving force was his deep Christian faith: in his undergraduate days at Cambridge he had been president of the Nonconformist Union: later he became a member of the Church of England, but he never lost sympathy with his many Nonconformist friends.'

No less devoted a son of Stortford was A. G. Doggart. A remarkable all-round athlete of international repute, who was especially brilliant at cricket and soccer, Graham Doggart never made a fetish of games either at school or at Cambridge. This is not the place to recount his career as a sportsman: but it is notable that his services to both cricket and soccer in an administrative capacity were outstanding. He became vice-chairman and finally, in 1961, chairman of the Football Association; and he was on the finance committee of the M.C.C., as well as being a member for three years of the full M.C.C. committee.

A man of such administrative experience could not fail to be a tower of strength to the School as a member of the Governing Council and, more particularly, as chairman of its Finance Committee. This office he held for more than twenty years, a period which included the difficult war period. 'I doubt whether anyone who has not served on that committee or on the Governing Council', wrote S. D. Herington, his vice-chairman, 'can fully appreciate the work that Graham did for the School for so many years and continued to do till the time of his death.' And he ended: 'He never spared himself, and we depended more than we can yet fully realize on his wise counsel, which was always based on sound professional judgment but also illumined by his own broad humanity and great devotion to the School.'

The new chairman of the Governing Council in succession to Mr W. E. Palmer was Professor John Morley, who carried on for the next three years, handing over in 1965 to Mr T. K. Collett—the fourth Old Stortfordian in succession to hold this office.

In 1962 J. S. D. Allen joined the staff. In that year B.S.C. lost the services of Claude Covill, than whom no groundsman can have been more popular. 'Grounds have been available', wrote the Stortfordian, 'when it has not seemed humanly possible to prepare them; white lines, flags, oranges, the pavilion boiler, first-aid kit—all have been Claude's care, as well as the maintenance of our thirty-five acres of fields and their attendant draining, ditching and hedging.' Claude was succeeded as groundsman by Ted Witherden, a Kent county cricketer who had later moved to Norwich, where he was the professional of the Norfolk County C.C., and therefore had had wide experience as a coach.

In the following year Mr P. ('Pip') Carlaw retired, after more than forty years' service as carpentry instructor; he worked at first in confined quarters at the west end of the Old Gym; later in the slightly better premises of what is now the Prep Day Boys' headquarters; and since 1939 in the then new Manual Workshop. His place was taken by Mr F. G. Stones.

It was in 1963 also that K. A. Hearne left, after eight years as senior history master, during which he carried on the fine tradition started by W. A. Jones in the matter of university awards. He was assistant housemaster for a time in the School House and then at Alliott's: he presided over the Debating Society, and latterly took over from H. E. Wall the running of the Archaeological Society. Above all, he was an enthusiastic coach of rugger, hockey and especially cricket.

In 1964 the School said goodbye to two more men who in their different spheres had contributed a great deal to its life: C. D. Ross Murray and Captain A. W. Mack. Charles Murray, an Old Boy of the School, returned to Stortford in 1957, having previously been teaching at Silcoates under S. H. Moore. He came as senior English master, and in that capacity became president of the Dramatic Society. Reference has already been made to his success as a producer of plays, and in 'Taking Stock' he has given his own account of the methods he followed. W. J. S. wrote of him in the *Stortfordian*: 'Charles Murray had an uncanny gift for casting: that, and his power to wring the best out of actors and back-room boys alike, were to my mind his outstanding characteristics. I would say that his two best productions were his first, *Hamlet*, and his last, *The Merchant of Venice*: like the month of March he "came in like a lion" but, unlike that month, went out in the same rumbustious way.' In addition to his work for the Dramatic Society, Charles Murray was treasurer of the *Stortfordian* and School Librarian: he also ran the printing hobby, whose press produced a series of tickets and programmes for various occasions and menus for various dinners.

The same term saw the departure of Captain A. W. Mack, a Polish international athlete who, after an adventurous career as an officer in the Polish Army during the war, came to England, took various courses in the coaching of boxing, lawn tennis and athletics, and in 1953 brought his tremendous enthusiasm to bear on the athletic activities of B.S.C. During the twelve years that he was with us he raised the School's standards both in individual performance and in inter-school fixtures. (In this connection, mention may be made especially of G. E. Bucknell, who was invited to throw the javelin for Hertfordshire Schoolboys, and of A. C. Webb, who broke both the quarter and half-mile school records, and also ran in the Hertfordshire Schoolboys' Athletics team). Mack also introduced basket-ball and, in the Prep, the popular game of 'Glosters'; he revived boxing and fencing, and indeed encouraged every form of athletic exercise. Since leaving B.S.C. he has taken on, in addition to other school work, the coaching of the Oxford University Athletics Club, with outstanding success.

With so many of the staff leaving, the autumn term of 1964 saw what the *Stortfordian* referred to as 'a huge influx of new masters': of these A. Lee (senior history master), J. C. P. Cole (who went into School House as assistant housemaster), and D. R. Main are still on the staff. The latter, who is a former Welsh rugger international, took over the gym and P.E. of the School, and shortly afterwards the rugger and swimming as well.

In 1965 a prominent member of the teaching staff and a biologist of outstanding ability, Arnold Darlington, left to become senior biology master at Malvern College. When A. D. came to Stortford in 1950, he found biology still very much the Cinderella of the sciences, and immediately set about raising it to its rightful position. It meant a long struggle to secure the laboratory accommodation and equipment that he wanted, and to establish an up-to-date curriculum in biology. But his enthusiasm, his expert knowledge of his subject and his capacity for sheer hard work soon bore fruit. One has only to look through the pages of *Coturnix*, the N.H.S.'s magazine to which we have already referred, to see the wide range of specialized lines of research which his boys covered, in addition to their basic work in school. Reference too has been made to the holiday parties which A. D. organized to various islands round our coasts for the purpose of biological study; to his surveys of Dernford Fen and The Naze; to the School's successes in the annual exhibitions of the Association of School N. H. Societies. For a year, shortly before he left, he was seconded to the Nuffield Foundation, for whom he carried out investigations, with the full support of the Department of Education and Science, into the methods and curricula of science teaching in English schools.

In addition to his biological work A. D., who is a gifted actor, more than once played with distinction in the Dramatic Society's productions, and with volunteer actors made tape-recordings of various English dramatic masterpieces. He is also an effective broadcaster, who from time to time was and is to be heard and seen on sound or television programmes.

In the same term Roger Beaufoy left after seven years, during which he made his mark in the English department of the School's work, as the pages of the *Stortfordian* or of his own special creation *New Wine* bear witness. The latter appeared for the first time in 1962: it is a purely literary magazine, consisting of original work in poetry and prose done by boys during the school year, with the accent on creative and imaginative writing; its pages are decorated with original graphic and calligraphic designs. This was only one of Roger Beaufoy's contributions to the School's activities: he was a keen supporter of the Architectural Society, and latterly was president of the Dramatic Society and School librarian.

It was about this time that the Prep finally said goodbye to a well-known figure in the person of W. Rogers, who first came to Grimwade House after being demobilized from the army in 1919. A small man pushing a large wheelbarrow laden with sacks of potatoes and other stores soon became a familiar sight for generations of Prep boys, for 'Wally' was to continue at the job for more than forty-five years. Indeed at the Prep he was everywhere: looking after the masters in the staff-room, the domestic staff in the kitchen, the boys in the common-room and classrooms. Rogers dealt calmly and effectively with any and every emergency: and boys and staff alike have grateful memories of his friendliness and unfailing helpfulness.

We have been recalling the names of men who in their time contributed much to the life of the School. In 1958 a dinner was held at the Stationers' Hall in London to do honour to one of B.S.C.'s best-loved personalities, F. S. Sutton, on the twentieth anniversary of the closing down of Waytefield. In his reply to the toast proposed in warm and appreciative terms by Sir Dick White, F.S.S remarked (and how typical of Bobby the remark was!) that he 'couldn't deny that there was a certain pleasure in wearing a halo for a short period, even if it didn't really belong to one!'

We have spoken of the new buildings and amenities which marked the earlier years of Mr Rowe's headmastership, and of senior masters retiring and younger men joining the staff. At the same time various changes in the school routine, some of them avowedly experimental, were introduced. Mr Rowe is a man who is always prepared to try out a new idea, whether the suggestion is his own or comes from the staff or from the boys: some of these innovations we may now consider.

In 1960 the first of the post-'A' Level courses was organized, during the last two or three weeks of the summer term, for the benefit of senior boys whose G.C.E. examinations were over. It proved most successful; and during recent years the idea has been developed on a wide basis, to include lectures from well-known speakers (a number of prominent Old Stortfordians amongst them), as well as expeditions to places of special cultural interest. The scope of these courses is continually extended: they are usually built up round some central theme. For example, one year the theme was Communications, including teaching, public speaking, industrial relations, planning: another time it centred round the Outward Bound type of activities: yet another subject was Design, which was studied in its various applications.

Mr Rowe has always encouraged the musical side of the School. At Stortford this was by no means an innovation; but the expansion of musical activities in the early sixties was so remarkable as to constitute a major advance in that sphere of achievement. This was due to Rowe's appointment of a man of great energy and drive in the person of Mr C. S. Bishop, the new Director of Music. During the next five years not only did the number of boys learning musical instruments increase phenomenally, but a First and Second Orchestra as well as a Preparatory School Orchestra were formed, in addition to a flourishing Choir, Choral Society, Madrigal Society and, finally, an Opera Group.

At the same time, inter-house music competitions were successfully organized: perhaps one should rather say that they were revived, for it may be remembered that they had been originally started, albeit necessarily on a less ambitious scale, by Mr Tidmarsh in the years preceding the First World War, but had long since lapsed. The Lyre Trophy which he had then presented was now retrieved from a store cupboard in Elgar House and awarded to the successful House. It was fitting too that the revival of the School's orchestral activities should have been made possible largely through the A. G. Tidmarsh Memorial Fund, which purchased a considerable number of musical instruments for the boys' use.

Not only was the amount of music played and sung in the School greater than ever before, but the standard of performance, more especially perhaps of choral works, under Mr Bishop's baton was very high indeed: one recalls with delight school performances of Mozart's *Requiem Mass* or, by way of contrast, of Gilbert and Sullivan's *H.M.S. Pinafore*; or the singing of the choir at the Carol Services. A successful recording was made of some of the Christmas carols sung by a special choir.

It was in the early sixties that the Carol Service was transferred from the Memorial Hall to St Michael's Church. The Carol Service undoubtedly lost thereby its former more intimate character as part of the School's own celebration of the Christmas festival; but it had become a function to which many of the School's friends in Stortford looked forward with appreciation each year, and it was of course possible for more people to attend in St Michael's. Similarly, concerts now began to be given from time to time in other local churches—at All Saints', Hockerill, for instance, and in the beautiful church at Thaxted, where in 1968 the School choir and orchestra joined with those of the Herts and Essex High School in a very enjoyable Haydn concert conducted by Mr Warburton.

In 1964 the first Careers Convention was most successfully launched by Mr Charlwood in his capacity as Careers Master. At this Convention senior boys and their parents were invited to meet more than a score of 'consultants', many of them Old Stortfordians, who were men of standing in their various walks of life. After giving a general talk about the nature of their work, the consultants met the boys and their parents individually, answering the questions of those who were interested and giving personal advice. The Careers Convention has now become a regular school assignment.

Two years later, mainly through the efforts of Mr T. A. Davies, a Language Laboratory was installed in one of the new Library Block classrooms (previously the music-room). Stortfordians of earlier generations may be interested to know what exactly is indicated by this term, familiar as it now is in educational circles. A Language Laboratory has been described as consisting basically of a battery of tape-recorders controlled and co-ordinated from a central switchboard. The equipment consists of a console with a high-quality tape-deck and inputs for microphone, radio and gramophone: from one or other of these sources (usually the tape-recorder) the chosen programme is fed to the acoustic-lined booths in which the boys sit. The remainder of the console consists of a complicated-looking switchboard, which enables the master in charge to operate the booths in various ways and to connect the programme and himself to them individually as required. The boys wear earphones, and in each booth a tape-recorder registers on one track the programme from the console and on another the boy's own reply to what he hears: thus a self-correcting dialogue is maintained between the student and the master tape. Indeed this continuous talk is the *raison d'être* of the laboratory.[1]

Striking results have been claimed for this method of language teaching, though with some reservations, in the U.S.A. and elsewhere as well as in this country. There is no doubt that this and other audio-visual aids to teaching have come to stay: the precise part they should eventually come to play in the curriculum and the extent to which they should supersede the more traditional methods is still under dis-

[1] The above paragraph is a shortened version of an article by Mr Davies in the *Stortfordian.*

cussion. It would seem to be ultimately a question of approach, depending on whether one regards the ability to speak a language fluently as the chief object in view, or familiarity with the literature and culture of the country concerned: in short, whether one is aiming at a practical skill or an educational discipline.

The winter term of 1966 saw the establishment of the first School Council: this was largely the outcome of a brief visit by the Headmaster earlier in the year to the U.S.A., where he became interested in the Student Councils that are usual in American schools. The present Council consists of the Headmaster (chairman), with Mr Soady (Second Master) and Mr Davies; the prefects and monitors; and one elected member from each House (in whose election councillors do not vote, the idea being that the House members should be representative of the School below monitorial level). There are also a few co-opted members. The Head of School acts as secretary. The Council meets once a fortnight, and is mainly a deliberative body: an Executive Council, consisting of the Headmaster, Mr Soady (the latter representing the housemasters) and the prefects, meets weekly, and has the job of taking certain decisions, subject of course to the Headmaster's approval.

It will be seen that, unlike the Students' Councils in the U.S.A., the Council is not (apart from House members) elected by the School. But Mr Rowe had felt that the old monitorial system tended to be a hierarchy, as he put it, 'too narrow at the top', so that there was apathy amongst the masses, who felt that decisions were taken over their heads. Further, the monitors, as opposed to the prefects, had felt that their responsibilities ended with their Houses, whereas they should regard themselves as school functionaries as well. He therefore hoped that the Council would be more in touch with a wider body of school opinion, while at the same time it would work in closer co-operation with the staff than is the case in American schools. The Council's main purpose would be to promote the wellbeing of the school community, by helping to improve leadership and discipline: though he would welcome constructive suggestions as to how that might be reconciled with as much individual freedom as possible. He hoped for free and frank discussion of all school problems, while making it clear that, naturally, final decisions must rest with him. There seems every reason to suppose that the School Council will make an increasingly important contribution to the running of the School.

One result of the Council's deliberations has been the appointment of a Chapel Committee, under the chairmanship of Dr Gregory, the Congregational minister, consisting of Rev. J. Sykes, curate of St Michael's Parish Church, the Director of Music, and a number of boys representing the Council. This committee discusses with the Headmaster suggestions in connection with the Sunday evening chapel services and also the weekday morning assemblies, for which different individuals make themselves responsible; Friday assemblies being of a more secular nature, when readings, recitations, short dramatic episodes or music recitals may be given.

The sixties saw two Stortfordian anniversaries of some interest. The year 1962 was the fiftieth anniversary of the Norfolk Stortfordians' gatherings at Church Farm, Happisburgh, more commonly referred to simply as 'Hasbro'; and a jubilee dinner, organized by G. H. Day, was held at Great Yarmouth. After proposing the toast of 'our Pious Founders, A. G. Tidmarsh and N. P. Wood', George called on Charles Mellows, the president; and Chas in reminiscent mood reminded us of games of 'lurkey' and puddox in the old days at Church Farm, of cricket matches against the Norwich 'loonies', of a hundred and one incidents on Hasbro' beach, or in the sea, or on the Broads. The following morning a short service was held in the church hall at Walcot, near Hasbro', in memory of the Club's Founding Fathers: and the roll was called of those Club members who had fallen in two world wars, and of many others who had died peacefully during the previous half-century. It is of course only a minority of Old Stortfordians, albeit a considerable minority, who have been members of the Hasbro' club. If we have written about it at some length, it is because we believe Hasbro' to be a uniquely Stortfordian institution, which had its roots in that 'family spirit' which was fostered by F. S. Young in the school which he was building up more than half a century ago.

The second anniversary was another jubilee, that of Alliott House, in 1964; and at the beginning of the autumn term of that year the present housemaster, W. E. Clare, invited Old Boys of Alliott's to a sherry party in the House, followed by a dinner in the School dining-hall. This was attended by forty-six present boys and eighty-four Old Boys of Alliott's, by the Headmaster and seven housemasters and assistant housemasters, past and present, of A.H., and also by H. M. Wagstaff, then president of the Old Stortfordians' Club. Two of the original members of the House when it was opened under C. S. Colman in 1914, S. D. Herington and S. N. Salmon, were able to be present in 1964.

In these days of consumer research, it was gratifying to find that in 1965 Bishop's Stortford College was placed, by the Advisory Centre of Education, twenty-fifth in a list of the seventy-five best public schools, judged on their 'A' Level results—'one of the best of the so-called cheaper public schools'. In that year eight boys gained admission to Oxford or Cambridge.

During the sixties it became a common practice, which still continues, for senior boys who have finished their 'A' Levels to put in a year, before going on to the university, with the Voluntary Service Overseas organization. In this way a number of Stortfordians have carried out social work of the most varied kinds, though mainly in the sphere of education, in countries as far apart as Labrador, Gambia, Malawi and the Malayan peninsula. In every case they have enjoyed the work immensely, and have felt that, quite apart from the intrinsic value of the work done, they themselves have benefited greatly from the experience, which has given them first-hand knowledge of some of the world's political, social and economic problems. More recently the School has formed its own link with Starehe School, in the centre of the African quarter of Nairobi: O.S. have been teaching at Starehe, and African boys from Starehe have spent a couple of terms at B.S.C.

In the post-war period, the academic side of the School's activities continued the tendency already noted in favour of history, modern languages and science at the expense of the classics—a tendency, of course, common to many of the public schools. Most of the open awards gained at Oxford and Cambridge were for the two subjects first named: at the same time increasing numbers of boys were going to the 'red brick' universities, though the shortage of places to meet the demand has made entry more and more difficult.

We have said little so far about the academic work of Old Stortfordians as senior members of the universities, whether in this country or abroad: perhaps this is a suitable point at which to make brief mention of the contributions these men have made and are making to scholarship and scholastic studies, both in the arts and the sciences. At Oxford E. G. Collieu is Senior Fellow and Tutor at Brasenose College and Lecturer in History; W. G. Moore is Fellow and Senior Tutor at St John's and Lecturer in Modern Languages. At Cambridge D. E. D. Beales is Fellow and Tutor at Sidney Sussex College and University Lecturer in History; D. J. Cove is Fellow and Tutor at Trinity Hall (the first Fellow in Biology to be appointed there) and University Lecturer in Genetics; R. A. Wisbey is Fellow and Librarian at Downing and University Lecturer in Modern and Medieval Languages, specializing in medieval German and the history of the German languages.

At London University, N. R. Callan is Professor of English Language and Literature; J. P. Shillingford is Professor of Angiocardiology; V. D. Logue has recently been appointed Professor of Neurosurgery; and W. H. A. Larrett is Assistant Lecturer in German at University College. J. Morley was for many years Professor of Surgery at Manchester University, but has been 'Emeritus' for more than twenty years now. At Bristol C. J. Beedell is Lecturer in Education. At Leeds A. W. de Rusett is Senior Lecturer in International Relations. At Edinburgh F. F. Bonsall is McLaurin Professor of Mathematics, having previously been Professor in the same Faculty at Newcastle: he was recently in the U.S.A. as visiting Professor at Yale. At Aberdeen M. R. Wilson is Lecturer in Thermo-Dynamics. At Durham P. J. Whyte is Lecturer in French, and at Newcastle G. C. J. Midgley is Lecturer in Philosophy. At the University of Essex P. F. Thompson is Lecturer in Social Studies. At the University of East Anglia C. Scott is Assistant Lecturer in French. At Leicester University R. F. Jameson is Assistant Lecturer in Astronomy; and in this connection we might mention that Jameson's father, J. D. Jameson, also an O.S., who died a few years ago, was for a time Dean of the Faculty of Agriculture at Makerere College, the University College of East Africa. At Loughborough University of Technology, of which D. B. Collett is Senior Pro-Chancellor, A. N. Strachan is a Lecturer in the Department of Chemistry. And finally D. Stanton is Assistant Lecturer in Economics at Brunel University, Uxbridge.

Old Stortfordians are to be found too teaching in various university cities abroad. In Paris E. R. Pratt is on the modern languages staff of the École Normale Supérieure. In the U.S.A. J. C. Ward is Professor of Physics at the Johns Hopkins University of Baltimore: he has also gained the high distinction of being elected a Fellow of the Royal Society, in recognition of his work on the systemization of nuclear particles. At Rochester, N.Y., C. A. Poulter is Professor of Radiotherapy. Also in the States is J. Ferguson, who previously, after holding Lectureships in Classics first at Newcastle and then at Queen Mary College, London, had, for ten years, been Professor of Classics in the University of Ibadan, Nigeria; he was for two years Visiting Professor of Classics at the University of Minnesota in Minneapolis, U.S.A., but in 1968 went in the same capacity to the Hampton Institute, Virginia, which is a Negro university of high standing, founded a century ago. In Canada, R. H. Grice is Assistant Professor of Engineering at McGill University, Montreal; and M. J. Bennett is Assistant Professor of Inorganic Chemistry at the University of Alberta, Edmonton. In Australia, N. Glanvill Smith is Lecturer in Plant Physiology in the Department of Agronomy at the University of New England, Armidale, N.S.W. And in Africa, the Faculty of Agriculture in the University of Khartoum was organized and established on a firm basis by F. Coleman as Senior Lecturer, but he has since retired from this post. C. R. Oldham was for some years a Lecturer in History at the same university.

From this list it will be seen that Old Stortfordians are playing their part in the sphere of higher education, in a wide range of subjects and in universities scattered throughout the world. And in addition to those mentioned others, too numerous to list here, have held research studentships and fellowships, both in this country and abroad, in English, modern languages, mathematics and science. It may fairly be claimed that our academic record, at the end of the first century of the School's existence, is one of which a comparatively small school such as Stortford can be proud.

To return now to the School: in 1961 the Athletic Sports were transferred to the summer term: this arrangement leaves more time for hockey in the spring term, and facilitates athletics fixtures with other schools. In 1963 a change was made in the running of the school games. The Headmaster felt it wise, in order to maintain continuity, to leave major decisions on policy in the hands of members of the staff, subject of course to his approval. With this in view the Games Committee was reconstituted, to consist mainly of the masters responsible for the various games, including a representative from the Prep. (The present chairman is W. E. Clare, and the secretary J. S. D. Allen.) This is to some extent a return to the practice in the earlier years of F. S. Young's time, when both boys and masters sat on the Games Committee: now, however, boys are members of the sub-committees of the various sports, but not of the Games Committee itself. It is recognized that the initiative and co-operation of the boys are absolutely essential to the successful running of the school games: their suggestions are welcome at the various sub-committees, and are passed on, after discussion, by the master in charge to the Games Committee.

Both in the Main School and in the Prep the last few years have seen considerable achievements in sport. In 1965 the 1st Hockey XI lost only one match out of thirteen played, and that to a strong Hockey Association team: indeed out of a total of fifty-four matches played by the six school teams only four were lost in all. In that year B. N. F. Mills[1] was chosen to tour Australia, Canada and the U.S.A. with the Swifts' schoolboy hockey team; and A. C. Webb, the school captain, also captained the Hertfordshire Schools XI. The following season, some sixty matches were played, of which forty-two were won. In 1967 the School entered a team for the International Junior Hockey Festival at Amsterdam: B.S.C. took fourth place out of an entry of ten competitors. In cricket during the 1965 season, out of sixty-four matches played by the various school teams, only twelve were lost.

The Prep too were doing well, especially in rugger under the skilled

[1] In 1968 Mills played in an England trial.

coaching of E. J. Cussell: in 1964 their 1st XV won seven out of eight matches played, and were runners-up in the Seven-a-Side tournament organized by Mr Cussell, in which sixteen teams from ten prep schools took part. So enjoyable did this tournament prove that it has since become an annual event, to which prep schools from a wide area are glad to send one and sometimes two teams. When in 1966 Mr Cussell, to the Prep's great loss, left to become headmaster of Waterside Preparatory School in Bishop's Stortford, Mr Campbell took over the running of these tournaments, handing over in 1968 to Mr Stonehouse.

Finally, in swimming also 1965 was a most successful year, the 1st VII losing only three fixtures out of fourteen. The School reached the finals in both the Bath Club Cup and the Public Schools Medley Race.

In that year Mr Clare handed over the responsibility for the swimming to Mr Main:[1] and it is worth noting a few of the achievements of the School in swimming during the eleven years when Mr Clare was running it. The polo VII was unbeaten in school matches for three successive years (1958–60), in the two latter of which the swimming team also remained undefeated in school fixtures. In 1954, 1955 and again in 1960 the School won the Public Schools Medley Relay, and in the latter year were runners up for the Bath Cup.

These years also saw the revival or introduction, often only ephemerally, of various minor sports. In 1957 Captain Mack restarted boxing lessons and fencing, and in the same year Mr J. W. Kerr O.S. presented a House Squash Racquets Cup. Basket-ball was widely played; inter-House table-tennis was revived; golf lessons were instituted as a regular activity; a school team of three won the local Schools Riding Championship. More recently, in the winter term of 1967 these minor sporting activities were encouraged by the institution of an experimental 'Cock House' competition, for which each House had to produce teams for badminton, squash, table-tennis, basket-ball, cross-country running, golf, skittleball, swimming, junior seven-a-side rugger and chess. Apart from the rugger there was no distinction between seniors and juniors, but a boy could only represent his House in one activity. This new competition (which was won by School House 'A') proved very enjoyable, and it is hoped that it may become a regular annual activity.

Hobbies continued to play an ever-increasing part in the School's life. A Canoe Club was formed in 1958: camping week-ends were organized during the summer term. A Social Service Unit represented a new departure: boys have helped local inhabitants, chiefly old folk or pensioners, by renovating or decorating houses, clearing up gardens that had got out of hand through long neglect, assisting the W.V.S.

[1] Mr Clare still runs the water-polo.

either as drivers or as helpers in connection with 'Meals on Wheels', taking for drives old people who would otherwise be house-bound, and visiting the General Hospital, where they have helped to cheer the patients in various ways, e.g. by reading aloud to those who for any reason were unable to read themselves.

The Debating Society continued its activities to such good effect that in 1963 its two best speakers, W. J. Bolland and A. A. Jiwa, reached the final in the competition organized by the Public Schools Debating Association.

We have referred already to W. J. Strachan's enthusiastic championing over the years of Italic handwriting: it was a fitting climax to his efforts when in 1962 the School's team of calligraphers won the £100 prize offered by the Platignum Pen Company for competition amongst English schools. The award also included a lightning continental trip for the successful team, who with W. J. S. and a representative of the Platignum Company visited Belgium, Holland, Germany, Luxembourg and France all in a trip of ten days.

'Civics lectures' have recently been revived by Mr Lee: each term a subject of general interest is chosen—Mass Media, International Relations, the Political Parties, Contemporary Art, to mention some recent topics—and men of note in these various spheres have been invited to give informal lectures and to answer questions: modern writers and painters, for instance, have spoken of their work and of the aims of the *avant-garde* movement in this country.

In 1966 Dr R. P. Gammie left Stortford after forty-two years, for thirty-eight of which he had been Medical Officer at B.S.C. As the school M.O. (we quote from W. J. S. writing in the *Stortfordian*) 'his services have extended over an unusually lengthy period, which included the polio emergency and the difficult years of the last war. As school doctor he struck a happy medium between feather-bedding and over-strictness, so that every parent could feel complete confidence in his care and judgment'. Dr Gammie was interested in all sides of the School's life. We have referred already to the cup that he presented for inter-House tennis: he was a keen supporter too of the school rugger, being more often than not present on the touchline at 1st XV home matches. He now lives in Cambridge: his place as M.O. to the School was taken by Dr I. Ross Russell.

The autumn term of that year saw various changes in the Houses. In the School House, Mr Potts having left to go into industry, Mr A. E. Charlwood with his wife and family moved in as housemaster. At the same time Mr G. K. Bond moved out of Grimwade House to one of the masters' houses in Maze Green Road, and Mr Dawson took over the charge of the boarders at Grimwade House.

Mention has been made of Professor John Morley's retirement from the chairmanship of the Governing Council in 1965: in 1966 the fiftieth Northern Dinner, held as usual in Manchester, was made the occasion of doing honour to this distinguished O.S. To him Stortfordians are grateful not only for his work on the Governing Council for many years, but for his energy in organizing, year by year, from the beginning of his brilliant career as a surgeon in Manchester more than fifty years ago, the O.S.C. Northern Dinners in that city. He is indeed the doyen of Old Stortfordians in the north of England, and all were sorry when in the following year he decided for health reasons to retire from the Governing Council.

The later sixties saw an increase in the number of boys, reaching 470 by 1967 (the highest figure before the sixties had been 380, in 1928, just before the slump [1]): this was made possible by the extra accommodation available in the Houses after the building of the new dining-hall, and by the new classroom facilities in the Library Block. The increase was, however, chiefly in the Prep, where for the first time the day boys now outnumbered the boarders. This led to the decision in 1967 to revert to the practice of nearly forty years previously and to organize the Prep day boys in a separate House. The new House was named Monk-Jones House, to commemorate N. M. J.'s long connection with the Prep both as headmaster and as housemaster of Grimwade; and in the summer term of that year 'M. J. H.' was officially opened at a short inaugural ceremony attended by both Mr and Mrs Monk-Jones. The old Recreation Hut was extensively altered, to become the headquarters of the new House until such time as a more permanent building can be provided. Mr J. T. Campbell was appointed as housemaster, and under his enthusiastic leadership the House got off to a good start.

Meanwhile a somewhat similar reorganization of the day boys had taken place in the Main School, where in 1965, the number of day boys having for some time passed the hundred mark, it was decided to abandon the X and Y division of Hayward House and to form two completely separate Houses: and the obviously appropriate name for the new House, now installed in that part of Waytefield where Mr Sutton had formerly lived, was Sutton House. Mr T. A. Davies remained housemaster of Hayward's, and Mr F. D. Bryan-Brown became the first housemaster of Sutton's.

This is perhaps an appropriate point at which to summarize the history and comment on the position of the Day Boys at B.S.C.[2] There were of course day boys at the old N.G.S. from its foundation in 1868,

[1] See footnote on p. 10 for earlier figures.

[2] We are indebted here to an article on the Day Boys by S. E. Linsell in the *Stortfordian*.

though as we have seen they had at first no corporate existence apart from the boarders. The first day boy to become Head of the School was S. G. Organe, who held office from 1899 until 1902. But even after the 1914–1918 war the boarders still tended to regard themselves as the School, and merely to tolerate the 'day bugs', who were very much in the minority, as outsiders—witness the hostile and opprobrious cries of 'Out, scab!' whenever a day boy had the temerity to show his face in one of the Houses.[1] Those days, however, are long past: and for more than half a century the day boys have made invaluable contributions to the athletic and especially to the academic successes of the School.

We have already traced the vicissitudes of the Day Boy House under various housemasters up to their occupation of Waytefield after the 1939–1945 war. The Day Boys at that time moved into the ground floor of what had been the boys' side of Waytefield, with their housemaster Mr Hayward occupying what had been Mr Sutton's private quarters when he was running the boarding house: the upper storeys on each side were turned into masters' flats.

The evolution of the Day Boy House into two finally separate Houses was a gradual process. In 1934 it was split for administrative purposes, and this division, applied to the Yeo Cup competition in 1937, was by degrees introduced into other forms of inter-House sport. The two halves were named X and Y.

In 1956 occurred the death of the housemaster who since 1929 had done so much for the Day Boys, and it was most fitting that the House was now, in his honour, renamed Hayward House. Mr Hayward was succeeded for a short period by Mr L. G. Soady, but in 1957 the present housemaster, Mr T. A. Davies, took over. Mr Davies did much to cope with the reorganization needed for increasing numbers, and to provide or to improve the necessary amenities in the House. In 1960, as we have seen, he was able to utilize space in what had at one time been Mr Hayward's flat for a library, a monitors' common room and a Sixth Form library. And with the completion of the new School dining-hall it became possible for the day boys to have lunch there with the boarders, so that what had been the dining-room at Hayward's was now available as a second common room. (But many old Day Boys will remember the 'good old days' when their lunch was provided from the School House kitchens, and was trundled down to the old Day Boy Hut, or later across to Waytefield, in the famous 'Chariot' of blessed memory.) In 1965, as we have seen, the day boys were finally divided into two separate Houses.

[1] Not that this Shakespearean mode of address was confined to day boys, being applied also to intruders from any other House.

On the last Saturday of each winter term the Day Boys now join the boarders for Christmas dinner in the School dining-hall, after which all boys return to Houses for the Christmas parties. At the end of the summer term, when the leavers from the boarding houses have a sort of buffet supper in the Houses, the day boy leavers hold their supper in the School dining-hall.

That the Day Boys have always been prominent over the years in the academic life of the School a glance at the Honours Boards will show. Not only have an increasingly large proportion of university scholarships and exhibitions been won by day boys, but of the thirty Old Stortfordians mentioned earlier as senior members of various universities, twelve were former day boys.

In the field of sport, the Day Boy House at one time experienced difficulties in inter-house competitions, simply through lack of numbers. But by the thirties we find a day boy, J. K. Tee, captaining the school rugger XV: a couple of years later his brother A. S. Tee was captain both of rugger and cricket, and later still G. J. Adams was captain of both games. In 1936 the Day Boys won the rugger, the Yeo Cup, and both the junior and senior swimming competitions. And since that time they have played their full part in all school activities: at the moment of writing once again the Head of School is a day boy.

13. Fifty Years in Retrospect

The following reminiscences were written by H. E. Wall at the time of his retirement in 1968.

MY PERSONAL association with Bishop's Stortford College just reaches back into the first half-century of the School's existence. So much has changed since the days of the Jubilee, celebrated as we have seen in 1919, that my memory, similar to an archaeological site, has layer after layer of relics of various kinds, which need very careful sorting to give a historical picture of the buried past. But what a busman's holiday for a teacher of history and a dabbler in archaeology! No: I propose to deal with different aspects of school life just as they occur to me.

Until 1919 the 'Schoolroom' (now the School House Senior Common Room) was used for morning Assembly, Sunday evening service, lectures, concerts and Prize Givings. At morning Assembly, members of School House Common Room sat at their desks, and the rest of the School sat in form order on lockers which were against the wall round the room. Every Sunday evening after tea there was a tidying up of the Common Room, after which chairs from the dining-hall (the present Junior Common Room) were brought in to provide seats for masters and their wives, matrons and other adults who attended what was very much a service for the whole school, the boys filing in after a roll-call. (This reminds me how few roll-calls there are now compared with the past; when there is one, boys answer 'yes' or 'here' instead of the old invariable 'sum', which now lingers on, apparently, only in the Prep.)

There was a sermon every Sunday evening. I wonder whether we were more or less religious than boys today? We certainly appeared more so in outward observance: not only were both Sunday services compulsory for all boarders, and Sunday evening services for day boys, but there were House prayers morning and evening in addition to prayers at Assembly. On Sunday evenings the hymn 'Ere I sleep' was sung in all the Houses. (In School House Mr Young habitually sat on the side-lockers during the hymn, which we sang sitting, and always got up to go to the master's desk at the words 'Let me rise'!) Furthermore at four-thirty on Sunday afternoon there was a scripture class for all forms, taken by form masters. It is true that, as time went on, some masters put their own interpretation on what 'scripture' meant, but in my young days the Bible was with most masters the basis of this period. A small group used to gather for a prayer-meeting in one of the classrooms on Sunday after tea: this was a movement among the boys, not sponsored by any master or outside religious organization. It was already in existence when I came in 1916 and was still flourishing more than ten years later. (On one occasion something more immediately practical than prayer was required when Fordham, the school porter, on his rounds locked us in by mistake!) Personal prayers were also said by most boys as a matter of course at bed time: having 'five minutes' was a sort of inverted euphemism. This was recognized in the bed-time routine in School House: at nine-fifty a monitor would shout 'Ten to now, please!', and the first monitor in the bathroom would repeat the call. (That delightful humourist J. A. Hall in his leaving speech said that, by the end of his first term, he had learnt that this meant 'Attend to your washing now, please!') The call demanded silence, which was rigidly enforced; boys on returning to the dormitory would kneel by their beds and pray before getting into bed. Some did the same in the morning, but most boys regarded this as an unnecessary extra.

I record these religious habits not to raise a smile on the faces of a more sophisticated generation, though they may well do so, but as an interesting comparison in outward religious behaviour.

The official bed time for all seniors was 9.45 p.m. (altered to 9.30 in the thirties): monitors, apart from those who were having a bath, had to be in bed by 10.15 (ten o'clock from the thirties to the fifties). Those who were not monitors had to be in bed by ten o'clock, when the lights were turned out. At 10.15 F. S. Young (for until quite recently the Headmaster was also Housemaster of School House) would come inside the door of the senior dormitories and say 'Quarter past ten now, please!'—even when, as sometimes happened, he was delayed, until perhaps 10.25: this was the signal to stop talking. (Under Leo Price, and for many years after, the same routine was followed, but a quarter of an hour earlier; so that a later generation became familiar with 'Ten o'clock now, please!')

In those days we used to be waited on more. There were half a dozen housemaids who laid the tables, served us at meals and cleared away. They also made our beds, and a boot-boy cleaned our boots (shoes were worn as yet only by a few). In School House there was also a butler: for twenty years this post was filled to perfection by the imperturbable Albert Carter. But the 1939 war brought about many changes; boys and masters made their own beds, helped with the washing up and so on. The last three butlers followed each other in a swift and somewhat ominous succession of names: Hoy, Wolf and D'eath.

There have been also, of course, big changes in school food. At breakfast there was no alternative to porridge, but you had the choice of tea or coffee. A rasher of bacon, or an egg, or a sausage on fried bread were provided, along with bread and margarine, as well as (occasionally) marmalade. The midday meal was a substantial one, though always cold on Sundays. Tea was 'high' in timing, but not in content; there was bread and margarine, and jam about twice a week, but no 'course', so boys were allowed to bring in such additions as sardines. (It was not till the thirties that Leo Price introduced a 'course' at high tea.) In the summer we used to buy eggs up at the waterworks (whose tall chimney, for years a conspicuous landmark, now no longer exists), and hand them in to the kitchen to be boiled for us; and we would walk over to the Cherry Farm on the Stansted Road, where cherries were cheap. Most boys had their own pots of jam and marmalade, carefully named, and stored between meals in the jam cupboard. During the latter part of the 1914–18 war bread at tea time was rationed to three whole slices for those over sixteen and two for the juniors. Tuck of course helped, but until the wooden tuck-shop was built in the twenties, the tuck-shop was, as has been related in an earlier chapter, merely a tiny brick building attached to the Racquets Court block (the present office block), which had room only for a man sent up from (I think) Holland and Barrett's on half-holidays: the boys queued up at the counter outside. In the boys' Common Room, two or three friends would group themselves into a 'tea-co', and on half-holidays and Sunday evenings would heat up soup or baked beans on the Common Room fire, and perhaps finish off the meal (taken on someone's desk) with a tin of fruit and sweetened condensed milk. A favourite was 'swine mixture'—cocoa powder mixed with condensed milk—first class! It was customary for senior boys to invite members of the Common Room up to study tea on half-holidays, a treat much appreciated by the juniors of those days. Housemasters and assistant housemasters regularly had boys to tea on half-holidays and Sundays. But of course the most radical change in the School's eating habits has been that brought about by central feeding which, though an economic necessity, perhaps in some respects compares unfavourably with the old system of meals taken in the Houses.

Fire Drill, as has been mentioned in an earlier chapter, was a regular ritual in School House. On one occasion we all went upstairs as usual, when H. A. Wilson realized up in the 'C' dormitory that he still had his boots on (boys had to go down the shute in gym shoes or in their socks). He promptly took them off, and to save himself the trouble of coming up for them afterwards, walked out of the dormitory and dropped them over the banisters. Just at that moment there was the familiar click of the latch of the dining-hall door, as Mr Young came through to ring the signal bell. Hilary dashed back to the dormitory, while his boots fell with an acceleration of 32 feet per sec. per sec. on to the Headmaster's head as he emerged into the open well of the staircase. Mr Young came up the three flights of stairs at great speed to discover the culprit!

The fall of Hilary Wilson's boots prompts me to digress and refer to another, far grimmer fall. Norman Garwood, who had come from Grimwade House to the 'C' with a reputation as a sleep-walker, dreamt one night that he was throwing books out of the window: he woke when he hit the concrete floor of the courtyard, thirty feet below. With a broken thigh (which later bore the imprint of the stippled pattern of the concrete), a broken pelvis and a broken arm and fingers, he dragged himself to the bootroom door. It was a frosty night, and he might well have died from exposure, but mercifully Jim Hardyman, the 'C' dormitory monitor, was awakened by his cries for help, and managed to carry him upstairs. Only after helping to get him up the narrow, twisting staircase to the sick-room did I realize what had really happened. Leo Price immediately rang up Dr Gammie, and in spite of our well-meant but ill-conceived attempts to help him, Garwood made a complete recovery, and was playing rugger again the following season.

And now what of our school work? Greek, of course, disappeared from the curriculum about thirty years ago. Latin used to be compulsory for all. More subjects have been introduced into our 'A' Level (the old Higher Certificate) course; geography, English, Spanish, economics, pure mathematics, Russian. Meanwhile the language laboratory and other audio-visual methods—film strips, radio, television—have come in over the years as teaching aids. During the twenties, owing to shortage of space, we used to go to a hall in the town to take our School Certificate ('O' Level) examinations. Nowadays there is much more specialization in school classes; forms as such only just survive. In the old days boys were in sets only for mathematics and French. Up to School Certificate all boys did general science. The form-master usually taught his form in several subjects; for a number of years, as form-master, I taught an Upper Fifth English, history, Latin and scripture—how different from today, when boys are 'setted' for almost all subjects, with no form orders and therefore no form prizes, nor the reading out of form orders at the final Assembly each term.

The arrangement of periods and the number taught were basically similar to those of today, but for twenty-five years and until fairly recently there was a long break of forty minutes in the middle of every morning, when the Houses did P.T. in squads under the control of the monitors. Evening prep in the boarding houses was divided by prayers and supper, the first hour and a half being supervised by a master—something of an ordeal for some members of the staff in the School House Common Room, where between seventy and eighty boys did their prep together. (There was a time when, for several evenings, the Common Room piano mysteriously played a few notes whenever a boy went up to the master's desk. Chas, whose firm discipline was unquestioned, remained impassive. Eventually the culprit was discovered by Ralph Arnold to be a mouse, which had made its nest in the piano!) In the summer term, from the time when I was a boy until the thirties, evening prep was shortened by half an hour, the time being made up by morning prep from 7.20 to 7.50. But the introduction of Daylight Saving during the 1914 war tended to make this a cheerless and chilly proceeding on a May morning, and, like cold baths, it has proved too spartan for the modern boy—and master.

The methods of punishment have changed considerably. 'Whackings' (the older name for 'beatings') were common, and in my schooldays were inflicted by monitors without needing the housemaster's permission. Otherwise, 'tracks', usually twelve or sixteen, were the stock punishment imposed by monitors. Forms that misbehaved would be 'kept in' by the master concerned for part of a half-holiday. In the middle twenties Detention was introduced as a method of strengthening classroom discipline and standards of work. In the summer term tracks were replaced by 'weedings', under the eye of Sergeant Salmon, or of Jack Nichols on Upper Field; or at Alliott House by 'rollings'—a period of time spent in pulling a roller to and fro across A. H. square. ('Chores' were introduced by Chas at Alliott's instead.) Punishment Drill was used by masters and boys over a long period: this was at first run by the P.T. master, and later by the prefects, and it fluctuated greatly over the years in intensity and effectiveness. Occasionally, when a number of boys were involved in some escapade, Mr Young decided on some communal punishment to hold them up to ridicule. I remember about twenty boys walking round the Track in single file, in complete silence except that the leader was required at intervals to ring a handbell!

The internal combustion engine has had a big effect on school habits and school rules. For my first away match we travelled to Saffron Walden in a horse-brake, dutifully getting out and walking up the final long hill. Teams later went in open charabancs, the 1st XV arriving at U.C.S. or Berkhamsted cold and a trifle dispirited. Because few people had cars, practically all boarders came by train: vast piles of trunks down at the station were a feature of the beginning and end of term. Visits from parents were rare except on Prize Day, though Sunday visits by parents with cars gradually increased in number; but for many years they were not supposed to take their boys away from the Bishop's Stortford area. There were no half-term week-ends, but a half-term whole holiday instead. Before motor-cars became common, most boys got a packed lunch and went out cycling or for walks. At one time the river at Sawbridgeworth was popular in the summer, a group of enthusiasts enjoying boating and bathing in an unpolluted Stort. Half-holidays used to be on Wednesdays and Saturdays, and on occasions Monday afternoon was given as a 'Merit Half', a privilege granted only when the School's record of behaviour had been satisfactory

In games, the most noticeable changes have been the disappearance of soccer, the introduction of hockey, the transfer of athletics to the summer term, and the greater emphasis now laid on minor sports. The abolition of compulsory games for boys over sixteen, with a variety of choices in the summer term, has only developed recently: it is interesting to note the revival of keenness on soccer, to the extent of unofficial House matches and matches against scratch sides. In a less specialized age boys played water-polo and swam for the School even though they were in the 1st XI at cricket: in my time H. L. Price, A. S. Hall and H. J. Wright were all Captains of Cricket and also fine water-polo players. The last boy to be awarded both cricket and swimming colours was R. F. A. Sharp: this was in 1934.

The O.S. week-ends on Whit Monday (a whole holiday) and on the occasion of the rugger matches against the Old Boys were so popular that in the twenties beds were put up in the gym for the considerable numbers who wished to stay overnight. The O.S. cricket match on Whit Monday attracted almost the whole School: in the evening, as well as a water-polo match there was an informal puddox match—O.S. *v.* the School, for as many as wanted to play—and finally an enthusiastic chantey. But the motor-car took boys away from the School on Whit Monday, and made it easier for O.S. to bring their womenfolk and children to the School and return the same night.

Leisure times, particularly whole holidays and Sunday afternoons (when no games or cycling were allowed) were perhaps tedious for some: we had no billiard tables, no television, and until the thirties no radio or table tennis. But boys read, played fives, chess or knucklebones, and practised their respective skills in the music rooms and the gym; or expended their superfluous energy constructing imposing 'mountains' of rock and attractive water-lily ponds down in the rock gardens. The Indoor Bath was crowded most Sunday afternoons and, when the Outdoor Pool came into existence, it was naturally a great draw in the summer. In both pools we bathed naked, boys and staff; for swimming matches until after the 1939 war bathing costumes as well as slips were worn.

In modern times school numbers have risen greatly, but the distribution is different. The most striking increase has been in the Prep, which has trebled its numbers to one hundred and fifty, and in the Day Boys, once twenty and now about a hundred and twenty strong. The distribution of boys through the School has likewise changed, the numbers in the Sixth Forms being far larger now, and their average age lower.

The regulations governing school clothes have naturally varied to some extent with fashion. In 1916 we wore suits of our own choice during the week, but on Sundays we had to wear black coats (a few Eton jackets were still to be seen) and stiff collars. Later the blue suit came in for Sundays: on weekdays there were grey flannel trousers, blue blazer and a white shirt open at the neck. The wearing of school caps or straw hats was, until recently, compulsory outside the school grounds (apart of course from Maze Green Road).

Until the thirties there was prep on Saturday evenings, after which outside lecturers came occasionally. But most of our entertainments were home-made—in my early days chiefly debates and chanteys. The Musical Society ran concerts contributed by local talent. The Dramatic Society has flourished for very many years; the chief difference is that inevitably performances have become more professional. In the past, not only scenery but lighting and costumes were home-made: expenses were kept down, and there was no charge for admission. School plays were, much more than now, domestic occasions, and this was also true of concerts and of the carol service at Christmas. After the concert at the end of the summer term, when it was fine, we all—boys, parents and staff—joined hands in a vast circle round the oak and sang 'Auld Lang Syne', with Tid conducting from the centre and leading the singing. The carol service on the last Sunday of the Christmas term, whether in the old Schoolroom, or later the Hut, or later still the Memorial Hall, had very much the atmosphere of Christmas, the buildings in question being decorated with holly and, later, with a Christmas tree on the platform of the Hall.

I will not write here of the additions to the School buildings during this last half-century, for they are shown on the front end-papers of this book.

Inevitably many of the changes I have recalled reflect the changes in society generally. Imagine a boy today starting his school career with five shillings in his purse, and sixpence or perhaps only threepence a week pocket money! But then we were not living in the affluent age.

14. Centenary Year: 1968

In the New Year's Honours list of 1968 there appeared, appropriately enough, the name of T. K. Collett, Chairman of our Governing Council, whose knighthood was awarded 'for services to the City and for Export'; an honour which gave great satisfaction to the School and to Sir Kingsley's many Stortfordian friends.

Meanwhile a Centenary Committee under the chairmanship of D. F. Cock O.S. had already been active, and a building programme had been put in hand to complete the Development Plan first initiated, as we have seen, in 1960. This second phase included a new entrance gateway at the bottom of the Drive; alterations to the Memorial Hall;[1] a Technical Centre, to be built east of the Outdoor Swimming Pool and to be named after Charles Mellows; a new one-storey sanatorium, to be situated immediately to the north of the old (Westfield House) sanatorium; and the extension and conversion of the latter, to provide accommodation for Sutton House and eventually for Hayward House as well, and also for a Sixth Form study centre. A start was made on this building programme in the spring term: in the summer term an additional item was the erection of a new 'mobile' classroom of a prefabricated type for the Preparatory School, situated at the moment immediately west of the Prep classroom block. The increased numbers at the Prep made this additional accommodation a necessity.

The chief items of the actual celebrations, very efficiently organized by D. F. Cock and the Secretary of his Committee, C. I. M. Jones, were the visit of Her Majesty Queen Elizabeth the Queen Mother at the end of May, and, during the afternoon of Speech Day at the end of the summer term, a Centenary Open Day, with Lord Soper as the guest speaker, when the School would entertain the town.

We were indeed fortunate to be honoured by the visit of the Queen

[1] The urns on the outside of the Hall were found to be in a dangerous state and were taken down. Inside, the western or platform end was completely reconstructed, the lapis lazuli and the gallery being removed. The coats of arms now painted on the cartouches, in addition to those of the School are, reading from east to west: (south wall) The Leys, Felsted, Mill Hill: (north wall) Aldenham.

Mother, and 28th May 1968 will remain a memorable day both for the members of the School, and for the Governors, parents, Old Stortfordians and numerous invited guests who assembled, some three thousand in all, to welcome Her Majesty to Stortford. Just before the proceedings were due to start the clouds dispersed, and for the rest of the day the school grounds were at their loveliest, bathed in sunshine beneath a blue sky. Punctually at midday a large red helicopter of the Queen's Flight was seen approaching from the south: it came down low over the Library Block and made a perfect landing on Middle Green. Her Majesty was officially greeted by the Lord Lieutenant of Hertfordshire, Major-General Sir George Burns, after which she and her party were escorted by the Chairman of the Governors, the Headmaster and Mr S. D. Herington, Deputy Chairman, to a dais which had been set up on the south side of the Memorial Hall. Here, after she had been presented with a bouquet by the Head Boy of the Preparatory School,[1] Her Majesty was welcomed to the School by the Chairman.

'There is a rather charming custom in this country' (we quote from Sir Kingsley's speech) 'that when a British subject reaches the age of a hundred, he or she receives a telegram from Her Majesty the Queen. For an individual a hundred years is a great age, and though in the historical context of these islands a century may seem but a short chapter, in the life of a school it is something about which all concerned can be justly proud and, let us not be unduly modest, something to celebrate. The receipt of a telegram by any centenarian is the confirmation of the hall-mark of longevity: for us here today the actual presence of Her Gracious Majesty Queen Elizabeth the Queen Mother allows us to claim royal recognition for our centenary celebrations, and we are as honoured as we are proud.

'Here in this country public schools still remain an integral part of national education. A school's reputation is made up not by the age nor indeed by the modernity of its buildings—its shell—but by the impact the products of the school have on the world at large. We would not claim to be amongst the oldest or indeed the greatest of public schools, but during the last hundred years we have provided our share of well-known and respected citizens, who have endeavoured to maintain and uphold the traditions and values first acquired in formative years at the College. We can hazard a guess at the future of the public schools and say, as this particular school enters upon its second century, that there is every likelihood that it will still be here at the end of it.

'We are met here in the merry month of May, not only to celebrate

[1] N. H. Adams.

evelopment of the Library Block

1929. (*Right*)

From 1936 to 1960. (*Middle*)

1962. (*Bottom*)

The New Dining Hall, 1962

THE OPENING CEREMONY. *From left:* Mr V R. Price, Mrs R. O. Foster (wife of the Arch Mrs A. G. Doggart, Mrs S. D. Herington, Mrs P. W. Rowe, Mr S. D. Herington (Vice-Chairman of Gove Council), Mr T. K. Collett (Chairman of the Centenary Development Fund), Mrs T. K. Collett, Mr Doggart, Mr P. W. Rowe.

Exterior

Interior

XI HOCKEY, 1965. S. J. Lander, R. J. S. Steel, P. G. V. Smith, A. Coates, J. B. M. Tidd, D.W. Fell. *ting:* T. J. Martin, B. N. F. Mills, A. C. Webb (Capt.), J. Townsend, A. J. Faure. Played 13, Won 9, Drawn Lost 1.

HE 'HARD SURFACE': used for Hockey Practice and Tennis Courts. Beyond on left, part of the brary Block, centre, the Leo Price Gymnasium, on right, the Art Room (previously the Gym).

GRIMWADE HOUSE NEW WING, 1964.

FIRST SCHOOL COUNCIL, 1966. *Right at back:* S. J. V. McDonald, M. A. P. Richards, J. H. Cleghor
J. C. Logan, C. J. Padfield, R. W. French, G. D. S. Jones, A. P. P. Smith, R. F. Walters, A. J. Smith. *Mixed ro*
on ground and behind: C. D. Harrison, D. Ellison, J. Foley, R. B. Kirby, J. C. Fitch, R. W. Arend, D. W. Fe
N. J. K. Hawkyard, S. J. Arthurell, J. G. R. Perry, A. R. W. Lefevre, J. W. Collett, D. M. Rona, D. S. Linse
B. J. Leach, P. F. Samson, C. Moy, R. Bertschinger, R. J. Thomas, N. D. Backwith, H. D. Gibbs, R. N. Goo
child, J. Gloster-Smith, J. P. N. Minto, N. F. Hawker, M. J. Houlder. *Sitting:* R. D. Harrison, M. J. Wa
S. F. Knight, Mr Strachan, The Headmaster, Mr Wall, W. Morris, B. G. Sturrock, T. H. Wall.

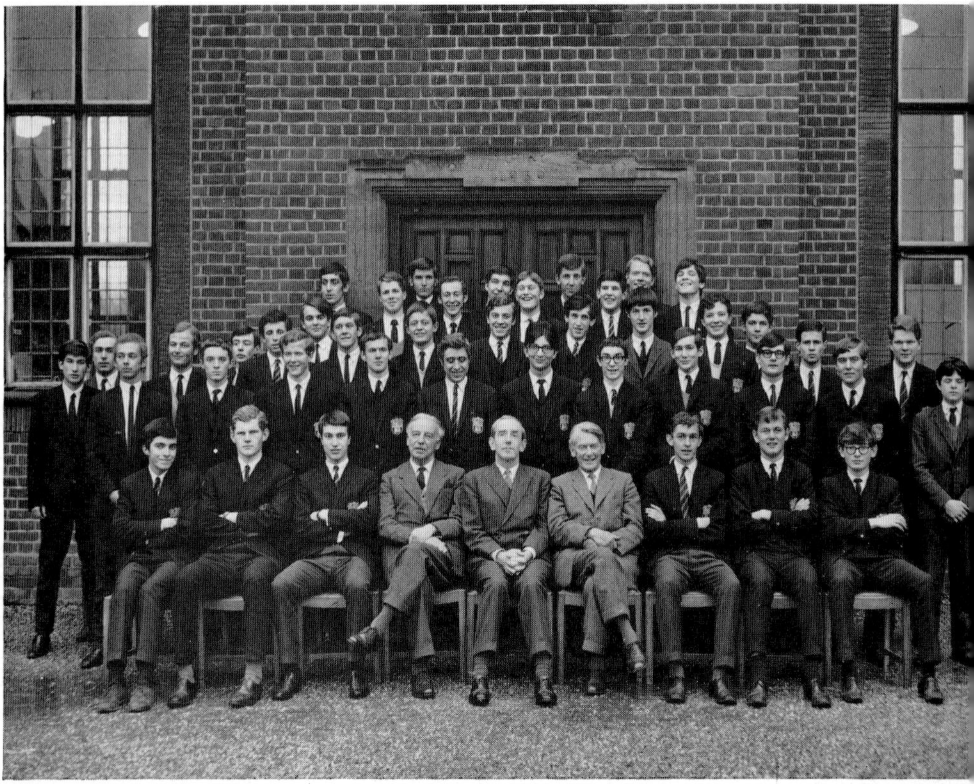

Miss G. E. Parsons.
Mistress, Preparatory School 1910–46.

A. O. Ward. Master 1927–60.

W. J. Strachan. Master 1924–68.

H. E. Wall. Master 1927–68.

Mr T. A. Davies in the Language Laboratory.

THE NEW SCIENCE LABORATORIES, from in front of the Dining Hall across Maze Green Road

ACHING STAFF, 'Open Day', 1968. *Back row:* R. McKean, D. R. Main, G. E. J. Simpson, J. M. H. ımphrey, A. Lee. *Next row:* J. B. Wordsworth, T. Stonehouse, J. T. Campbell, P. C. Thompson, G. D. aam, D. N. Banks, Rev. J. C. Sykes, J. C. P. Cole, Rev. J. K. Gregory. *Next row:* M. A. Roberts, M. S. xwell, C. I. M. Jones, J. S. D. Allen, F. G. Stones, Mme G. Castaing-Jones, H. L. Jones, D. C. Deeley, D. Taylor, C. G. B. Rees, M. A. Easterman. *Sitting:* F. D. Bryan-Brown, G. K. Bond, T. A. Davies, H. E. ll, P. W. Rowe, W. J. Strachan, L. G. Soady, J. H. P. Dawson, W. E. Clare, A. E. Charlwood.

HOOL HOUSE, Summer 1968. *Back row:* N. W. Morris, L. J. Adendorff, J. B. Thoday, P. L. Hunt, J. R. einberg, G. C. Wilkerson, R. M. Lockie, C. W. G. Goddard, I. D. C. Kew, C. P. Wayman, R. H. Knee, I. C. rquhar, V. Chang, J. Goulding, D. A. Pinnell, J. C. Dalton-Golding, M. Ray, L. M. B. Byres. *Next row:* A. M. ll, M. G. Miller, P. M. Taylor, P. S. Davis, T. R. M. Johnstone, A. R. Menhinick, J. Yiasoumi, N. J. D. ıridge, W. J. Wells, J. Jermyn, R. T. Steele, R. H. Haynes, C. J. Eccleston, C. J. Booth, J. W. Corke, N. J. ıter, C. J. Carter, M. C. R. Tattersall, R. W. Pinder. *Next row (standing on ground):* D. A. Leyton, C. R. E. James, A. Collett, P. E. Lukies, P. W. Croft, A. J. L. Sharp, S. C. Huddle, I. E. C. Gregg, R. F. Bilane, S. J. Boling-ke, P. L. Hale, J. P. Warren, M. R. Claridge, B. C. Jameson, G. H. Collett, N. M. R. Arnold, D. B. P. Arya, H. Leftwich, B. Basseghi, R. H. Fairer, K. A. Davis, P. F. Gibbons. *Sitting:* R. C. Fell, J. Ray, M. B. Parker, Bolingbroke, J. P. Eyres, C. M. Norris, P. B. Hillling, Mr G. R. Balaam, Miss J Marshall, Mr A. E. Charlwood, s Charlwood, Mr J. C. P. Cole, Mr M. A. Easterman, W. J. Moore, A. J. Blake, A. N. Fry, T. M. Brick, C. R. he. *In front:* J. H. West, J. Bolingbroke, M. Buckley, C. Buckley, A. R. Woodyatt, A. M. Bull, P. A. Bentall, H. Baylem, P. A. Soper, J. C. Read, M. G. Creasey, N. E. Brick, S. R. Douglas, A. J. Elleray, A. W. L. Hollis, L. Clarke, S. C. Ross, J. F. Clark, R. W. Burgess, G. J. Cobbett, N. K. Staton, C. F. Corke.

The smaller photograph was
taken by A. O. Russell with
Brownie Box Camera in 192
and is the earliest known ae
photograph of the school.

B.S.C. from the Air,
1968

PREPARATORY SCHOOL PHOTOGRAPH, Summer 1968. *Back row:* A. M. Green, M. R. Hoare, N. C. H. Tointon, S. A. Broughton, K. Wilkinson, J. G. Barr, M. J. J. Peasnall, R. A. Carter, D. P. Rees, N. D Holland, M. Grant, S. K. Todd, D. J. D. Wallace, P. G. M. Stockley, A. G. Hunter, S. W. Blades, M. J. D Arnold, C. J. W. Williams, C. G. Drew, P. W. Holland, A. J. Humphreys, E. J. Pelham, N. V. Jeremy, G Buttenshaw, R. Karthigasu, R. G. Tippen, P. N. B. Moss, W. J. Greenall, M. R. Gurr. *Next row:* T. R. Padfield M. C. Elderfield, C. M. Rowlands, R. A. Brittain, J. S. Carter, A. W. Musgrove, N. A. Shryane, C. P. Rice J. T. McCloskey, N. J. Hull, M. A. Purves, P. D. A. Rossiter, J. P. Oyston, P. C. Preston, J. M. Armitage, G Hulks, M. L. Hunter, A. R. Maclean, C. W. Gysin, P. R. Berendt, R. C. Anson, J. M. Tonkin, I. Slater, J. S Johnston, D. B. Johnson, D. J. H. Bush, R. N. Elwell, A. D. MacGillivray, R. A. Calvert, P. R. Chapman, T. D Howard-Smith. *Next row:* G. E. Robson, R. Tinner, G. G. Thomas, G. N. Tee, K. A. Wall, I. H. H. Magnay N. R. Scott, J. T. Benfield, D. H. Thomas, J. M. G. Upton, R. J. Gozzett, R. A. Nichols, D. R. Child, B. D Millage, C. A. Marr, D. G. Wigens, P. Hinkins, G. A. Barr, J. J. Horsford, A. Panayotopoulos, R. W. G. White-

HAYWARD HOUSE, Summer 1968. *Back row:* M. S. Harrison, G. A. Murdoch, D. J. Stott, D. B. Bate, R. L. Campbell, R. J. Dunn, T. A. Jenner, D. R. White, M. R. Samson, P. W. Edmondson, M. C. E. Evans, M. E. Wells, N. W. Hall, J. D. Briggs, V. M. P. Knight. *Next row:* G. J. Yates, G. D. Nicholson, H. E. V. Marchant, P. R. Dunn, H. D. Parnham, D. C. Johnson, P. M. Whalley, P. J. Savidge, A. G. Tooley, S. F. J. Tucker, A. P. Rogers, S. P. Chester, G. H. Cooper, P. L. B. Reid, B. D. Harvey, P. A. H. O'Donovan, P. R. St J. Boyanton, I. K. Braybrook, S. C. Rapkin. *Sitting:* L. Taylor, D. W. Wrightson, I. D. A. Johnson, Mr T. A. Davies, P. F. Samson, D. P. Dineen, W. L. Harris, P. J. W. Miller. *In front:* B. J. Child, A. W. Norrie, W. J. R. Sharpe, A. J. Wallace, S. J. Hurwitz, A. C. Kitchingman, D. G. Hall, N. M. Kerans, S. A. Coombe, W. C. Camplin, G. S. Rice, J. V. Howard-Smith, M. H. Swanzy, T. F. J. Reid. *Absent:* P. H. Carey, M. A. Gamon, P. A. Gooden, D. G. Hopkins, O. J. Plummer, J. I. Stephens, I. Turner, N. W. Whalley.

, S. G. Cozens, P. M. Norrie, D. H. Tee, P. L. Sidey, J. H. R. Heuch, J. I. V. Chuchla, J. P. M. Gray. *ding on ground:* M. S. Collinson, R. A. MacDonald, C. T. Page, M. D. Townley, S. D. Holdsworth, G. A. nie, P. S. Podgorski, M. G. F. Smith, R. H. Robertson, K. G. Gould, A. L. Courtman, R. G. E. Miller-liams, C. C. Trounce, R. P. Morgan, R. K. Merritt, D. M. Chester, R. J. R. Whitehair, R. C. Olney, S. C. man, C. R. Hislop, N. R. Seeley, M. R. Simpkins, C. K. Bond, N. St C. Morgan, I. J. White, J. C. Slater, . Gamon. *Sitting:* J. S. Hall, D. R. Croft, D. A. Davidson, W. H. Maycock, N. H. Adams, Mrs Tolley, Miss ey, Mr McKean, Mr Boumphrey, Mrs Dawson, Mr Dawson, Mr Bond, Mrs Bond, Mr Campbell, Mr Max-, Mr Thompson, Mr Stonehouse, J. S. Ramus, C. Rowe, I. B. Marsh, T. M. G. Gray, W. A. F. Minto, M. B. yne. *In front:* R. B. Fenwick N. P. D. Upton, H. M. Crowe, J. W. Napper, S. P. C. Ellis, P. Rowe, C. W. y, A. D. Snudden, S. J. Pugh, A. R. Holmes, W. J. Tee, S. H. Bosworth, J. T. H. Arthur, M. Franklin, V. West, H. V. Matthews, J. J. H. Grant, C. A. Bacon, G. R. Manly, A. M. W. Simmonds, D. J. F. Forrow, . Alvi. *Absent:* M. Fowler, J. W. Brigden.

TTON HOUSE, Summer 1968. *Back row:* K. V. Schroeder, N. St C. Morgan, C. H. Eaton, J. R. N. Pad-, M. C. Gayford, B. R. Blythe, W. E. Chapman, N. D. Trounce, P. C. Fish, N. H. Woods, N. A. Backwith. *(double) row:* P. L. Ramus, J. R. Tee, R. G. Lanham, T. J. Green, D. R. L. Bone, C. M. Parkin, M. J. pman, J. R. Shann, B. C. Baldwin, R. N. Starling, A. J. Hull, A. Tonkin, R. H. Joscelyne, I. R. Blades, V. Brooks, P. G. Coleman, A. S. Barnard, M. J. Thompson, S. V. Crane, T. J. M. Rossiter, P. Tonkin, D. M. nt, W. N. Avery, D. C. Andrews, J. A. Blenkin. *Sitting:* D. J. Oliver, T. G. Prior, P. A. Warner, Mr F. D. an-Brown, Mr D. N. Banks, A. F. Gebhart, A. P. J. Rea. *In front:* M. D. Avery, J. P. Martin, M. P. Harvey, Jones, J. S. Dorrington, N. C. K. Ballentyne, G. C. Brownridge, D. C. R. Hood. *Absent:* H. C. C. Minto, V. G. Ballentyne, P. S. Barnard, J. P. Bone, R. J. G. Bratt, W. J. A. Bullough, J. R. Burrow, J. P. Burrows, . Lanham, A. Marriott, J. C. Osborn, P. R. Pallett, G. B. Picken, M. J. M. Ridge, J. Q. Trounce.

ROBERT PEARCE HOUSE, Summer 1968. *Back row:* H. G. Stearn, J. J. Read, M. A. Jackson, P. Ba O. R. Burgess, S. C. Rycroft, T. J. Sharp, G. T. Minnis, R. P. J. Atkinson, R. C. S. Hale, C. Cheng, S. G. Rid A. J. Heuch, P. R. Seymour. *Next row:* J. D. Grain, A. G. Vingoe, T. G. Batchelar, P. Murdock, J. R. Toffl M. J. Barber, M. A. Ratcliffe, C. S. Salmon, P. R. Horsfall, M. Carter, R. G. B. Rowe, D. K. Reynolds, N Brodrick, V. Haroutunian, M. F. Halpern. *Sitting:* R. A. Palmer, R. O. Shillaker, N. R. G. Dawson, J. W. Rycro J. G. R. Perry, Mrs Soady, Mr L. G. Soady, Mr J. B. Wordsworth, J. C. Logan, S. T. Overy, P. L. J. Swaff R. C. Newman. *In front:* T. S. Smith, J. K. Merritt, M. H. Norris, A. B. Hilliam, S. M. Popowski, S. M. Sma S. B. Curnow, R. Preedy, M. J. Churchill, A. G. Batchelar, B. A. Horsford.

ALLIOTT HOUSE, Summer 1968. *Back row:* R. J. J. Walton, T. Tinner, M. J. Thomas, R. J. Hall, N. Carter, S. J. Bellamy, R. W. Tinckler, A. Ritsema, J. S. Farrow, S. K. Hossack, A. N. Child, R. S. Collyer. *Ne row:* H. D. Joslin, N. H. Kingston, T. M. Wayne, J. P. T. Irwin-Singer, R. J. Copping, A. G. Joslin, R. J. Chi M. H. Caton, D. G. Brown, R. S. Nicholls, C. J. Peters. *Sitting:* N. M. Whitaker, W. H. Taylor, R. W. Frenc Mr H. L. Jones, Mrs Clare, Mr W. E. Clare, Miss Hughes, Mr J. S. D. Allen, A. P. P. Smith, T. S. Ewart-Jam J. F. Wood, R. T. W. Arthur, *Kneeling:* R. H. Peters, G. M. Hale, E. Soti, D. Kirumbar, M. A. J. Brett, M. W. de Jong, P. W. Elder, B. G. P. Chase, P. F. Tizzard, G. P. Sutterby. *In front:* E. W. Lee, M. D. C. Hale, D. Tomlinson, J. G. T. Irwin-Singer, J. C. Harrison, J. R. F. Welch, J. Carson, R. W. Farrow, D. Ritsema, P. Matthews, A. C. P. Smith, S. Voon.

)MINISTRATIVE AND OUTSIDE STAFF, 1968. *Back row:* M. M. Phillips (Retired), Miss Gunton, Beckenham, Miss Stone, R. H. Wacey, Mrs Hurren, H. A. Wacey, Miss Smith. *Front row:* Miss Stedman, F. Turner, Mrs Steer, F. W. Jordan (Clerk of Works), A. C. Johnson (Bursar), Mrs Jordan, E. Witherden, Coakham, C. Hummersone.

ꞃEPARATORY SCHOOL ASSEMBLY HALL, 1968. Masters: C. N. C. Abram, T. Stonehouse, . S. Maxwell, J. H. P. Dawson, G. K. Bond, J. T. Campbell, P. C. Thompson, R. McKean.

ARRIVAL ON MIDDLE GREEN. Old Stortfordians are on the left in front of the Art Room (Old Gyr
Main School boys on the right by the Library Classrooms Block.

The Visit of H.M. Queen Elizabeth the Queen Mother

THE QUEEN MOTHER RESPONDS TO THE CHAIRMAN'S SPEECH OF WELCOME. On t
platform are Sir Kingsley Collett, Mrs Rowe, Lady Jean Rankin (The Lady in Waiting), The Headmaster, S
Martin Gilliat (Private Secretary to the Queen Mother), Lady Collett, Major General Sir George Burns (Lo
Lieutenant of Hertfordshire).

:E HEADMASTER CONDUCTS THE QUEEN MOTHER TOWARDS THE LIBRARY. On the ht is Sir Kingsley Collett and behind him J. G. R. Perry, the Head Prefect. Behind the Queen Mother is Col. A. F. Wilcox, the Chief Constable of Hertfordshire. Two boys on the left of the picture are R. W. nch and J. H. Leftwich.

V. J. GREGORY GIVING THE ADDRESS AT THE SERVICE in the remodelled Memorial Hall. : Bishop of St Albans is in the centre and Rev. D. Farmborough on the right. The Queen Mother is in the ıt row of the right-hand part of the congregation and Sir Kingsley Collett is next to her.

OPEN DAY, 1968. The Chairman of Bishop's Stortford U.D.C. (W. J. George, Esq.), Sir Kingsley Collet and Lord Soper making the commemoration speech.

THE NEW SANATORIUM with the Matron, Mrs Eaton.

THE CHARLES MELLOWS TECHNICAL CENTRE. On the left is the Manual Workshop.

but to do honour to the past, and to give our blessing and encouragement for the future: and how fortunate we are that you, Ma'am, have seen fit to accept our invitation and as it were to set the royal seal on this day of days, which means so much to us all and will remain, I know, a treasured memory in the years to come'.

In reply to the Chairman's address Her Majesty spoke as follows:—

'First of all, may I thank you for your kind welcome to me. Despite my rather unorthodox arrival, landing as I did almost literally at your feet, I feel that I am in familiar and friendly surroundings at Bishop's Stortford College. For I myself spent many happy years of my youth just fifteen miles from here at our home near Hitchin; and my brother, I know, took a keen interest in the School, and was a patron of your most successful Centenary Appeal. So I am especially pleased to share in your celebrations today. In congratulating you most warmly on achieving your Centenary, I wish you every good fortune in the years ahead.

'For a hundred years the boys of Bishop's Stortford College have made their mark in a wide variety of careers—in the service of the Crown, in the Church, the Law and in divers other callings, and many have played an important part in the affairs of this county and in the life of Great Britain. You who are at the School today are heirs of a great tradition—a tradition of service and loyalty of which you may be justly proud. The years ahead will be full of opportunity, and I know that the boys of the School will accept the challenge of the future, and in upholding by their prowess and example the high ideals of the past will add lustre to the great record of the School.'

Her Majesty ended by announcing that the Headmaster had agreed to her request for an extra two days' holiday, and this was loudly acclaimed by the School. The Head of School [1] then made a short speech of thanks, and presented to the Queen Mother a sheaf of poems, the work of Old Boys and of boys still in the School, written in the Italic hand by past or present members of the Calligraphic Society. This ended the more formal proceedings.

The Queen Mother now left the dais, and spoke with members of the Governing Council and of the staff as well as with a number of the senior boys as she walked across to the Young Memorial Library. Here Her Majesty handed to the Head of School a portrait of herself, as a gift to the School in commemoration of her visit.

The royal party took lunch in the Headmaster's house, while some three hundred invited guests enjoyed the hospitality of the School in the dining-hall: other visitors, including Old Stortfordians and parents,

[1] J. G. R. Perry.

lunched in two large marquees on Lower Green. Afterwards the Queen Mother visited many of the numerous exhibitions and 'activities' (such as audio-visual and language-laboratory demonstrations, swimming, drama and opera groups) before attending the Thanksgiving Service in the newly reconstructed Memorial Hall. The Headmaster was supported on the platform by the Bishop of St Alban's, the Vicar of St Michael's Church, Bishop's Stortford, and the Minister of the Congregational Church, who also gave the address. Dr Gregory ended with these words: 'Your fathers weren't afraid of controversy, and would want me to remind you that their nonconformity was for a certain belief in God; and that nonconformity in general had better be *for* something. I speak between thanksgiving and dedication, so, while I hope that the youngest of you does feel grateful for a past you never knew, I hope too that the oldest person present will join in dedication to a future he'll never see.'

On leaving the Memorial Hall the Queen Mother moved freely amongst Old Stortfordians, parents and other visitors during the afternoon garden party, speaking personally to many of them. After tea she was escorted down the Drive to the new gateway for the last official ceremony of the day, the unveiling of a plaque commemorating her visit. This plaque, together with that on the opposite gate-post, was presented to the School by the Old Stortfordians Club, and is the work of the well-known calligrapher, Mr Will Carter. The plaque reads:

This plaque commemorates the visit of Her Majesty

QUEEN ELIZABETH THE QUEEN MOTHER

on Thursday 28 May 1968, the Centenary Year

After the unveiling ceremony, Her Majesty drove up to Colman Field, where the School was awaiting her, and as her helicopter became airborne, the boys gave her a rousing farewell cheer.

So ended what all those who were present felt to be a memorable day. The proceedings throughout were a happy blend of formality and informal friendliness; and in a letter which the Headmaster afterwards received from Clarence House Her Majesty made it clear that she too had shared our enjoyment.

In the week following the Queen Mother's visit, two one-act operas by Elizabeth Maconchy were given their first performances by the

School in the Leo Price Gymnasium. The libretto of *The Strangers*, which was conducted by Ernest Warburton, is based on a short story by Thomas Hardy; that of *The Birds*, conducted by Christopher Rees, is an operatic extravaganza on the play by Aristophanes. Both operas were produced by John Cole, and the composer herself attended all three performances. *The Birds*, specially commissioned for our centenary, is, like its prototype, full of topical allusions which, since most of the dialogue is spoken, can easily be kept up to date or retailored to fit local conditions: for this reason, as well as for what one critic described as 'its attractive, inventive, even poetic score', it should readily commend itself for production at other schools.

The last performance was followed the same evening by the Centenary Ball, held in a large marquee on Middle Green: it was attended by just under five hundred Stortfordians with their partners and friends, and the dancing continued until breakfast was served in the early hours of the morning.

Meanwhile normal school activities continued as usual. In music a new departure was marked by the televising, in the church of All Hallows, London Wall, of a religious service prompted by the School's visit, the previous Easter, first to the Nuclear Power Station at Bradwell-on-Sea, Essex, and then to the ancient Saxon chapel near by. This was produced by the B.B.C. as a 'meditation' on Hidden Power, in which the Headmaster and Dr Gregory took part, and the School choir, conducted by Mr Rees, sang the hymns: folk songs were also introduced, sung solo to a guitar accompaniment. The programme was cleverly integrated with an exhibition of modern sculpture, and was broadcast on B.B.C. television during the Easter holidays.

In sport, the rugger season of 1967 (matches played, 12: won 8, lost 4) was the best since 1958. This was followed by an equally successful hockey season: indeed, in the opinion of those most fitted to judge, the 1st Hockey XI of 1968 was in some ways even better than that of 1965, even if the record of matches won and lost was not quite so impressive. The School put in a team for the Six-a-Side Tournament, organized at Beckenham by the Midland Bank (in which twenty schools took part), and were the winners; and if they were not so successful at the Public Schools Hockey Festival at Oxford, they ended a good season by winning the Bishop's Stortford Hockey Festival during the Easter holidays. Two members of the 1968 team (J. G. R. Perry, the captain, and W. J. Moore) won their Schoolboy International caps. Soccer, reintroduced on a strictly unofficial basis, continued to be played against scratch teams, and inter-House knock-out competitions were organized.

The School's centenary coincided with the retirement from the staff of two masters whose personalities loomed large in the life of the School for more than forty years—W. J. Strachan and H. E. Wall. Walter Strachan, a scholar of St Catharine's College, Cambridge, where he read Modern Languages and English, joined the staff in 1924. A man of immense energy and wide interests, he rapidly made his mark at Stortford, not only in the classroom but in various out-of-school activities. In 1926 he took over from N. P. Wood the Chairmanship of the Magazine Committee. In the following year he left to take up a post at Giggleswick School, but returned in 1928 to become head of the Modern Languages Department at B.S.C., and set himself at once to build up that side of the School's academic life. As he himself once put it, he regarded his language teaching, especially French, as a 'way of life' more than as a succession of school periods; and his classroom became the centre of varied studies connected with European but especially French culture in all its aspects. Its walls were soon covered with maps and plans of Paris, with photographs of French architecture and reproductions of French paintings, and surrounded with a colourful frieze of the heraldic shields of the old French provinces. Presently the School Honours Boards began to bear witness to the success of the Modern Languages specialists in gaining scholarships and exhibitions at Oxford or Cambridge. He himself maintained close links with the universities: at Cambridge he became a prominent figure at the yearly meetings of the Oliver Prior (Modern Languages) Society, of which he was a founder member, as he was also of the corresponding Sir Robert Taylor Society at Oxford.

From 1924 until 1927 Walter was assistant-housemaster to A. G. Tidmarsh at R.P.H. In 1929 he married Margaret Wood, whose father and brothers were Stortfordians, and from this time on he had her invaluable support in all his work for the School. It was at their first home in Pleasant Road that their two children, Jean and Geoffrey, were born: the latter was in due course to come to B.S.C. and to gain a scholarship at his father's old college at Cambridge. In 1937, when Mr Tidmarsh retired from R.P.H., Walter Strachan returned there as housemaster, and soon he and his wife were wrestling with the manifold difficulties of running a boarding-house in war time. In 1947, when he retired from the housemastership, the *Stortfordian* wrote of 'his fine guidance and support through ten years of turbulent times'. But he gave up the House only to intensify his other school activities, and for his last ten years he was Second Master and President of the M.C.R.

During his early days at Stortford Walter had been an energetic rugger forward who played regularly for the Town club and achieved an Eastern Counties trial. For some thirty years he coached and refereed rugger sides and for many years hockey also. But his main contribution to Stortford, apart from his class teaching, lay in his enthusiasm for the artistic side of the School's life. As early as 1927 he had founded the Architectural Society, and from then until his retirement more than forty years later he continued to run it with unabated energy, and with results that could be seen year after year in the exhibitions of architectural drawings, paintings, photographs and models which the Society mounted on successive Speech Days. We have seen too how his encouragement of the arts—of painting, of typography, above all of calligraphy—permeated the whole School as well as his Sixth Form enthusiasts.

Somehow he managed to combine his school work with a considerable output of original literary and artistic activity of his own, with what consumption of midnight oil one can only surmise. He produced two small volumes of verse, *Moments of Time* and *The Season's Pause*; he translated poems, short stories, novels and especially books on various aspects of art by French, German and Italian authors (some of his translations have been broadcast) and he wrote numerous articles in such well-known periodicals as *The Studio*, *The Connoisseur* and *Typographica*. Above all, through his regular visits to France (chiefly to Paris) during the holidays, he kept in touch with the work of modern French painters, spending many hours with them in their *ateliers*. As a result he has become the leading authority in this country on what the French call the *livre d'artiste*, and at the moment of writing we await with interest the publication of his book *The Artist and the Book in France*, which promises to be the authoritative work on this subject. In 1968 he was made a Chevalier de l'Ordre des Arts et des Lettres for his services to French art and literature.

It would be difficult to exaggerate the contribution that W.J.S. has made since the twenties to the academic, literary and artistic life of the School. His unquenchable enthusiasms, his personal gaiety and ready wit will assuredly be missed alike in the classroom and in the M.C.R.

H. E. Wall came to Stortford as a boy in 1916, returning to join the staff in 1927. His connection with the School as boy and master has only been surpassed in duration by that of Charles Mellows, for, having been preceded by three brothers at the School, he knew a number of Stortfordians well before the 1914–18 war.

At the Queen's College, Oxford, he switched from classics to history, and when, after two years at George Green's Secondary School in Poplar, he returned to B.S.C., he taught chiefly history and Latin with some English. He was at first assistant housemaster to Charles Mellows in School House, becoming senior housemaster when Charles moved to Alliott's in 1931. Altogether he was in School House for nineteen years: during twelve of these he was working in very close co-operation with H. L. Price, who discussed with him not only House questions but numerous matters relating to the running of the School in the difficult war years. Price shared with him his hopes and plans for the School and relied greatly on his loyal support.

During his early years on the staff, Teddy Wall played rugger frequently for the Eastern Counties. He also captained the O.S. team for two seasons. For some twenty years he was in charge of the school rugger, as well as regularly helping with the swimming, cricket and athletics. He ran the *Stortfordian* for an even longer period, only handing it over to C. D. Ross Murray in 1948. He was President of the ornithological section of the Natural History Society for nearly as long; for a time he ran the Chess Club; then after the war he started the Archaeological Society (which developed from the archaeological section of the 'Pioneers' scheme of the thirties). In the late twenties and in the thirties, for some ten years, he ran the Claremont camps, which he has described in an earlier chapter. He was president of the Old Stortfordians' Club in 1947, served on the O.S.C. committee for many years and is a vice-president both of the O.S.C. and of the O.S.R.U.F.C.

In 1946 he married Elizabeth Hartley, who had come to School House as assistant matron, and for four years Mr and Mrs Wall lived in Cricketfield Lane, where their children, Tessa and Tom, were born: the latter was recently Head of School.

In 1950 Teddy took over Alliott House, again, as in School House, following Charles Mellows: and he remained housemaster of Alliott's for the next eleven years. At no period can his work for Stortford have been of more value than during these years. A disciplinarian in the best sense of the word, he managed at the same time, with the indispensable help of Mrs Wall (who was matron during most of these years), to foster a most happy spirit in the House. No trouble was too much for him to take in helping individual boys, especially perhaps those who found school life difficult; and many of his boys, and their parents too, cherish a deep feeling of gratitude for what Mr and Mrs Wall did for them.

On giving up Alliott's in 1961, he built a house up Maze Green Road. In 1965 he took over the secretaryship of the Games Committee, as we have seen, and this office he continued to hold till he finally retired. In 1966 he joined the Headmaster and the Second Master as staff representative on the newly formed School Council.

His retirement will affect almost every aspect of the School's life: his sound judgment, based on long experience in teaching, in coaching games, and above all in running first School House and then Alliott's, has been invaluable both in the Masters' Common Room and at meetings of the School Council. Over the last half-century he has won the affection and the admiration of a wide circle of friends, whether school contemporaries, pupils, colleagues or Old Boys; and many will find it difficult to picture B.S.C. without him.

Of these two men the Headmaster, P. W. Rowe, spoke as follows at the 1968 London Dinner: 'Walter has done more than any schoolmaster I have known to sow a love of the arts—poetry and painting, sculpture and architecture—in the hearts of the young. Teddy has done more than any schoolmaster I have known to foster a sense of responsibility in every aspect of school life, whether it be in the timing of a pass in Rugby, the running of a boarding-house or a school society, the leading of the Student Council or the editing of the school history. With their capacity for those twin Olympian virtues, enthusiasm and loyalty, they have set a standard for us younger men to emulate. For many years we shall stand very much in their debt, and I know their former pupils here will want to say a heartfelt "thank you".'

Walter was succeeded as Second Master by Mr L. G. Soady. Mr T. A. Davies became Head of the German Department and a new master, Mr A. Gande, M.A.(Oxon), who came to B.S.C. from Loughborough Grammar School, was appointed Head of the French Department.

The end of the summer term saw the last of the main centenary celebrations. The final Assembly was held on 12th July, when the usual procedure was followed: after the singing of 'Lord dismiss us with Thy blessing', which generations of Stortfordians will remember as the traditional hymn for the end of term, the Solemn Charge to the leavers was read out by the Headmaster, and Assembly was brought to a close by the singing of 'Heroes'.

On the last day, 13th July, Speech Day was combined with an Open Day, when the College and its grounds were thrown open to the general public. The Prize Giving took place in the morning, the prizes being distributed by Mr W. G. Moore, Senior Tutor of St John's College, Oxford, the son of a former master of the College and himself an Old Stortfordian. The annual report usually given by the Headmaster was on this occasion given by Mr W. J. Strachan, to mark his last appearance as Second Master.

In the afternoon the School acted as host to the Town. The local residents had been invited 'to tour the buildings of the School where 471 boys and 34 masters work and play'. Once again the multifarious activities of the School were on view; but whereas 28th May had been in the nature of a family gathering of Stortfordians in honour of their Alma Mater, 13th July was rather a gesture of goodwill offered to the members of the local community with which the School has through the years become more and more closely integrated. The Guest Speaker was Lord Soper of Kingsway; amongst the local guests were Councillor W. J. George, Chairman of Bishop's Stortford Urban District Council, and other councillors; Brigadier T. F. J. Collins, Chairman of the Essex County Council; and Sir Derek Walker-Smith, M.P. for the East Herts Division. Once again the weather was kind, after storms which earlier in the week had wrecked the marquees; and our guests were able to wander round the school grounds, visiting not only the various exhibitions in the classrooms, but also two of the boarding-houses, Grimwade and Alliott's, that were thrown open for their inspection, and the 'new' Dining Hall that had already become a familiar feature of the School scene.

The Commemoration Ceremony was held in the open air on Middle Green, the speakers standing at the top of the steps on the south side of the Memorial Hall. Opening the proceedings, Sir Kingsley Collett welcomed the visitors from the Town, stressing the value that the Governors and the Headmaster placed on the ties of friendship that existed with the Urban District Council and with the County Councils of both Hertfordshire and Essex. Councillor W. J. George replied, thanking the Governors for their invitation to be present: he was glad that Town and School were no longer isolated communities, and felt that if the public schools generally followed the example of the College, they had a useful part to play in co-operation with the Local Education Authorities. The Headmaster, who spoke next, rejoiced that the 'Independent' schools were no longer independent of the local communities and their resources, upon which they were drawing more and more, and thanked the Chairman of the U.D.C. for coming. He ended by extending a warm welcome to Lord Soper, whom Sir Kingsley Collett then formally introduced—an Honorary Fellow of St Catharine's College, Cambridge; President of the Methodist Conference; and the most accomplished performer in the House of Lords—on the tin whistle! And Sir Kingsley went on to speak with appreciation of Lord Soper as a lunch-hour speaker at open-air meetings on Tower Hill.

Lord Soper, in congratulating the School on reaching its centenary, referred to its Nonconformist origins. Not everything in Nonconformity, he thought, would survive; but certain basic Nonconformist principles needed to be recalled. First, the Christian religion must be made relevant to everyday life, informing and transforming it. Secondly, the freedom which Whitefield and the Wesleys championed in the eighteenth century was just as important to the twentieth—the freedom to disagree: and Lord Soper illustrated his point with references to the hecklers whom he met on Tower Hill. Thirdly, education was no longer a matter of 'pushing in facts': here too we needed rather 'the fellowship of free controversy'. In this connection, the speaker referred to the highly topical question of 'student power': he thought that young people, even if uncertain as to just what it was that they wanted, could perhaps see with clearer eyes than their elders the wrongness of many of the things we tolerate, and the need, through education, to change the world. Finally, he believed that all education must be based on the Christian ethic 'It is more blessed to give than to receive'. He ended by wishing the School prosperity during its second century, at the end of which he would be very pleased to come and visit Stortford again!

Throughout his address Lord Soper combined eloquence with wit, illustrating his points with anecdotes that delighted his audience. A vote of thanks was proposed by Mr H. E. Wall, and the formal proceedings then ended. Tea was now served in the resurrected marquees and carried outside to be enjoyed in the open: many visitors stayed on to listen to a short concert in the Memorial Hall, or to watch the swimming in the Outdoor Pool: and it was not till well on in the evening that the last visitors had left, and the last boys gone home for the holidays.

The autumn term saw the completion of two buildings that added greatly to the amenities of the School—the Charles Mellows Technical Centre and the new Sanatorium, which, as we have seen, belonged to the second phase of the original Centenary Development plan. These buildings are similar in style, being of the Vic Hallam 'system-built' type, one storey high, walled with cedar-wood; the spacious windows giving a very pleasing effect both inside and out. The Technical Centre comprises rooms for the Archaeology, Architecture, Photography, Pottery and Printing hobbies, and a Technical Drawing room which can be used as a lecture-room and library; while a wide corridor will provide ample space for the show-cases needed for the exhibitions mounted from time to time by the various school societies. The architect's plans allow for a new Art Room to be built later, extending eastwards. The Centre is a fitting memorial to one who devoted so much of his spare time to the hobbies and outdoor activities of the School, and who himself for so many years ran the Natural History Society and later the Pottery hobby.

The new sanatorium is splendidly equipped: it has thirteen beds, with room for more in an emergency. The old (Westfield House) premises were taken over by Sutton House, still however retaining temporarily the music rooms and some accommodation for masters. The intention is eventually to transfer Hayward House also from the Hadham Road, so that all the Day Boys will then be accommodated in the same premises.

And so to September 23rd, when the School reached the hundredth anniversary of its foundation; for, as we saw in our first chapter, that was the date of the inauguration ceremony in 1868. The school flag was flying on School House to mark the historic day, which was celebrated by a special commemorative service, in which the Prep joined the Main School, instead of the usual morning Assembly. The service began, as had been the case a hundred years earlier, with the hymn 'Let us with a gladsome mind Praise the Lord, for He is Kind'. The Headmaster, after a few introductory remarks about Nevil Wood's long connection with the School as boy and master, then asked Norman Monk-Jones to read Nevil's account, compiled from a report in the *Bishop's Stortford Advertiser*, of the proceedings at the inaugural ceremony in 1868. After the reading, Mr Rowe in a short address referred to the militantly nonconformist attitude adopted by some of the speakers on that day, but pointed out that Mr Alliott himself, dissenter though he was, had from the first welcomed boys from Church of England homes; thus continuing in the Nonconformist Grammar School the non-sectarian spirit which had characterized the earlier Collegiate School, and has been distinctive of the College ever since, not least at the present time. The service ended with the singing of 'Heroes'.

Looking Forward

We have followed the fortunes of the School through a hundred years of steady growth and development, during which numbers have increased more than tenfold, and the buildings and playing fields and other amenities have been correspondingly extended to meet the demands of a modern public school. It is fitting that we should bring this chronicle to an end by looking forward rather than back: we therefore conclude with a few words by way of epilogue from P. W. Rowe, in which, as Headmaster, he has summarized his hopes and ideals for the School's future.

'No one would want me', he writes, 'to lay down a blueprint for the School to follow over the next hundred years. It has been the greatness of Stortford in the past to follow no blueprint, but to allow the distinctive form of the education it provides to become apparent essentially through the personalities who have chanced to be there at the crucial moments. No one foresaw this clearly. At the beginning someone talked of Stortford becoming the "Nonconformist Rugby"; Binney himself spoke in strongly sectarian terms at the inaugural service; while others thought of Stortford as one more of those nineteenth-century schools in which the children of one class would be educated to resist the social challenge of the one beneath. All these hopes proved very wide of the mark, because they were imposing on the simple educational process considerations which were foreign to its nature and which every schoolmaster knows it should not be asked to carry. People will look to Stortford with respect only if, in educational terms, it is helping individual pupils towards the good life, a life of fulfilment and of service. "I was grateful to Stortford because it helped me to find my true self": this is what one hopes former pupils will continue to say.

'It will require a number of essentials: a degree of personal and pastoral care amongst teachers not less than that exemplified by the great figures whose names are recorded in this chronicle; a professional competence that is ready to embrace novel modern devices of communicating skills to the young such as our predecessors would hardly have dreamt of; an intellectual vigour and a strength of will at all levels of the School, capable of rebuilding values in a morally splintered world; and the continuing provision of facilities—artistic, musical, technical athletic—comprehensive enough for boys of varying abilities to find their own road to a life of rich fulfilment.

'These are the essentials: granted these, the pressing problems of our day begin to lose their edge. Provided we retain the power to select, the provision of a proportion of our places for boys to be financed by the State would present us with no great difficulty. Indeed, amongst the independent schools we pride ourselves on a measure of integration already some way in advance of others. There is talk, too, of changing patterns of boarding education, of the need to relate the life of otherwise secluded boarding schools to the life of the locality. Here again Stortford has been well placed to experiment and to acquire valuable experience, both through its geographical position and through its policy from the beginning of accepting a good proportion of day pupils. Linked as we are closely to the life of the neighbourhood, the pressure for co-education evident in many circles this year is hardly, with us, more than an academic talking-point.

'The pressing problems of one year become the passing ones of the next. Education is constantly being subjected to the social and political pressures of the moment. It would be wrong for Stortford to brush them aside and complacently sit back, resting on her traditional values. Yet she can be proud of what she has achieved: she has held on to a personal quality of education in the context of a small-sized public school catering for both boarders and day boys—a quality which, it may be, the second half of this century will increasingly sigh for, if the trend towards larger and larger educational factories continues. There is clearly a vital role to be played by such a school, if the richly diverse pattern of educational provision throughout this country is to be maintained.'

Heroes

Thronging through the cloud-rift, whose are they, the faces
Faint revealed yet sure divined, the famous ones of old?
'What'—they smile—'our names, our deeds so soon erases
Time upon his tablet where Life's glory lies enrolled?

'Was it for mere fool's-play, make-believe and mumming,
So we battled it like men, not boylike sulked or whined?
Each of us heard clang God's "Come!" and each was coming:
Soldiers all, to forward-face, not sneaks to lag behind!

'How of the field's fortune? That concerned our Leader!
Led, we struck our stroke nor cared for doings left and right:
Each as on his sole head, failer or succeeder,
Lay the blame or lit the praise: no care for cowards: fight!'

Then the cloud-rift broadens, spanning earth that's under:
Wide our world displays its worth, man's strife and strife's success:
All the good and beauty, wonder crowning wonder,
Till my heart and soul applaud perfection, nothing less.

ROBERT BROWNING